C000283363

COMMERCIAL
LENDING

OTHER BOOKS AVAILABLE IN THE CHARTERED BANKER SERIES

Chartered **Banker**

COMMERCIAL LENDING

PRINCIPLES AND PRACTICE

ADRIAN CUDBY

KoganPage

Publisher's note

Every possible effort has been made to ensure that the information contained in this book is accurate at the time of going to press, and the publisher and author cannot accept responsibility for any errors or omissions, however caused. No responsibility for loss or damage occasioned to any person acting, or refraining from action, as a result of the material in this publication can be accepted by the editor, the publisher or the author.

First published in Great Britain and the United States in 2019 by Kogan Page Limited

Apart from any fair dealing for the purposes of research or private study, or criticism or review, as permitted under the Copyright, Designs and Patents Act 1988, this publication may only be reproduced, stored or transmitted, in any form or by any means, with the prior permission in writing of the publishers, or in the case of reprographic reproduction in accordance with the terms and licences issued by the CLA. Enquiries concerning reproduction outside these terms should be sent to the publishers at the undermentioned addresses:

2nd Floor, 45 Gee Street	c/o Martin P Hill Consulting	4737/23 Ansari Road
London EC1V 3RS	122 W 27th St, 10th Floor	Daryaganj
United Kingdom	New York NY 10001	New Delhi 110002
www.koganpage.com	USA	India

© Adrian Cudby, 2019

The right of Adrian Cudby to be identified as the author of this work has been asserted by him in accordance with the Copyright, Designs and Patents Act 1988.

ISBN   978 0 7494 8277 0
E-ISBN 978 0 7494 8278 7

British Library Cataloguing-in-Publication Data

A CIP record for this book is available from the British Library.

Library of Congress Cataloging-in-Publication Data

Names: Cudby, Adrian, author.
Title: Commercial lending : principles and practice / Adrian Cudby.
Description: London ; New York : Kogan Page, [2019] | Includes
   bibliographical references and index.
Identifiers: LCCN 2018031603 (print) | LCCN 2018034012 (ebook) | ISBN
   9780749482787 (ebook) | ISBN 9780749482770 (pbk.)
Subjects: LCSH: Commercial loans–Great Britain.
Classification: LCC HG1642.G7 (ebook) | LCC HG1642.G7 C83 2019 (print) | DDC
   332.1/7530685–dc23

Typeset by Integra Software Services, Pondicherry
Print production managed by Jellyfish
Printed and bound by 4edge Limited, UK

To Sarah, George and Sofia.

CONTENTS

ABOUT THE AUTHOR

Adrian Cudby runs his own financial training and consulting business based in Leeds. His clients range from international financial institutions to individuals who require one-to-one mentoring and coaching. He is a professional banker (ACIB) with over 30 years' experience in the industry. He has a Master's degree in Business Administration and a Postgraduate Certificate in Higher Education. He describes himself as an academic banker.

PREFACE

This book has been written to support banking students with their studies of commercial lending.

Lending is a key activity for the commercial banks in the UK, which in turn gives them one of their most significant risks. Lending money to commercial customers is a key part of the economy and, if carried out properly, gives those customers the ability to grow and prosper, whilst at the same time providing a strong source of profit to the banks.

Many of you taking this qualification won't be actively looking after customers who are borrowing money and may be working in different parts of your bank. Having an understanding of the key principles that inform good practice when lending money is vital for any banker even if you never actually deal with customers directly.

There is no assumed knowledge in the book and it has been written to support learners who are approaching this topic for the first time. The focus is on lending to commercial customers, and covers the fundamental areas that bankers need to understand in order to deal with these customers effectively. Each chapter contains learning activities which are designed to consolidate the key concepts and help you explore topics in greater detail.

Lending has sometimes been described as an art not a science. The truth is somewhere in between. The financial analysis of information requires a level of technical expertise, particularly around the interpretation of the figures, whilst the ability to assess management requires a very different set of skills which are much more qualitative in nature.

Bankers need to be knowledgeable, able to build strong and lasting relationships with their commercial customers, deliver products and services which are appropriate and be able to support their customers through good and bad times.

I hope this book helps you in your studies and your wider career.

ACKNOWLEDGEMENTS

There are many people I would like to thank.

Mark Roberts and everyone from the Chartered Banker Institute who made this book possible in the first place.

Particular thanks go to Melody Dawes from Kogan Page for her support and enthusiasm through the whole writing process and to my editor Katherine Hartle, whose encouragement, patience and guidance have been invaluable. Thanks too to Martin Huber for the excellent technical review.

Many friends have given me their time and energy and I am profoundly grateful to Alan Brook, Neil Rockett, Steve Shimwell and Sally Williamson.

Thanks also to Dave Jones for taking time to discuss the current asset based lending marketplace with me.

My final and heartfelt thanks go to my wife Sarah for putting up with me writing for a year, for her love and for always being there to listen.

LIST OF ABBREVIATIONS

CAMPARI	Character, ability, margin, purpose, amount, repayment, insurance
CFADS	Cash flow available for debt service
CSR	Corporate social responsibility
CVA	Company voluntary arrangements
DRO	Debt relief order
EBITDA	Earnings before interest, tax, depreciation and amortization
EFGS	Enterprise finance guarantee scheme
EI	Emotional intelligence
FCA	Financial Conduct Authority
FRS 102	Financial Reporting Standard 102
IBR	Independent business review
IP	Insolvency practitioner
IVA	Individual voluntary arrangement
LLP	Limited liability partnership
LPA receiver	Law of Property Act receiver
P2P	Peer-to-peer funding
PESTEL	Political, economic, social, technological, environmental, legal
PLC	Public limited company
PPARTSI	Person, purpose, amount, repayment, term, security, income
SME	Small- and medium-sized enterprise
SWOT	Strengths, Weaknesses, Opportunities and Threats

The relationship between the bank and the customer

INTRODUCTION

The focus of this chapter will be on lending to business customers that are small- and medium-sized enterprises (SMEs), with also a brief examination of micro-enterprises, mid-sized businesses, and corporates (PLCs).

SMEs will be specifically defined and their importance to commercial banks and the UK economy will also be explored.

Banks have rights and duties as do their customers and the legal basis for these specific rights and duties for both parties will be discussed in detail.

LEARNING OBJECTIVES

By the end of this chapter, you will be able to:

- define small- and medium-sized enterprises (SMEs), mid-sized businesses and micro-enterprises;
- assess the fundamental differences between the three legal entities of sole traders, partnerships and limited companies;

- evaluate the advantages and disadvantages of these three business structures;
- assess the key rights and duties banks have to their commercial customers (defined by legal precedent);
- assess the key duties commercial customers have to their bank (defined by legal precedent);
- assess the role of legislation and the Financial Conduct Authority in protecting the customer; and
- define the concept of unfair contract terms.

Defining small- and medium-sized enterprises (SMEs), mid-sized businesses and micro-enterprises

The importance of **small- and medium-sized enterprises** (SMEs) to the overall economy is underlined by the fact that in 2016 there were 5,490,470 SME businesses employing a total of 15,734,000 people with an estimated turnover of £1,824 billion (www.gov.uk, 2017).

The definition of an SME (by the government) is any business that:

- has fewer than 250 employees;
- has a turnover of less than £25 million; and
- has gross assets of less than £12.5 million. (www.gov.uk, 2017)

Within this definition are also **micro-enterprises** (0–9 employees), small businesses (10–49 employees) and medium businesses (50–249 employees).

The **Financial Conduct Authority** (FCA) defines a micro-enterprise as:

an enterprise which:

(a) employs fewer than 10 persons; and

(b) has a turnover or annual balance sheet that does not exceed €2 million.

In this definition, 'enterprise' means any person engaged in an economic activity, irrespective of legal form and includes, in particular, self-employed persons and family businesses engaged in craft or other activities, and **partnerships** or associations regularly engaged in an economic activity. (Handbook, www.fca. org.uk, 2017)

> **Small- and medium-sized enterprise**   A business that has fewer than 250 employees, turnover of less than £25 million and gross assets of less than £12.5 million.
>
> **Micro-enterprise**   A business that employs fewer than 10 persons and has a turnover or annual balance sheet that does not exceed €2 million.
>
> **Financial Conduct Authority (FCA)**   The UK regulator of conduct of 56,000 firms and financial markets in the UK.
>
> **Partnership**   Two or more individuals working together in a business to make a profit.

Mid-sized businesses are defined as entities that have turnover of between £25 million–£500 million (www.gov.uk, 2017). Many of these businesses will be structured as **public limited companies** (PLC), which we will look at in more detail later on in this chapter.

> **Mid-sized businesses**   Entities that have turnover of between £25 million–£500 million.
>
> **Public limited company**   A company that must have share capital with a nominal value of no less than £50,000. The shares can be purchased by the general public. Public limited companies are usually quoted on the Stock Exchange.

All of the UK commercial banks have segmentation criteria where they split their business customers into different categories based on their sales (often called turnover). Barclays Bank, for example, categorize a business customer as a business that turns over up to £6.5 million. At £6.5 million and above they then class a customer as one to which they would provide corporate banking services to (www.barclayscorporate. com, 2017).

The legal categorization of business customers

It is vitally important to the bank, when lending to its customers, that it establishes the legal status of each customer before lending. This is important for many reasons as the banker will need to feel satisfied that the customer has the ability to borrow and remain liable for the borrowing until it is repaid in full.

Often customers themselves, particularly if they are in partnerships, are unclear exactly who is responsible for bank borrowing. This can cause particular confusion in the event of a death of one of the partners or a dispute between the partners.

Sole traders

There is no specific banking legislation that banks need to be aware of relating to **sole traders**.

When entrepreneurs start new businesses, they often start up as what is known as a sole trader. These are individuals who run a business which may be run under a trading name which doesn't have to have the owner's name in the title, for example, it could be *The Country Kitchen* or it could be *Amanda's Country Kitchen*. The only restriction is that the customer must not use a trademark that is already in use or use the words limited, ltd or LTD in the title (the reason for this will be discussed shortly).

When a sole trader borrows money from a bank for their business, either to start it up or to expand it, they borrow in the same way as they would if they were borrowing for a personal loan (eg for a car or home improvements) and, in exactly the same way, they remain personally liable for any borrowing until it is completely repaid.

> **Sole trader** A single individual who runs a business in their own name. They have full personal liability for any business debts. They may have a trading name.

CASE STUDY

Amanda's Country Kitchen

Amanda Jones is opening a new café, near to the university in the centre of the city. She has savings of £5,000 and needs to borrow £20,000 from her bank to refurbish her new rented premises, buy equipment (oven), chairs, tables and cutlery. She is fully and personally responsible for this borrowing and the bank will lend to her in her own name.

Amanda is an example of what a sole trader might look like in terms of a personal and financial profile. This example shows the personal liability Amanda has when she borrows from the bank. This, and other examples will be revisited during the course of the book.

A sole trader's assets which include any property (usually their personal residence), cars, cash and investments (shares, premium bonds etc) cannot be held separately and if they default (or become bankrupt, which we discuss further in Chapter 9) the bank, potentially, would be able to get hold of these assets to try to recoup their borrowing.

The sole trader business will cease to exist on the death, mental incapacity or bankruptcy of the sole trader.

The advantages of being a sole trader are:

- It is very easy to set up as a sole trader.
- No documentation is required.
- Separate accounts for the business do not need to be submitted to Her Majesty's Revenue and Customs (HMRC).
- All the profits are retained by the sole trader.
- A sole trader is autonomous and does not need to defer to anyone else when making decisions.
- People who work for themselves often say they have the highest levels of job satisfaction.

The disadvantages are:

- Any finance to be raised is based on the strength of the sole trader (ie if they have had a poor credit history in the past this will have an impact).

- It can be fairly lonely with no one to share the burdens and pressures of running a business and often this means having to cover all the key roles in the business.
- Working hours – linking to the above point, most sole traders work long hours and often tasks like paying invoices, and administration are carried out in the evenings or at weekends.
- Personal assets (house/car) are at risk if the business fails.

Partnerships

> ### REGULATION
> *The Partnership Act [1890]*
>
>
>
> This legislation has been in place for a significant period and at the time of writing there is no indication any further legislation will be enacted at the present time.

The Partnership Act [1890], defines a partnership as 'the relation which subsists between persons carrying on a business in common with a view of profit' (www.legislation.gov.uk, 2017). This is rather old-fashioned language to describe two or more people working together in a business, to make a profit. The latter doesn't always happen, but it should be the aim!

In a similar way to sole traders, a partnership doesn't have to trade in the names of the partners and can use a trading name, such as *Cutting Edge Barbershop* or *Azreena and Kim trading as Cutting Edge Barbershop*. Again, the customer must not use a trademark that is already in use or use the words limited, ltd or LTD in the title. See the *Cutting Edge Barbershop* case study for an example of a partnership.

> ### CASE STUDY
> Cutting Edge Barbershop
>
> Azreena Khan and Kim Taylor have been running a barbershop called *Cutting Edge Barbershop* in Shoreditch in London for two years. The

business has been very successful and they have also made significant profits from selling hair grooming products, particularly beard oil. They want to start manufacturing their own men's grooming products and have provisionally leased premises above the existing shop. They have cash of £10,000 and want to borrow £40,000 to refurbish the premises and to buy equipment.

One of the misconceptions that partners often have with each other, and subsequently with the bank, is how the responsibility for new borrowing is divided between each partner. The partners will borrow the money in joint names and each partner is fully responsible for all the borrowing, so in this instance Azreena and Kim are both responsible *individually* for £40,000. The partners do not split the borrowing pro rata (ie £20,000 each). This is often known as 'joint and several' liability.

The actions that could be taken by the bank if Azreena and Kim, as a partnership, default on the borrowing will be discussed later in the book.

A key difference between a partnership and a sole trader is that, due to the *Partnership Act*, partners can have a partnership agreement (although they are not compelled by law to have to). The partnership agreement defines the relationship between the partners and covers key areas such as when the partnership commences (often the date of signing the partnership agreement), when the partnership ends and how disputes are to be resolved. It includes the names of the partners (and partners must be named here), the name of the partnership, what the partnership does, and where it is located (this may be the main site if there is more than one site). The agreement also covers key financial arrangements, including how partners will get back capital they have invested in the business, who the bankers are and who the accountants are.

The key point for the bank is that if it sees a copy of the partnership agreement then it is bound by it, so usually the bank will not ask to see it and rely instead on the **bank mandate** (which we will cover later in this chapter). The bank mandate covers all banking activity.

The death or bankruptcy of one of the partners will normally be a trigger for the dissolution of the partnership. At this point the bank would need to act to protect its position (this will be discussed later in this chapter).

> **Bank mandate**   A standard bank document used to detail the relationship between the bank and the customer. It sets out the signing arrangements for the sole trader, the partners or the directors (in the case of a limited company). For a limited company or a partnership, it may specify how many partners or directors need to sign banking instruments such as cheques.

The advantages of a partnership are:

- It is very easy to set up a partnership.
- No documentation is required although often partners will enter into a partnership agreement.
- Separate accounts for the business do not need to be submitted to Her Majesty's Revenue and Customs (HMRC).
- Decision making can be straightforward if there are only a small number of partners.
- A partnership allows people with complementary skills to work together.

The disadvantages are:

- Any finance to be raised is based on the strength of the partners (ie if they have had a poor credit history in the past this will have an impact).
- Working hours – partners will work long hours and often tasks such as preparing invoices, chasing outstanding monies and organizing the monthly management accounts are carried out in the evenings or at weekends.
- Personal assets (house/car) are at risk if the business fails.

Limited companies

The major difference between limited companies and either sole traders or partnerships is that limited companies are a legal entity which is completely separate to their shareholders and directors. There are a number of significant legal precedents and pieces of legislation which impact on limited companies and particularly the relationship between limited companies and banks. These will be discussed below.

REGULATION
The Companies Act [2006]

This is the key legislation in England and Wales covering all matters relating to limited companies. Any further updates will be published on www.legislation.gov.uk and learners are encouraged to keep up to date with current legislation.

Formation of a limited company – private limited companies

Companies in England & Wales are formed at **Companies House,** which is a simple process. There has to be at least one director and at least one shareholder. Other key information needed is the name of the company (existing names cannot be used or brand names infringed), and the address of the registered office.

When companies are formed they receive a **Certificate of Incorporation** (a little like a corporate 'birth certificate') which shows the date the company was formed and its company number. They also have another key document called the Memorandum and Articles of Association which sets out the 'rules' by which the company will be run. In the past, banks were particularly concerned about the defined activities of companies (ie exactly what they did) within the Memorandum and Articles of Association. This was because if a bank lent funds for an activity which wasn't defined they could potentially struggle to enforce the borrowing in the future. These companies are known as **private limited companies.**

Companies House The government body in England and Wales that maintains a central register of all information pertaining to limited companies.

Certificate of Incorporation A document issued by Companies House, which shows when a limited company began and is the proof of the company's existence.

Private limited company A legal entity, owned by a shareholder or shareholders. The liability of the shareholders is limited to the amount of the share capital. It has the same rights as a person and can enter into contracts as a person would. They must have at least one director and one shareholder.

The limited company as a separate legal entity

Salomon v A Salomon and Co Ltd [1897] established this important legal principle. It stated that once a limited company is formed it has the same rights as a person. It is a legal entity in its own right and can contract in the same way as a person. It is completely separate to the directors and shareholders (which in private limited companies are often the same individuals).

This is an important principle for banks, because any assets that the business has are deemed to be owned by the limited company rather than the directors (this is important when the bank is taking security to protect its borrowing, which we will discuss further in Chapter 6). It is also an important principle for directors and shareholders as their personal assets (particularly houses) are not part of the assets of the business and cannot be called upon if the limited company gets into financial difficulties in the future.

In the *Hat Enterprises Ltd* case study below, an example is given of the type of customer that a commercial banker will deal with and shows the split between corporate and personal liabilities and the importance for the banker in understanding this distinction.

CASE STUDY
Hat Enterprises Ltd

Hat Enterprises Ltd, a family business set up by Bonny and her husband Max, imports millinery materials from all over the world. It was established 10 years ago and has a significant need for increased warehousing space. The directors are looking to buy new premises, in the company name, outside of Peterborough for £3 million. They have cash of £750,000 that has been built up as a cash purchase and want to borrow the balance from their bank. A new loan of £2.25 million in the name of the limited company will only be the legal liability of the company and the directors will have no personal liability for the loan.

The advantages of limited companies are:

- The directors and shareholders are able to keep their personal assets separate from the business.
- The liabilities of shareholders are limited to their share capital (which is often a nominal amount).

- Directors can change (retire, resign etc) and this does not affect the existence of the limited company.

- In the same way, the death of a director does not impact on the existence of the limited company.

- It is possible to use assets that the business has such as trade receivables (debtors) and inventory (stock) to raise finance for the business.

The disadvantages are:

- Financial statements must be filed at Companies House on an annual basis and the directors can be fined if they aren't.

- These financial statements are available to the public (and to competitors).

Public limited companies

Public limited companies (PLCs) are companies that must have share capital with a nominal value of no less than £50,000, and the shares can be purchased by the general public. PLCs are often quoted on the stock exchange (although they don't have to be). It is highly likely that at a commercial level any business dealt with will be quoted on the Alternative Investment Market (AIM), which is part of the London Stock Exchange: 'As companies grow, the initial external capital usually provided by friends and family, and angel investors, is often not sufficient to sustain their capital requirements; yet these companies are not necessarily ready for a traditional listing.' (www.londonstockexchange.com, 2017).

Limited liability partnerships (LLPs)

Banks will usually deal with this type of business where they have professional firms that bank with them, such as solicitors and accountants. **Limited liability partnerships** (LLPs) have similar characteristics to private limited companies.

Limited liability partnership (LLP)   Introduced in April 2001 (via the *Limited Liability Partnerships Act [2000]*) they are a hybrid of private limited companies and partnerships. They have members rather than shareholders and directors. The personal liability of members is limited.

ACTIVITY 1.1
Bank segmentation criteria

All of the banks in the UK who lend to commercial customers have different segmentation criteria. Research how your own bank segments different types of commercial customer. Compare this to one of your competitors.

The banker/customer relationship

Bankers often know how to carry out tasks for their customers and how to protect the position of the bank. What bankers often lack is the knowledge that explains why they need to carry out certain duties and why they have certain rights.

Rights and duties

Banks and their customers need to build their relationships on mutual trust if they are ever to be truly effective. Customers have the right to demand certain things from their bank (such as secrecy about their financial affairs) and banks also have the right to demand certain things from their customers. Many of the rights and duties on both sides have been established by legal precedent.

When does a customer become a customer?

According to the *Bills of Exchange Act [1882]* (www.legislation.gov.uk, 2017), a customer actually becomes a customer when either the account is opened in the customer's name, or when the bank receives an instruction to open the account with a deposit which is credited to the new account.

The duty of reasonable care

The Supply of Goods and Services Act [1982] (www.legislation.gov. uk, 2017), states that one of the primary duties of a bank is to use 'reasonable' care when providing banking services. The bank in this instance is classified as a supplier and Section 13 states 'there is an implied term that the supplier will carry out the service with reasonable care and skill'.

The phrase 'reasonable' is used a number of times with cases related to banking, although no definition is offered. The Concise Oxford English Dictionary defines reasonable as 'moderate, tolerable and sensible' (Stevenson and Waite, 2011).

The duty of secrecy

The other primary duty of a banker is to maintain confidentiality of their customers' affairs at all times. This duty remains in place even when the customer has closed their accounts. There are often exceptions to any principle and a key legal case which impacts on this duty is *Tournier v National Provincial and Union Bank of England [1924]*:

> It is an implied term of the contract between a banker and his customer
> that the banker will not divulge to third persons, without the consent of the
> customer express or implied, either the state of the customer's account, or any
> of his transactions with the bank, or any information relating to the customer
> acquired through the keeping of his account, unless the banker is compelled
> to do so by order of a Court, or the circumstances give rise to a public duty of
> disclosure, or the protection of the banker's own interests requires it.

The key exceptions to the duty of secrecy are therefore:

- an express consent given by the customer;
- court order;
- public duty; and
- the bank's interest.

We will now go on to explore what may impact on the above exceptions.

An express consent given by the customer

The most obvious and regular request that the banker receives is to provide information to the customer's accountant on an annual basis. This will be so that the accountant can prepare audited accounts for the last year (which in the case of a limited company is a requirement from Companies House). The customer will sign some form of audit letter request, which is an explicit request for information to be provided, such as balances held at the audit date, security held and any other information that is considered pertinent to the audit.

Court order

A court order may arise for a number of reasons; however, with the increasing focus on crime (especially money laundering) and terrorism by governments nationally and globally, banks may be compelled to comply with requests under specific legislation. This is likely to include legislation such as the *Anti-terrorism, Crime and Security Act [2001]*, the *Proceeds of Crime Act [2002]* and *Money Laundering Regulations [2007]* (www.legislation.gov.uk 2017). Banks must provide information if they are asked for it, and in practice, they will need to be given a reasonable time to comply with the request. Banks are likely to refer any such request to their own legal department to ensure the veracity of the request.

Public duty

One of the specific times this may impact on banks is in a time of war, where citizens of other countries, who had been legitimately carrying out business transactions before the war, when war is declared become known as 'enemy aliens' and the banks may have to disclose information to the government (ie that would be a UK bank having to provide information to the Bank of England or one of their agent organizations).

The bank's interest

The most common example of this would be where the bank is being taken to court by one of its customers and needs to be able to give information about its dealings with the customer in order to defend itself. This highlights the risk that banks must ensure that the information they hold on their customers is factually accurate and any personal opinions bank staff may have about their customers is kept to a minimum.

Other duties of the banker

The bank mandate

The bank mandate is a standard bank document used to detail the relationship between the bank and the customer. It usually sets out the signing arrangements for the sole trader, the partners or the directors, in the case of a limited company (depending on the type of entity). For a limited company or a partnership, it may specify how many partners or directors need to sign banking instruments such as cheques, payment transfers or Bills of Exchange (usually used in international trade transactions). The bank must comply with the mandate otherwise it will be in breach of contract.

ACTIVITY 1.2
Customer mandates

Look at the standard bank mandates that your own bank uses, compare and contrast the differences between sole trader, partnership and limited company mandates.

Joachimson v Swiss Bank Corporation case

A key case in banking law is *N Joachimson v Swiss Bank Corporation [1919]* (*Joachimson*), which established a number of key principles that bankers need to adhere to:

- repayment on demand of monies deposited by the customer;
- reasonable notice to close an account;
- the duty to collect funds;
- the duty to make payments;
- the duty to provide regular statements;
- the right to charge for services provided; and
- the right to 'stop' a current account.

We will now consider each of these in turn.

Repayment on demand of monies deposited by the customer

The bank must repay any monies that the customer has deposited if the customer demands this. This will often be in writing; however, with an increasing use of electronic means, this could be via electronic banking or even the use of some form of debit card.

Reasonable notice to close an account

Reasonable notice needs to be given by the bank if it wants a customer to close their account. For personal customers, a month's notice should be reasonable, particularly with the introduction of the Current Account Switch service, which was originally launched in 2013, and encouraged a smoother process for customers wanting to move their accounts (www.currentaccountswitch.co.uk, 2017).

For business customers, particularly larger corporate customers, one month is likely to be considered unreasonable, bearing in mind the likely complexity of their affairs and three months is more likely to be stipulated by the bank (and considered to be reasonable). This would be particularly true if the customer has a number of lending facilities and services it takes from the bank.

The duty to collect funds

According to the *Joachimson* case, the bank has an obligation to 'receive money and collect bills'. Increasingly, many business customers receive monies electronically, and even if they are in the retail sector, with the decline in the use of cash and cheques for purchases, many customers are using debit and credit cards which ensures funds are credited to the customer's account electronically. As mentioned above, bills refers to bills of exchange, which were a very common form of payment method historically but tend to be confined now to international trade transactions.

The duty to make payments

If a fundamental duty is to collect funds for a customer, it is logical that a duty on the other side of the coin is to make payments for a customer (if they conform to the mandate held by the bank as discussed above). This duty was established in *Barclays Bank plc v W J Simms & Cooke (Southern) Ltd [1980]*. The proviso to this principle is that the customer must have sufficient 'cleared' funds or have an overdraft facility with sufficient room in it to make the payment.

The principle of cleared funds is an important one for banks, and we'll return to the example above of Hat Enterprises Ltd (HE) to illustrate this point. When a customer (in this instance it is HE) pays funds into their account, it depends on what the payment is as to how long it is before the bank allows HE to 'draw' on these funds. Cash can be accessed immediately; however, in this instance, as HE is paying in a cheque then this needs to be processed through the clearing system (a central system used by all banks in the UK to settle cheques between them) which takes up to five working days to ensure that the cheque has cleared. In the time between the cheque being credited to HE's account and it being fully cleared, if the bank allows HE to use the funds, and the cheque is not paid, HE's bank will need to reverse the original transaction by debiting the amount of the cheque to HE's account. Depending on the amount of the cheque this could cause an unauthorized overdraft on HE's current account that the bank may not have normally granted.

The duty to provide regular statements

The bank must provide regular statements to their customer, and this will usually be a minimum of once a year. As banks move increasingly to providing information electronically, they will often ask their customers whether they want their statements in a paper format or online via an electronic banking system. Banks will usually keep information on their customers for a maximum of seven years.

THE IMPACT OF ELECTRONIC BANKING

The majority of commercial customers are likely to use electronic banking products, particularly when they need to make payments. They will be able to access banking services via a desktop computer, a laptop, tablet and phone. Often there will be an 'app' that is downloaded with various security features built-in. This allows customers to search transactions and to be able to download transactions into accounting software packages such as Sage, Xero and QuickBooks. Whilst the bank may not physically post out a paper statement, customers can of course print out paper statements themselves, and this may be required by their accountants when preparing annual accounts.

The right to charge for services provided

This is recognized under *Joachimson* and must be commensurate with the service provided. Where a business customer has more complex and sophisticated needs, especially in a retail business that deals with high levels of cash, then the bank will be entitled to charge a higher level of fees due to the services provided.

The right to 'stop' a current account

A case from over 200 years ago still has an impact on banks today. *Devaynes v Noble [1816]*, often referred to as *Clayton's Case*, impacts on bankers where there is a current account in operation, and in this particular case it was a partnership that had the bank account.

REGULATION
Clayton's Case [1816]

The actual legal case is *Devaynes and Noble [1816]* but is often referred to as *Clayton's Case*. It requires banks to stop current accounts on partnership or sole traders to ensure the bank doesn't incur further liability and is able to protect any outstanding lending position.

It requires some form of 'trigger event' such as bankruptcy or death in order for the bank to have to take action.

As mentioned in the Regulation Feature above, there then needs to be a 'trigger' event such as a partner becoming bankrupt, wishing to leave the partnership, retiring or dying. The key principle that was established and discussed above under the Partnership section was for 'joint and several' liability but this is only applicable if the partners are all in the partnership. Once the trigger event occurs, and using the *Cutting Edge Barbershop* as an example, if one of the partners dies and there is an overdrawn position, once the bank is informed of the death, then the bank should 'stop' the account and not allow any more credits or debits into or out of the account.

This needs to happen because the bank may want to call on the estate of the deceased partner for the repayment of the outstanding balance. The 'first in-first out principle' was a legal principle established in *Clayton's Case*. This means that at the date of being advised of the death, from that point onwards, any new credits into the bank account will reduce the outstanding debit balance on the partnership current account, until they have extinguished the original debt. Any further debits will create what is effectively new debt. Whilst on the face of it, the position is the same from the remaining partner's point of view and the bank is no worse off, because the original debt has been in effect repaid, the bank will not be able to claim on the deceased partner's estate. This is because the court ruling from *Clayton's Case* was very specific and said that the original debt must be preserved until the position with an estate can be dealt with.

On the face of it, this may seem like a bank is being very unhelpful, especially at a very difficult time for the surviving partner; however, the bank will do all it can to make the period following the death as easy as possible for the partner that remains. A new bank account will be opened, and this can be used to deal with new credits. Any debits (particularly cheques) that are in the clearing system will need to be reconfirmed by the surviving

Table 1.1 Cutting Edge Barbershop January accounts

Date		Credits	Debits	Balance	Limit
Date	10 January			−5000	10,000
	11 January	2000	3000	−6000	
	12 January	1500		−4500	
	13 January	1000		−3500	
	14 January	1500		−2000	
	17 January	1500		−500	
	18 January	1000		500	
	19 January		2000	−1500	
	20 January		1000	−2500	
	21 January		2000	−4500	
	22 January		1000	−5500	

partner as the old mandate will no longer be valid and they can then be debited to the new account.

Table 1.1 shows the position of the Cutting Edge Barbershop business in January. The bank is informed of the death of one of the partners on 11 January, and at that point, it should stop the current account. In this instance it does not and subsequent credits reduce the initial overdrawn position until it is completely repaid. The further debits create new debt.

The bank will need to review the financial position of the business and of the surviving partner and will need to ensure that the business can continue (they will need to review the roles that each partner carried out) and that any outstanding lending facilities can be repaid.

The right of 'set-off' – combining accounts

Most customers will operate a number of bank accounts with the same bank, that at any one time will be in credit or debit. A business customer may have a current account with an overdraft facility, a deposit account (tax bill saving) and a loan account. A business that operates on more than one site (perhaps where it has five depots) may have different current accounts for the different depots and they may have a 'group' overdraft facility which combines all the debit and credit balances into a 'net' group position.

The bank has the right, if it wishes, to combine all the accounts for a customer into a net position, so that the bank is not in a disadvantageous position. The case of *Garnett and McKewan [1872]* set out the principle that banks have not only the right to combine accounts, but they do not have a legal obligation to tell their customer.

For the bank to be able to combine accounts, the bank accounts must be in the same name and the same 'right'. It would not be possible, for example, to combine limited company accounts with partnership accounts, and even if the directors of the limited company and the partnership are the same individuals, because the limited company is a separate legal entity, they are not the same 'right'.

The bank is only likely to take the steps of combining accounts if it is concerned about the customer's position. If, for example, a customer had a large unauthorized overdraft or was exceeding an overdraft, had funds in another account (perhaps a deposit account) and was not correcting the position after being asked to do so by the bank, the bank could move funds from the deposit account to correct the position.

The right to combine accounts is often used by banks where there is an insolvency situation.

Duties of the customer to the bank

We have now discussed in detail the duties that banks have to their customers, and it is also important to investigate the duties that customers have to the bank. The *Joachimson* case, discussed earlier, not only has implications for the bank to its customers but also impacts on the certain duties customers have to the bank; we will now go on to consider each of these in turn.

Pay reasonable charges for services provided by the bank

The word 'reasonable' is used again here and this will very much depend on what the service is that is being provided. Banks have come under increasing pressure in recent years to not charge unreasonable fees when customers go overdrawn and the customer is unaware of this.

Repay on demand sums due on an overdrawn current account

Banks can demand that customers repay overdrawn balances on current accounts. There are various circumstances under which this may occur; for example, it may be because the relationship has broken down or because the customer is in financial difficulties. Making a demand on the customer is a precursor for taking action to recover monies lent.

Customers may often have to refinance in order to comply with such a demand, and the bank would need to give the appropriate time period depending on the type of customer. For a business customer this may be three months. If a loan agreement is in place, and the customer is acting in accordance with the terms and conditions of this agreement, then the bank cannot demand repayment of the loan.

Duty to inform the bank of any fraudulent activity

Further to the two important principles above, customers have a duty to inform their bank if they are aware of any fraudulent activity on their account. This is particularly important where the customer has prior knowledge of another party forging their signature on cheques (this may be a wife or a husband) and allows the cheques to be presented as if the customer themselves had signed the cheque. They cannot then take subsequent action against the bank to recover monies that have been paid out as the bank will argue that the customer themselves was aware of the fraudulent activity and had a duty to inform the bank of this. This principle was established in *Greenwood v Martins Bank Ltd [1933]*.

Duty not to facilitate fraud

Customers also have a duty to ensure that by their own actions they do not assist fraudsters. Much of the case law is based on drawing cheques and bills of exchange in such a way as to allow fraud to take place. In the case of *London Joint Stock Bank v Macmillan [1918]*, a member of staff significantly increased the amount on a petty cash cheque signed by the customer. The cheque was completed in such a way that the member of staff could change the amount of the cheque. The payee (ie the beneficiary of the cheque) was also left blank, which enabled the dishonest member of staff to make the cheque payable to themselves. It was held that the customer had facilitated this fraud by their actions and could not subsequently claim the monies back from the bank.

Legislation

Banks, by their very commercial nature, tend to have a much stronger position in contractual relationships than their customers and legislation has evolved to reflect this. The disparity in this relationship is also recognized by the courts.

The *Consumer Rights Act [2015]* (CRA) came into force in March 2015. Before this legislation, unfair contract terms were covered by the *Unfair Contract Terms Act [1977]* (UCTA) and the *Unfair Contract Terms in*

Consumer Contract Regulations [1999] (UCTCCR). The CRA has had an impact on both pieces of legislation by replacing completely UCTCCR and amending UCTA, so that it (UCTA) in the future only relates to business-to-business contracts. It is useful to consider briefly both earlier acts.

REGULATION

Consumer Rights Act [2015] (see www.legislation.gov.uk/ukpga/2015/15/enacted for current updates)

This is legislation which has an impact on contracts between banks and customers. In the context of commercial lending, it will have an impact on relationships with smaller customers. It defines what an 'unfair' contract term can be:

- Services are to be performed with reasonable care and skill (Section 49).
- A reasonable price is to be paid for the service (Section 51).

Principles may also be applied to larger businesses to ensure that business customers are being treated consistently and to ensure that previous case law is also being respected.

The Unfair Contract Terms Act [1977]

The provision of bank services is considered to be captured under this legislation and the UCTA stipulates that terms within a contract must be 'fair and reasonable'. The reasonableness test, under Section 11 of the Act states: 'the term shall have been a fair and reasonable one to be included having regard to the circumstances which were, or ought reasonably to have been, known to or in the contemplation of the parties when the contract was made' (www.legislation.gov.uk, 2017).

Unfair Contract Terms in Consumer Contract Regulations [1999]

This act replaced the *Unfair Terms in Consumer Contracts Regulations 1994* and has similar aims to the UCTA. Its primary aim is to restrict the use of terms in contracts which puts the customer (consumer) at a disadvantage, particularly where the customer has not been involved in the negotiation of the terms (www.legislation.gov.uk, 2017).

CRA sets out a number of principles regarding the provision of services (and banking services will fall under this definition) and these complement the duties set out in case law (discussed earlier):

- Services are to be performed with reasonable care and skill (Section 49).
- A reasonable price is to be paid for the service (Section 51).

Unfair terms in a contract

The definition in the CRA for unfair terms in a contract [Section 62(4)] is: 'A term is unfair if, contrary to the requirement of good faith, it causes a significant imbalance in the parties' rights and obligations under the contract to the detriment of the consumer.'

The challenge for banks is defining what a consumer is: '"Consumer" means an individual acting for purposes that are wholly or mainly outside that individual's trade, business, craft or profession' [Section 2(3)]. The impact of this, according to this new legislation, is that it will only include small businesses such as sole traders, small partnerships or micro-enterprises under £1 million turnover.

However, it is very likely that the principles may also be applied to larger businesses to ensure that business customers are being treated consistently and to ensure that previous case law is also being respected.

Financial Conduct Authority

The Financial Conduct Authority (FCA), as we have touched on earlier, plays a significant role in how banks treat their customers. Whilst much of the FCA's focus is on consumers the point made above about applying these principles to larger businesses is relevant: 'We have powers to challenge unfair terms in financial services consumer contracts' (FCA, 2017).

The continuing theme in this chapter is that banks must treat customers fairly. The FCA has six key consumer outcomes:

- Outcome 1: Consumers can be confident they are dealing with firms where the fair treatment of customers is central to the corporate culture.
- Outcome 2: Products and services marketed and sold in the retail market are designed to meet the needs of identified consumer groups and are targeted accordingly.
- Outcome 3: Consumers are provided with clear information and are kept appropriately informed before, during and after the point of sale.
- Outcome 4: Where consumers receive advice, the advice is suitable and takes account of their circumstances.

- Outcome 5: Consumers are provided with products that perform as firms have led them to expect, and the associated service is of an acceptable standard and as they have been led to expect.

- Outcome 6: Consumers do not face unreasonable post-sale barriers imposed by firms to change product, switch provider, submit a claim or make a complaint. (FCA, 2017)

Onerous clauses

In the case of *Tai Hing Cotton Mill Ltd v Lui Chong Hing Bank Ltd [1985]*, three banks in Hong Kong imposed onerous clauses on their customer, and attempted to enforce a clause on Tai Hing Cotton Mill that it must tell the bank within seven days of any items on its statements that were considered to be fraudulent. The courts ruled that this was an unreasonable clause and was too onerous on the customer.

Specific clauses in loan documents will be explored later in the book; however, for business customers it is worth reflecting on a simple example of what might constitute an unfair contract term.

Unfair contract terms in loan agreements

Returning to Hat Enterprises Ltd again, if the bank lent the money to develop the business, one of the conditions the bank is very likely to impose is for the provision of regular financial management information showing how the business is performing against budgets and forecasts. It would be considered unreasonable to ask the directors to produce information within one week of the month end; however, asking for information within a month of the month end should be considered reasonable (ie management information for, say, the end of June would be expected at the end of July).

CASE STUDY
The impact of treating customers unfairly

Banks sell a variety of products to their customers and following the financial crisis, there was an examination of interest rate hedging products (IRHPs). These products were designed to protect customers in the event of interest rates increasing; however, when the Bank of England lowered interest rates (base rate) to a historical low of 0.5 per cent following the financial crisis, many customers were left paying high interest rates linked to the IRHPs, which meant they did not benefit from the lower interest rates. There was also significant cost for 'breaking' (in other words cancelling) the IRHP contract, which customers, in many cases, were not informed of.

When the review began there was an attempt by the banks to categorize customers into 'non-sophisticated' and 'sophisticated' businesses. If a business was categorized as sophisticated, then there was much more of an onus on the customer to prove that they weren't aware of the implications of the product (particularly the downside risk if bank base rates were lowered).

The Financial Conduct Authority (FCA) and the successor to Financial Services Authority have been concerned about businesses being treated unfairly by their banks. The British Bankers Association (replaced from 1 July 2017 by UK Finance) said in 2013, 'where customers have been treated unfairly, they will be compensated' (BBC News, 2017).

Questions

1 Using the FCA website (www.fca.org.uk), review the current position about interest rate hedging products.

2 How many banks have been impacted and is your bank included in the review?

3 What is the amount that has been paid out to customers in redress?

4 How does your bank protect customers against interest rate rises?

5 Research what products it currently uses.

6 See the end of the chapter for commentary regarding 1) and 2).

Chapter summary

In this chapter we have explored:

- the criteria the government uses to define different sizes of business;
- the key differences between the legal business entities of sole traders, partnerships and limited companies and their relative advantages and disadvantages;

- the rights and duties of commercial banks to their customers;
- the duties commercial customers have to their banks; and
- the principle of unfair contract terms in agreements between banks and commercial customers.

Objective check

1 Define an SME and explain how it differs from a mid-sized business and a micro-enterprise.

2 What is the difference between the personal liability the owner of a Sole-Trader or a Partnership has compared to the director of a Limited Company related to the bank borrowing of each entity?

3 What do you feel are the advantages and disadvantages of Sole-Traders, Partnerships and Limited Companies?

4 What do you consider to be the three main duties and three main rights that banks have in relation to commercial customers?

5 What do you consider to be the three main duties commercial customers have to their banks?

6 How do legislation and the FCA protect the customer?

7 Explain the principle of unfair contract terms.

Further reading

Financial Conduct Authority: https://www.fca.org.uk/
Financial Conduct Authority – Banking Conduct of Business Sourcebook: https://www.handbook.fca.org.uk/handbook/BCOBS.pdf
UK Finance: https://www.ukfinance.org.uk

References

AIM – London Stock Exchange [accessed 12 June 2018] [Online] http://www.londonstockexchange.com/companies-and-advisors/aim/aim/aim.htm
Anti-terrorism, Crime and Security Act 2001 [accessed 12 June 2018] [Online] http://www.legislation.gov.uk/ukpga/2001/24/contents
Barclayscorporate.com [accessed 12 June 2018] [Online] https://www.barclayscorporate.com/
BBC News [accessed 12 June 2018] Banks to pay for 'swap' mis-selling, FSA demands [Online]http://www.bbc.co.uk/news/business-21272606

Bills of Exchange Act 1882 [accessed 12 June 2018] [Online] http://www.
legislation.gov.uk/ukpga/Vict/45-46/61

Business population estimates 2016 [accessed 12 June 2018] [Online] https://www.
gov.uk/government/statistics/business-population-estimates-2016

Companies Act 2006 [accessed 12 June 2018] [Online] http://www.legislation.gov.
uk/ukpga/2006/46/section/382

Currentaccountswitch.co.uk [accessed 12 June 2018] The Current Account Switch
Service – your guarantee to a successful switch [Online] https://www.
currentaccountswitch.co.uk/Pages/Home.aspx

FCA – Fair treatment of customers [Accessed 12 June 2018] [Online] https://www.
fca.org.uk/firms/fair-treatment-customers

Micro-enterprise – FCA Handbook [accessed 12 June 2018] [Online] https://www.
handbook.fca.org.uk/handbook/glossary/G2623.html

Mid-sized businesses [accessed 12 June 2018] [Online] https://www.gov.uk/
government/collections/mid-sized-businesses

Money Laundering Regulations 2007 [accessed 12 June 2018] [Online] Available
at: http://www.legislation.gov.uk/uksi/2007/2157/contents/made

Partnership Act 1890 [accessed 12 June 2018] [Online] http://www.legislation.gov.
uk/ukpga/Vict/53-54/39/section/1

Proceeds of Crime Act 2002 [accessed 12 June 2018] [Online] http://www.
legislation.gov.uk/ukpga/2002/29/contents

Stevenson, A and Waite, M (2011) *Concise Oxford English Dictionary*, Oxford
University Press, Oxford

Supply of Goods and Services Act 1982 [accessed 12 June 2018] [Online] http://
www.legislation.gov.uk/ukpga/1982/29

Unfair Terms in Consumer Contracts Regulations 1999 [accessed 12 June 2018]
[Online] http://www.legislation.gov.uk/uksi/1999/2083/contents/made

Legal case references

Barclays Bank plc v WJ Simms & Cooke (Southern) Ltd [1980] 1 QB 677

Devaynes v Noble (Clayton's Case) [1816] 1 Mer 572

Garnett v McKewan [1872] LR 8 Exch 10

Greenwood v Martins Bank Ltd [1933] AC 51

London Joint Stock Bank v Macmillan & Arthur [1918] AC 777 242, 296–298,
325, 487

N Joachimson (A Firm) v Swiss Bank Corporation [1919] J 707, 1289

Salomon v A Salomon & Co Ltd [1897] AC 22, HL 94, 652

Tai Hing Cotton Mill Ltd v Lui Chong Hing Bank Ltd [1985] 2 All ER 947

Tournier v National Provincial and Union Bank of England [1924] 1 KB 461

Suggested answers for activities

Activity 1.1 – Bank segmentation criteria

RBS segment their customers, for example, as commercial (£2 million–£25 million turnover) and mid-corporate (£25 million +).

Learners should devise their own answer for Activity 1.2. No model answer is supplied.

Suggested answers for case study questions

Case study – The impact of treating customers unfairly

1) The nine UK banks included in the review were:

- Allied Irish Bank (UK);
- Bank of Ireland;
- Barclays;
- Clydesdale & Yorkshire Banks;
- Co-operative Bank;
- HSBC;
- Lloyds Banking Group;
- Royal Bank of Scotland; and
- Santander UK.

2) At the time of writing in excess of £2.2 billion has been paid out by all of these banks to 13,900 customers.

02

The financial analysis of businesses

INTRODUCTION

Financial information produced by a business is fundamental to the management of that business. It is primarily used by the owners of the business to ensure their business is making money, has sufficient cash and is performing against targets. Banks who lend to businesses will expect to receive financial information on a regular basis and will use this information to check the financial 'health' of the business.

LEARNING OBJECTIVES

By the end of this chapter, you will be able to:

- apply key financial ratios to analyse the performance of a commercial business;
- explain the significance of financial ratio analysis and identify the main categories: liquidity, profitability and financial strength;
- explain the key differences between annual accounts, management information and projections and when they would be used by a bank;

- assess the performance of a business by identifying year-on-year trends in financial information;
- define the accounting standard FRS 102 and explain the revised accounting terminology; and
- differentiate between financial and non-financial information.

Learner introduction to accounting

A number of you reading this book are likely to be tackling this subject for the first time with no prior experience of either business studies or accounting. Some of you may be studying this subject following a career change or having worked in financial services for a number of years and decided to gain further qualifications. It is not necessary to be an accountant in order to study this part of the book nor is it necessary to have prior experience of any formal business studies. The material covered in this chapter has been written in a logical and common-sense manner and whilst you are required to learn the key concepts and be able to apply them no previous knowledge is presumed.

The origins of accounting

Accounting and bookkeeping originated thousands of years ago and coincided with when man first began to trade. A key development was the introduction of a technique called 'double-entry bookkeeping' by the Venetians in the fifteenth century.

You will be relieved to know that it is not necessary to learn the techniques of double-entry bookkeeping, simply to understand the principles that it is based on as these inform modern-day accounting practices.

Accountancy became significantly more important to businesses (and their bankers) associated with the increase in industrialization across the UK and Europe in the eighteenth and nineteenth centuries. As a profession, it was formally recognized in Scotland in 1854 by a Royal Charter with the formation of the Society of Accountants in Edinburgh (Lee, 2002) and the Institute of Chartered Accountants in England and Wales was similarly recognized by Royal Charter in 1880.

The rationale for the analysis of financial information

There is often a misconception from the owners of SME businesses that it is only banks that either want or need financial information. Without it of course, it is very difficult, if not impossible, for banks to decide whether or not they should lend money to their customers. However, the owners of businesses need to be able to manage their businesses effectively and regular, accurate financial information will enable them to do just this. This is particularly true of management information (to be explored later in this chapter), which allows businesses on a monthly and quarterly basis to monitor financial performance including – most vitally – their cash position.

The techniques now available enable businesses to produce financial records on a regular basis, that are cumulative (ie profits and losses can be passed on to the next accounting period) and allow comparison with different accounting periods.

Annual accounts, management information and projections

In order to have consistency when preparing sets of accounts, accountants have accounting standards which allow for the treatment of certain accounting items in a similar way. It is not necessary to have a detailed knowledge of accounting standards to cover this part of the book; however, there is one standard you need to be familiar with that does impact on the way businesses report their financial information; this is **Financial Reporting Standard 102 (FRS 102)**. This accounting standard replaces a number of previous standards and comes into effect from any new accounting period that starts after 1 January 2016. For example, a business with a year end on 31 July 2016 will adopt FRS 102 from 1 August 2016.

> **Financial Reporting Standard 102 (FRS 102)**   An accounting standard that affects businesses that have accounting periods commencing after 1 January 2016. It replaces a number of other accounting standards. It introduces new accounting terminology.

There are some exemptions for businesses that are classified as 'small', defined as:

- employees – 50 or less;
- turnover – £6.5 million (or less); and
- balance sheet – £3.26 million (or less).

One of the key changes that companies need to be aware of is the change in accounting terminology, and much of this is a change from the language used in the various Companies Acts. Table 2.1, whilst not a definitive list, identifies the key changes that you need to be aware of.

Some of the new terminology is more logical and explains more clearly the nature of an asset or a liability. For example, trade creditors are monies that a business owes for goods it has bought but hasn't paid for yet. A supermarket will buy goods from its suppliers to sell in its stores and will not pay for them for, say, 30–45 days. The FRS 102 replaces this with trade payables, which seems to be more logical.

In a similar way, debtors are goods or services that have been sold by a business on credit terms and the business selling them hasn't received the

Table 2.1 Accounting terminology defined by FRS 102

Original terminology	New FRS 102 terminology
Accounts	Financial statements
Balance sheet	Statement of financial position
Capital and reserves	Equity
Cash at bank and in hand	Cash
Debtors	Trade receivables
Financial year	Reporting period
Interest payable and similar charges	Finance costs
Interest receivable and similar income	Finance income/investment income
Profit and loss accounts	Income statement (under the two-statement approach)
Stocks	Part of the statement of comprehensive income
Tangible assets	Inventories. Includes: property, plant, equipment, investment property
Trade creditors	Trade payables

SOURCE © Financial Reporting Council Ltd (FRC). Adapted and reproduced with the kind permission of the Financial Reporting Council. All rights reserved. For further information, please visit www.frc.org.uk or call +44 (0)20 7492 2300.

monies yet. Again, with the new terminology, trade receivables, rather than debtors or trade debtors, seems to make more sense.

The components of annual accounts

Financial accounts produced by businesses are usually produced on an annual basis (there is a legal requirement for limited companies to produce annual accounts – see below) and provide:

- information on the profits or losses in a particular accounting period;
- information on the assets and liabilities that the business has; and
- details of the share capital and retained profits in the business.

Statement of comprehensive income (SOCI)

Table 2.2 shows an example of a **statement of comprehensive income** (profit and loss account) for a business (The Luxury Goods Company). It doesn't matter what sector a business operates in (eg Retail, Transport, Professional Services), the principles behind producing financial accounts are that they are stated in a consistent manner, regardless of the type of business. All of the items shown in this statement are used to indicate how much money a business has made (or lost) in the period in question, which in this example is 12 months.

Statement of comprehensive income – detailed explanation of each item

This is a retail operation, selling luxury retail goods:

1 **Turnover** – this is the sales for the business in this period.

2 **Cost of sales** – this is costs that the business has incurred in order to generate the turnover. These include the variable costs incurred such as purchase of **inventory**, wages and other costs.

3 **Gross profit** – this is the profit the business has made after the deduction of variable costs.

4 **Distribution costs** – costs incurred to distribute the company's goods within a network.

5 **Administrative expenses** – these are costs incurred and will include head office costs which are fixed.

6 **Other operating income** – this is any other income the business may have.

Table 2.2 The Luxury Goods Company (SOCI)

Statement of comprehensive income	year ended 20XX £k	Notes
Profit and loss account		
1) Turnover	9735	
2) Cost of sales	–4579	This is deducted from turnover to produce gross profit
3) **Gross profit**	**5156**	
4) Distribution costs	–4306	
5) Administrative expenses	–904	
6) Other operating income	115	
7) **Operating profit**	**61**	
8) Interest payable and similar charges	–11	
9) **Profit on ordinary activities before taxation**	**50**	
10) Tax on profit on ordinary activities	–15	
11) **Profit for the period/year**	**35**	

7 **Operating profit** – this is the profit the business has made after the deduction of all of its costs but before the deduction of **finance costs** and taxation.

8 Interest payable and similar charges – this relates to borrowings that the business has and is the costs that are incurred in that period.

9 **Profit on ordinary activities before taxation** – profit before taxation is paid.

10 **Tax on profit on ordinary activities** – the tax payable for that period.

11 **Profit for the period/year** – The final profit after all costs have been deducted.

Statement of financial position (SOFP)

Table 2.3 shows a breakdown of items in a **statement of financial position**.

Statement of financial position – detailed explanation of each item

1 **Fixed assets** – These are assets that the business owns which are used to run the business and are divided into **intangible assets** and tangible assets.

- Intangible assets: these are usually items such as intellectual property (eg patents/software) and are called intangible because it is not possible to touch them or see them.

- Tangible assets: these are assets the business has (eg property, such as factories/offices/shops) which are used to run the business.

2 Current assets and current liabilities.

- Current* assets: these are assets that the business needs to trade on a day-to-day basis and are separated into inventories, trade receivables and **cash**. (*The definition of current – in accounting terms this means that for a liability, it is payable by the business within 12 months and for an asset it is due for payment to the business again within 12 months.)

- Inventories: this is stock that the business owns, and depending on the type of business, this will contain raw materials, work-in-progress and also finished goods. A manufacturing business, for example, is likely to have all three types of stock, whereas a supermarket chain is only likely to have finished goods (ie they do not get involved in any stages of the manufacturing process and only deal in completed goods).

Table 2.3 The Luxury Goods Company (SOFP)

Statement of financial position		year ended 20XX
1)	**Fixed assets**		
2)	Intangible assets		12,285
3)	Tangible assets		633,286
			645,571
4)	**Current assets**		
5)	Inventories	1,731,603	
6)	Trade receivables	1,920,613	
7)	Cash	115,506	
		3,767,722	
8)	Creditors: amounts falling due within one year	2,227,308	
	Net current assets		**1,540,414**
			2,185,985
	Creditors: amounts falling due after more than one year		−17,250
	Provisions for liabilities		
9)	Deferred tax	−28,353	
			−28,353
			2,140,382
10)	**Capital and reserves**		
11)	Called up share capital		143,042
12)	Profit and loss account		1,997,340
	Total equity		**2,140,382**

- Trade receivables: this is money due to the business and arises when a business sells goods or services on credit terms and is to be paid in the future. Normal credit terms may be 30 days (ie the purchaser must pay within 30 days of the invoice date).

- Cash: this is funds that the business holds in either the current account or a deposit account.

- Creditors: this is monies that the business needs to pay and the main component of current liabilities is trade payables.

- Trade payables: these arise when a business buys raw materials or other goods on credit terms from its suppliers. Normal credit terms may be 45 days (ie the materials or goods must be paid for within 45 days of the invoice date).

- Deferred tax: tax that is not paid immediately in this period.

Liabilities are deducted from assets in order to arrive at a net asset figure. This is then one part of the balance sheet.

The other side of the 'balance sheet' is a total of what the owners have invested in the business, or the **equity**.

1 Capital and reserves: this shows what capital and reserves the business has and constitutes two items:

- Called up share capital: this is the issued share capital of the business and often in SMEs can be at a relatively small level relative to the size of the business.

- Profit and loss account: this is the cumulative position of the business at the date of the accounts. It is a cumulative position because it takes the profitability position of the business from the previous accounting period and is then adjusted depending on if the business has made a profit, or suffered a loss in the current accounting period.

Administrative expenses　These are fixed costs incurred (and will include head office costs if applicable).

Cash [new FRS 102 term]　The cash a business holds (in bank accounts or in petty cash).

Cost of sales　Costs the business has incurred in order to generate turnover (these include the variable costs incurred such as purchase of inventory, wages and other costs).

Distribution costs   Costs incurred to distribute the goods of a business.

Equity [new FRS 102 term]   The value the shareholders have, usually expressed as the share capital owned.

Finance costs [new FRS 102 term]   The costs incurred by a business in a specific period.

Finance income/investment income [new FRS 102 term]   Interest paid to a business for any deposits it may have had in the period in question. Any other investment income is also recorded here.

Financial statements [new FRS 102 term]   The financial accounts for the business, usually covering a 12-month period.

Fixed assets   These are assets that the business owns, which are used to run the business and are divided into intangible assets and tangible assets.

Gross profit   The profit the business has made after the deduction of variable costs.

Intangible assets   Items such as intellectual property (eg patents/software). They are called intangible because it is not possible to touch them or see them.

Inventories [new FRS 102 term]   The raw materials, work-in-progress and finished goods that a business has to sell (but hasn't yet sold).

Net profit   The profit made after all costs have been deducted from sales income (the costs include interest, tax and dividends).

Other operating income   Any other income.

Operating profit   Profit a business has made after the deduction of all of its costs and before the deduction of finance costs and taxation.

Profit on ordinary activities before taxation   Profit before taxation is paid.

Profit for the period/year   The final profit after all costs have been deducted.

Reporting period [new FRS 102 term]   The time period covered by the financial statements.

Statement of comprehensive income   The profit or loss a business has made in a particular period. It details all of the costs incurred in that period including depreciation, amortization, interest, tax and dividends.

Statement of financial position [new FRS 102 term]   The assets and liabilities of the business, stated at a particular point in time (usually the year end).

Tax on profit on ordinary activities   The tax payable for a specific accounting period based on the profits in that period.

Turnover   Sales of a business.

The differences between annual accounts, management information and projections

Annual accounts

Annual accounts, as mentioned above, particularly for limited companies, are a statutory requirement under Companies Act legislation. They need to be submitted to Companies House by specific dates each year, otherwise the directors can be fined for non-compliance with Companies Act legislation.

Sole Traders and partnerships, as discussed in Chapter 1, do not have legislation to get them to produce accounts (and there is no legal requirement for them to be submitted to a central location such as Companies House); however, they will need to produce accounts for both tax purposes and also the bank.

Annual accounts are a permanent record of the financial performance of a business, covering a specific period of time (usually 12 months). They contain useful information about the activities of the business and information such as staff numbers and have usually been prepared by an accountant. As such, they are a useful source of information for a bank.

The main problem with annual accounts is that by the time they are produced they are relatively historic and any bank would not rely on them as the only place for financial information about any business they are lending to.

Annual accounts   The financial statements for a business covering a year. A statutory requirement under Companies Act legislation.

Management information

There is often a misconception with the owners of businesses that, when they are asked to produce monthly or quarterly reports for the bank to show how the business is performing, this information is only useful for the bank. This is simply not true and good practice for any business is that the owners understand on a regular basis how the business is performing. Many owners just focus on the day-to-day cash position and whilst this is eminently sensible, and to be encouraged it is only one part of the broader picture of how the business is performing financially.

Management information, in its simplest sense, is information produced on a regular basis (often monthly), that shows the financial position of the business in a 'mini' version of the annual accounts. It should show the profits or losses in the month and will enable businesses to see over a period if the financial ratios (discussed in depth below) are being met. It will also show the balance sheet position (the assets and liabilities of the business).

Many businesses are subject to **seasonality** (see Activity 2.1), and this can have a big impact on the monthly figures. For an established business, this helps the planning process as the business can use the previous years' experiences as a guide to how the figures are likely to be in the current year. This allows better communication with the bank and means that if profit margins are low, or that a profit is not made in a particular period due to seasonality, this can be dealt with effectively.

Management accounts usually show the performance for the period in question, with a comparison to the same time last year and also a cumulative position for the business (ie if the start of the year is 1 January and the accounts are as at 31 August, the cumulative period will be for eight months). There will also be a comparison with any projections that have been produced, to show whether these targets have been met or not and details of any variations.

Management information   Financial information produced on a regular basis by a business (often monthly or quarterly). It shows the financial position of the business in a 'mini' version of the annual accounts. It will show the profits or losses in the month (or quarter) and show the assets and liabilities of the business.

Seasonality   The impact during the year of certain events (such as Christmas for retail businesses).

ACTIVITY 2.1
Seasonality in different sectors

Consider how seasonality impacts on different types of business and think of three very different businesses:

1 A seaside hotel.

2 A retailer of luxury goods (based on Oxford Street, London).

3 A care home for elderly people.

Will seasonality impact on these very different businesses and why?
Write down your own answer and review these at the end of the chapter.

Projections

Businesses usually produce **projections** of performance over at least a 12-month period. The bank will usually need these if either new borrowing is required or if an increase in borrowing is requested.

These will comprise a projection of the profits of the business, and what the assets and liabilities will be in the future. There will also be a projection of the cash position of the business and this is particularly important to show the peaks of the cash requirements of the business. The projections will show the periods when the demands on cash are the greatest (and the level of any overdraft needed).

The bank will normally apply a level of sensitivity to the projections, and particularly where a large increase in sales is projected, the bank will apply a sensitivity which shows how the business will perform if a similar pattern of sales is achieved using the last 12 months' performance as a baseline. They will also apply a sensitivity for a rise in interest rates (at the time of writing interest rates in the UK are at a historical low).

An obvious point about projections is that the further into the future they are prepared, the greater the level of uncertainty about whether they will be achieved due to changes outside the business (the impact of external factors will be explored later in the book).

> **Projections** Management forecasts of the future financial position of a business. They will forecast profits/losses, asset/liability position and the cash position.

Key ratio analysis

The financial information provided by businesses can be analysed to ensure, from a banker's perspective, that the business is in good financial health and that key metrics are being met.

> **Key ratio analysis** The important financial ratios that are used to analyse the financial performance of a business.

Financial analysis of a business can be divided into different categories and whilst all of the ratios that can be produced are useful, they measure different elements of the business, depending on what a bank may be focusing on. They need to be viewed holistically.

A useful point when considering ratio analysis is that the calculations also need to be linked to the actual amount of money involved. We will discuss profitability margins later and a small change in, for example, gross margin may not appear on the face of it to be particularly important or significant, but for a large business the impact may be hundreds of thousands or even millions of pounds.

Financial ratios are separated into three different categories as they measure three very different but important aspects of the business:

- **Liquidity** – this is a measure of liquid funds that a business can access. Cash is vital in any business and these ratios help the bank to calculate how quickly current assets can be turned into cash to cover current liabilities.

- **Profitability** – businesses cannot survive if they do not generate sufficient profits and the ratios in this category are used to identify where profits are made and to also analyse the costs within the business.

- **Financial strength** – the bank is concerned with the financial resilience of the businesses that it lends to and the ratios in this category show the actual or potential vulnerabilities that a business has in relation to its ability to repay its bank and other borrowings.

> **Liquidity** A measure of liquid funds that a business can access to cover current liabilities.
>
> **Profitability** The measure of how much profit a business generates, being the difference between income generated and the costs incurred.
>
> **Financial strength** The financial resilience of a business. It shows the actual or potential vulnerabilities that a business has in relation to its ability to repay bank and other borrowings.

The key point of ratio analysis is that it is a dynamic process, requiring regular information and regular reassessment. Banks are often prepared to accept financial ratios that are higher than they would prefer if there are mitigants against the potential risks identified and that there is a clear plan or strategy for a particular ratio to improve (eg **gearing**). The importance of these vital elements will be explored more fully in the next part of the chapter.

The first part of the process is to actually calculate the key ratios that the bank is concerned with and we will now go on to consider how to actually calculate each ratio.

> **Gearing** It measures the relationship between what the bank (and any other lenders) have committed to the business and the financial commitment of the shareholders/directors/owners.

Liquidity

Cash is arguably one of the most important aspects to consider in any business; it is often the lack of cash that causes the failure of many businesses rather than the lack of profitability. Ratios help to identify how quickly a business can turn its assets into cash and also show how, in the **working capital cycle,** cash is either generated or used.

Working capital cycle

Working capital is the capital businesses need on a day-to-day basis to run themselves effectively. Cash, as identified above, is the lifeblood of any business and whatever the business does, via its sales, it must generate cash, which is then used within the business. Let's return to the example introduced in Chapter 1 of Hat Enterprises Ltd (HE) to illustrate this point. The working capital cycle is a process that happens, in a business such as HE, when goods (and in HE's case these goods are imported) are purchased for eventual re-sale, become inventory, and at the same time a trade payable is also created (as HE will not need to pay their suppliers for the goods immediately). The inventory (the stock now held) will be used to generate sales within the UK, and some of these sales will be for cash (or credit card etc which is a cash equivalent) and a proportion will become **trade receivables** (the goods are not paid for immediately as a period of credit is given to the purchaser). The two further movements in the working capital cycle are for the trade receivables to become cash when they are paid, and the trade payables to be paid by the HE, which will need cash to pay them. Figure 2.1 shows an illustration of a typical working capital cycle.

Working capital cycle The capital a business needs on a day-to-day basis to run itself effectively.

Figure 2.1 The working capital cycle

Using Amanda's Country Kitchen as a different example (also introduced in Chapter 1), we can see that the dynamics of this business are very different. Amanda will buy mainly perishable goods (flour, eggs, sugar etc) as well as longer dated goods such as tea and coffee. She will make cakes, scones and other items for the café and these will be sold, for cash, and the profits generated will be used to purchase further stocks.

She will probably use a wholesaler and therefore not have to pay for the goods immediately, and this in turn creates a trade payable, which allows her to trade the café and, using the profits generated, to pay the outstanding liability in the future. Unlike HE she will not generate any trade payable items as all the sales will be for cash (this includes debit and credit card sales).

The whole process is a continuous process and the management of all the elements of the working capital cycle is fundamental to how the cash is managed and whether or not a business has enough working capital to run the business effectively. We will revisit the working capital cycle in Chapter 3.

Key liquidity ratios

Current asset ratio

Calculation: $$\frac{\text{Current assets (X)}}{\text{Current liabilities (Y)}} = X{:}Y$$

The components of the **current asset ratio** are:

Current assets = cash + trade receivables + inventory
Current liabilities = trade receivables + overdrafts + borrowing commitments (due within 12 months)

Overdrafts are always classed as current liabilities as they are payable on demand (covered in Chapter 7) and the usual way of accounting for longer term liabilities such as term loans is to put the payments that are due during the 12-month period as current liabilities and the balance as a longer-term liability.

Current assets comprise the items discussed above in the working capital cycle and is all of the assets that are due within 12 months divided by all of the liabilities that are due within 12 months. This indicates how quickly the business can access cash in order to cover its liabilities. A ratio of at least 2:1 is usually what the bank will be looking for and anything less than 1.5:1 will cause the bank to have concerns, as it would suggest that the business might have a problem paying its liabilities when they are due.

Liquidity ratio (often referred to as the acid test ratio)

The **liquidity ratio** or **acid test ratio** is very similar to the current asset ratio; however, the fundamental difference is that it removes the inventory (the stock) in the business from the calculation.

$$\text{Calculation:} \qquad \frac{\text{Current assets} - \text{inventory} \ \ (X)}{\text{Current liabilities} \ (Y)} \quad = \quad X{:}Y$$

The components of this calculation are:

Current assets   =   cash + trade receivables (minus inventory)

Current liabilities   =   trade payables + overdrafts + borrowing commitments (due within 12 months)

The theory behind stripping out inventory is to review the liquidity when inventory is not being considered. Businesses can sometimes build up high levels of stock, some of which is very slow moving, or not sold at all.

Banks will normally look for a ratio of around 1.5:1, and if the ratio is less than 1:1 it would suggest potential liquidity problems for the business.

Inventory turnover

$$\text{Calculation:} \qquad \frac{\text{Average inventory}^*}{\text{Cost of goods sold}^*} \times 365 \quad = \quad X \text{ number of days}$$

$$\text{Average inventory is calculated by:} \quad \frac{\text{Opening inventory} + \text{Closing inventory}}{2}$$

*If opening inventory isn't given then it is acceptable to use the closing inventory.

The **inventory turnover** is used to calculate the number of times that inventory (stock) turns over in a particular period. Certain businesses will turn over stock much more quickly than others and a degree of logical reasoning will need to be applied by the banker. Inventory is an asset of the business and needs to be turned into sales in order to generate profit for the business. If there is slow-moving or out-of-date stock, this will impact on the ability to generate profits. A retailer of sportswear, for example, will need to ensure that last season's football stock is sold before the start of the next season, particularly where a football club changes sponsor.

There is always a fine balancing act between not having enough stock and having too much stock – holding too much stock can have serious implications on the cash position of the business.

ACTIVITY 2.2
Inventory turnover in different sectors

Consider the difference between stock turnover in two very different businesses – a supermarket chain and a luxury car dealership.

Why are they likely to be different and what impact might that have on the liquidity of each business?
Write down your own answer and review these at the end of the chapter.

Trade receivable days

Calculation $\dfrac{\text{Trade receivables}}{\text{Sales}} \times 365 = \text{X number of days}$

The trade receivable days calculation is used to establish the relationship between the amount of **trade receivables** outstanding and the level of overall sales. The number of days outstanding indicates how quickly the business is able to collect in the monies owed to it where it has given credit to its customers. There is a direct relationship between the change in the number of days it takes to receive monies and uses/applications of cash within the business.

Returning to HE Enterprises again, if it usually gives 30 days' credit to its customers, this means that from the point of issuing an invoice and delivering the goods, HE will expect to receive monies within that period. If the accounts show that this period is, in fact, 35 days, then it may mean that the trade receivables are not being chased when they become overdue, and there could be potential bad debts (where the customer will not pay what is owed). There could also be a larger customer that has been given more advantageous payment terms and this is impacting on the number of days' figures. This is where a comparison with previous years is vital.

An increasing number of debtor days also has an impact on cash. It will mean that the business is having to use more of its cash resources in order to finance the increase. Conversely, a decreasing number of days means that there is less pressure on cash resources as trade receivables are paying more quickly.

Trade payable days

Calculation: $\dfrac{\text{Trade payables}}{\text{Purchases*}} \times 365 = $ X number of days

* If purchases are not available then cost of sales can be used.

The **trade payable days** calculation is used to establish the relationship between the amount of **trade payables** outstanding and the level of purchases or cost of sales. The number of days outstanding indicates how quickly the business is able to pay monies owed by it where it has been given credit by its suppliers. In a similar way to the trade receivables calculation, there is a direct relationship between the change in the number of days taken to pay monies out and uses/applications of cash within the business.

If HE usually takes an average of 45 days' credit from its suppliers (and all suppliers will be different), this means that from the point of receiving an invoice and the goods, HE will be expected to pay monies out within that period. If the accounts show that this period is, in fact, 50 days, this could result in cash flow issues for HE as it is taking longer credit from its suppliers than it should. The major risk is that suppliers decide to reduce the credit terms given or even take draconian measures by stopping supplies until the outstanding monies have been paid. This could have disastrous implications for HE. On the other hand, if the number of days is falling, the business may be using more of its cash resources then it needs to. Again, this is where a comparison with previous years is vital to ascertain trends.

Acid test ratio   Another term for liquidity ratio.

Current asset ratio   The relationship between current assets and current liabilities.

Inventory turnover   This is the number of times that inventory turns over in a particular period.

Liquidity ratio   The relationship between current assets (having subtracted inventories from current assets) and current liabilities.

Trade payables [new FRS 102 term]   These arise when a business buys raw materials or other goods on credit terms from its suppliers.

Trade payable days   The number of days it takes a business to pay monies that it owes.

> **Trade receivables** [new FRS 102 term] Funds owed to a business, which arise when a business sells goods or services to its customers on credit terms. These funds are due to be paid at a future date.

Profitability

Key profitability ratios

Figure 2.2 shows how profits within a business are split into different categories. Ratio analysis often requires a logical progression through a set of similar calculations and the way businesses show how much money they are making impacts on the different types of calculation that are important.

Gross profit margin

Calculation: $\dfrac{\text{Gross profit}}{\text{Sales}} \times 100 \;=\; X\%$

The **gross profit margin** ratio measures how much money a business makes after it has taken into account the variable costs incurred for achieving the sales in that period. At this point there is not a calculation of all the costs in the business, as this is one of the further calculations.

The aim of any business is to make a profit and the principles for making a profit are identical for a small or a large business. A retail business makes money on the difference between the cost of sourcing its products and the price it sells them for. A simple business such as a fruit stall in the market makes money by buying its apples, pears, potatoes etc from a wholesaler and then selling to the general public at a higher price.

Figure 2.2 Profit progression

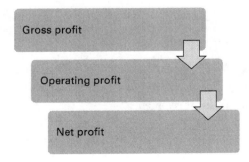

The gross profit margin in a business very much depends on the type of business that is being reviewed and if we use the example given in Activity 2.2 of the supermarket, where they have a high-volume business, the gross profit margins are likely to be relatively low, as the business model for a supermarket relies on selling goods (often called fast moving consumer goods) at low prices, but at very high volumes. The luxury car retailer, on the other hand, relies on selling a much smaller number of higher value items, and the difference between what a vehicle is bought for from the manufacturer and the price it is sold to the customer will obviously be much greater.

Operating profit margin

Calculation:
$$\frac{\text{Operating profit}}{\text{Sales}} \times 100 \;=\; X\%$$

The **operating profit margin** is the next part of the profit analysis. It measures how much money the business is making after variable and fixed costs have been deducted. All businesses have fixed costs, and whether that is a small shop lease with the added costs of business rates tax, insurance and electricity bills or if it is a large head office, these costs need to be covered whether or not the business makes a profit.

Net profit margin

Calculation:
$$\frac{\text{Net profit}}{\text{Sales}} \times 100 \;=\; X\%$$

The **net profit margin** ratio forms the final part of the profit analysis cycle. It considers the profit margin for the business after all costs have been deducted. This includes profit after financing costs (interest) and tax have been deducted.

Gross profit margin This is a ratio of gross profit to sales. It is a measurement of how much money a business makes after it has taken into account the variable costs incurred for achieving the sales in that period.

Net profit margin This is a ratio of net profit to sales. It is a measurement of how much money a business is making, after the deduction of all costs including interest, tax and dividends.

> **Operating profit margin** This is a ratio of operating profit to sales. It is a measurement of how much money a business makes after it has taken into account the variable costs and fixed costs incurred for achieving the sales in that period.

Financial strength

Key financial strength ratios

These ratios could be described as the foundation ratios for a business. As with any structure, if there is strength within the foundations then that structure can withstand shocks. Conversely, if there are weaknesses, then any shocks will cause a disproportionate amount of damage.

From a bank's point of view, in a similar way to the profitability and liquidity ratios already discussed, the fundamental issue is whether or not the business is sustainable and can continue to repay any borrowing facilities that it has.

Gearing

Calculation: $\dfrac{\text{Borrowing}}{\text{Total capital employed}} \times 100 = X\%$

In the above calculation, the borrowing is a total of all borrowing that the business has, both short term and long term. It also includes any hire purchase or lease commitments that the business has (both these lending products will be discussed in Chapter 7).

Total capital employed is calculated by adding together the share capital of the business (and for a small business this could be as low as £100!) and the retained profits of the business. The key difference with retained profits that are shown each year is that this figure is a cumulative figure. The principle about each year's figures being a 'snapshot' is slightly different here as what is shown is an amalgamation of profits (and/or losses) over a period of time.

The gearing ratio measures the relationship between what the bank (and any other lenders) have committed to the business and the financial commitment of the shareholders, directors and owners. Sometimes the phrase leverage might be used, such as a 'highly leveraged deal'.

A ratio that is higher than 50 per cent would suggest that the business is higher risk from a bank's perspective. The nearer to 100 per cent, the higher the risk the bank is taking. At anything over 100 per cent, then the bank is taking more risks than the owners.

There may be certain situations where the bank will be comfortable with this, but this is likely to be in circumstances where there has been a management buy-out. This would be where a number of directors or employees buy a business from the existing owners and repayment is based on the future profits of the business, with the initial transaction being 'geared' to a much higher level initially.

Debt interest cover

Calculation: $\dfrac{\text{Profits (before interest and tax)}}{\text{Total interest paid}} = \text{X number of times}$

The **debt interest cover** ratio is a measurement of how many times interest is covered by the profits of the business. Banks will normally look for two to three times. If the business can only achieve one times cover this means that there is enormous pressure to cover the interests cost of the business on an ongoing basis. There is a direct correlation between the interest cover ratio and the gearing ratio. The higher the level of gearing, the higher the interest costs are likely to be.

Other risks for the business are linked to the potential change in bank base rates, particularly an increase, which will increase the amount of interest paid and worsen the ratio.

> **Debt interest cover**   A measurement of how many times interest is covered by the profits of the business.

Break-even

The final issue to consider when analysing financial statements is what is referred to as the break-even point in a business. This is the point at which a business knows it can cover all its variable *and* fixed costs. A manufacturer will have an output in units (of what it makes). It will know that it has variable costs that relate to the manufacturing operations (eg wages/inventory/utilities etc) and it will also have fixed costs which it still has to pay (eg rent, loan payments, director salaries etc), regardless of its output.

At the break-even point the business is not making a profit but it is not losing any money either! See the Garden Furniture Ltd case study for an illustration of this point.

> ### CASE STUDY
> Garden Furniture Ltd
>
> Garden Furniture Ltd makes upmarket garden furniture (tables) from exotic woods. The business has fixed costs of £350,000 per annum and variable costs of £195 per unit. The tables retail for £700 each. Each table therefore contributes £505 to fixed costs.
>
> Its breakeven point for sales is 693 per annum (£350,000 divided by £505).

The use of financial ratios

Financial analysis also requires three fundamental and logical steps to be of any use to a bank:

- calculation;
- analysis; and
- interpretation.

Many banks will use internal systems to collect and analyse information but these are only of any use if the inputs are understood first.

- Calculation – this requires an understanding of which figures from either the income statement or the statement of financial position need to be used to calculate a particular ratio. It also requires an understanding of how a particular ratio is calculated.
- Analysis – this requires the figures from two or three time periods to be compared to each other to identify if the specific ratios have changed and by how much.
- Interpretation – this requires the use of the ratios that have been calculated to assess what the impact is on the financial position of the business and also its ability to repay its bank borrowings.

The Hotel Company Limited accounts are shown in Table 2.4. These show one year's accounts (the most current year). The initial figures are shown at an amalgamated level and what businesses often do is to show more detail in the notes to the accounts. The further breakdown for debtors and creditors is a good example of this.

Table 2.4 The Hotel Company Limited – current year's accounts
SOCI & SOFP 30 September 2017

Turnover	1,841,150
Cost of sales	−1,302,263
Gross profit	**538,887**
Admin expenses	−395,658
Other operating income	732
Operating profit	**143,961**
Interest payments	−38,300
Pre-tax profit	**105,661**
Taxation	−50,427
Profit after tax	**55,234**

Fixed assets

Tangible assets		102,889

Current assets

Inventory	235,478	
Debtors	286,045	(more detail on next page)
Cash	41,747	
	563,270	

Current liabilities

Creditors (amounts due within one year)	482,033	(more detail on next page)
Net current assets	81,237	

Total assets

(Less current liabilities)	184,126	
Creditors (amounts after more than one year)	4,841	
Net assets	**179,285**	

Share capital and reserves

Called up share capital	20,000	
Profit and loss account	159,285	
	179,285	

(continued)

Table 2.4 (Continued)	
Debtors	
(More detail)	
Trade receivables	252,212
Other debtors	17,412
Prepayments	16,421
	286,045
Creditors	
(More detail)	
Overdraft	249,316
*Bank loans (current)	22,700
Trade payables	124,875
Other creditors	14,669
Accruals/deferred	70,473
	482,033

*The loan is repaid during the current year

Profitability ratios

Gross profit margin	538,887/1,841,150 x 100 = 29%
Operating profit margin	143,961/1,841,150 x 100 = 8%
Profit after tax margin	55,234/1,841,150 x 100 = 3%

Liquidity ratios

Trade receivable days	252,212/1,841,150 x 365 = 49 days
Trade payable days	124,875/1,302,263 x 365 = 35 days
Inventory turnover	235,478/1,302,263 x 365 = 66 days
Current asset ratio	235,478 + 286,045 + 41,747/249,316 + 22,700 + 124,875 = 1.41:1
Liquid ratio (acid test)	235,478 + 286,045/249,316 + 22,700 + 124,875 = 1.31:1

Financial strength ratios

Gearing ratio	249,316 + 22,700/179,285 x 100 = 151%
Debt interest cover ratio	143,961/38,300 = 3.76 times

All of the key ratios explained earlier have been calculated. At this point, it is difficult to comment on some areas of performance as there is nothing to compare the current year to.

The one ratio that is a potential concern is the gearing ratio which is shown at 151 per cent. The loan is due to be repaid in the current year and therefore by the year-end there is the potential for this to be lower than it is now. If the level of overdraft was the same and no profits had been made this would drop to 139 per cent.

The previous year's accounts are shown in Table 2.5. At this point it is possible to start making comparisons with two financial periods.

Table 2.5 The Hotel Company Limited – previous year's accounts SOCI & SOFP 30 September 2016

Turnover		1,601,000
Cost of sales		−1,154,800
Gross profit		**446,200**
Admin expenses		−350,669
Other operating income		893
Operating profit		**96,424**
Interest payments		−36,630
Pre-tax profit		**59,794**
Taxation		−21,526
Profit after tax		**38,268**
Fixed assets		
Tangible assets		109,920
Current assets		
Inventory	216,876	
Debtors	267,391	
Cash	64, 099	
	548,366	
Current liabilities		
Creditors (amounts due within one year)	504,024	
Net current assets		44,342

(continued)

Table 2.5 (*Continued*)

Total assets

(Less current liabilities)	154,262
Creditors (amounts due within one year)	30,211
Net assets	**124,051**

Share capital and reserves

Called up share capital	20,000
Profit and loss account	104,051
	124,051

Debtors

(More detail)

Trade receivables	233,612
Other debtors	16,393
Prepayments	17,386
	267,391

Creditors

(More detail)

Overdraft	274,285
Bank loans (current)	18,200
Trade payables	121,407
Other creditors	14,559
Accruals/deferred	75,573
	504,024

Creditors

(More than one year)

Bank loans	22,700
Deferred tax	7,511
	30,211

(*continued*)

Table 2.5 (Continued)

Profitability ratios

Gross profit margin	446,200/1,601,000 x 100 = _____
Operating profit margin	96,424/1,601,000 x 100 = _____
Profit after tax margin	38,268/1,601,000 x 100 = _____

Liquidity ratios

Trade receivable days	233,612/1,601,000 x 365 = _____
Trade payable days	121,407/1,154,800 x 365 = _____
Inventory turnover	216,876/1,154,800 x 365 = _____
Current asset ratio	216,876 + 267,391 + 64,099/274,285 + 18,200 + 121,407 = _____
Liquid ratio (acid test)	267,391 + 64,099/274,285 + 18,200 + 121,407 = _____

Financial strength ratios

Gearing ratio	274,285 + 18,200 + 22,700/124,051 x 100 = _____
Debt interest cover ratio	96,424/36,630 = _____

ACTIVITY 2.3
Ratio analysis

Using the information provided for **2016**, calculate the ratios in the same way as they have been calculated for **2017**. A table is shown at the end of the chapter (Table 2.6), which summarizes both years.

Having calculated the ratios for 2016, consider the below commentary on both years.

Commentary – profitability

All the key profitability ratios have improved in the last year.

Commentary – liquidity

Trade receivable days have lessened, which suggests that the company is improving its debtor collection processes. This will have improved the cash position of the business.

Trade payable days have also lessened, which means the business is potentially paying creditors more quickly than they need to. This will have worsened the cash position.

Inventory is turning over more quickly, which is good and will be an improvement in the cash position.

The current asset ratio has improved in the last year which is very positive and suggests that the business is in a better position to cover its current liabilities. A similar position is shown with the acid test ratio.

Commentary – financial strength ratios

The gearing ratio is a concern for this business and whilst there has been a significant improvement in the last year, it is higher than the bank would normally like to see. The overdraft is substantial and going forward it may be beneficial to place part of the overdraft onto a loan to be paid off over, say, five years.

Debt interest cover is very positive and is improving due to the reduction in borrowing in the business.

Trade payable and trade receivable analysis

There is a further level of analysis that banks will carry out when examining these particular assets and liabilities of their customers, particularly where the bank is lending against the trade receivable book.

As identified earlier, trade receivables are monies that are owed to the business. Whilst they are an asset to the business, they need to be funded as part of the working capital cycle, and as such need to be carefully and robustly controlled.

Businesses should run, as part of their accounting package, a report which breaks down the funds they are owed into different time periods (ie 30 days, 60 days etc) which will allow a view of the 'age' of the different funds owed. It is a simple and effective way of checking whether there are problems with any of the customers that owe monies to the business. It is also a way of seeing where the concentrations of risk might be as, for example, one particular customer may be more than 50 per cent of the monies owed to the business, and if they face financial difficulties then this can have a disastrous impact on the business that is being lent to.

The impact of the failure of a large business has been a hard lesson to learn for many SMEs who have been suppliers to these businesses.

In 2008, MFI failed, owing their suppliers millions of pounds. MFI were a competitor to Habitat and IKEA selling 'flat-pack' furniture.
(www.telegraph.co.uk, 2017)

Depreciation

If something depreciates then it normally reduces in value over a period of time. From an accounting perspective, businesses need to account for the fact that assets they use (eg machines, vehicles etc) will reduce in value due to the use that they have, and if they are used constantly in, for example, a manufacturing process, then they are likely to reduce relatively quickly.

It is not necessary to know the different types of accounting **depreciation** policies that are used; the example given in the box below is a very basic one.

Depreciation   The measurement of a reduction in value of a fixed asset owned by the business.

DEPRECIATION

A machine is bought for £200,000, has a five-year life span, and a value at the end of the five years of £30,000. If the machine is depreciated on a 'straight line basis' then the amount of depreciation over the five years will be £170,000 (£200,000–£30,000). The machine in question is deemed to have reduced in value in each year by £34,000 (£170,000/5).

In the statement of comprehensive income, this then shows as a cost for the year and reduces the profits in that period by the amount of the depreciation. It is really important to appreciate that this is an accounting item only and does not create an item that takes cash out of the business. The benefit to the business is that by reducing the profits it will reduce its tax liabilities.

Dividend policies

Dividend policies are the ways that limited companies can pay out their profits to the owners (shareholders). The business must make profits in a period in order to be able to pay dividends and these payments are paid on a pro rata basis relating to the shareholdings. If the shareholding split between two directors is out of 100 shares, one has 80 shares and one has 20 shares, then a dividend payment of £5,000 will be split £4,000 and £1,000 respectively.

In many SMEs the shareholders are often also directors and they are also likely to be taking a regular salary from the business.

The key issue for the bank is that there is a balance between taking all the profits from the business in salary and dividend payments and leaving monies in the business for future investment. A good example of this is that even in small businesses, such *as Amanda's Country Kitchen*, she will need to replace items in the café (chairs, tables etc) and also ensure that the décor (including painting) is refreshed on a regular basis. This requires capital and if Amanda has taken all the monies out of the business then she will have to borrow from the bank rather than use her own financial resources.

> **Dividend policies**   This is the process a business uses to distribute profits of the business to the shareholders.

Capital expenditure

Linking closely to the points made above, all businesses have requirements for **capital expenditure**. The nature of the business will often dictate what is required.

For example, businesses in the leisure sector (hotels, public houses) require a significant level of ongoing capital expenditure for carpets, curtains and other soft furnishings. Hotels will need to ensure that beds are changed on a regular basis, that the bedrooms and en-suite facilities are kept fresh.

> **Capital expenditure**   The purchase of fixed assets used to continue to run the business. Sometimes shortened to Capex.

ACTIVITY 2.4
Capital expenditure

QHotels is a UK based hotel group which owns 26 four-star hotels.

It announced a major capital expenditure plan in 2015 to spend £50 million across the whole hotel chain to upgrade the bedrooms, bathrooms, furnishings and other areas of the hotels.

(www.QHotels.co.uk, 2017)

Think of another business, such as a commercial printer, that carries out work for a wide commercial customer base.

What capital requirements are they likely to have on an ongoing basis?
Write down your own answer and review these at the end of the chapter.

Financial and non-financial information

This chapter has been very focused on **financial information** (provided by customers) and the interpretation of this information. This is only one element (albeit an important one) of information that is available about a customer.

Non-financial information includes everything else about a business that is important in order to make a balanced and informed decision about whether or not to lend money. A large part of the lending decision is to assess the external environment that the business operates in, using strategic tools such as PESTLE and Porter's Five Forces (which will be examined in Chapter 5), the management of the business (which will be examined in Chapter 8), and the products or services that the customer provides.

If a business has a chain of retail stores then it is important to know the exact details about the portfolio of shops regarding location, size, and how each shop is performing. Many businesses have different divisions and it is vital to understand how each one operates in order to gain a holistic view of the business, and how each part operates.

Some information will be in the public domain (web articles or newspaper articles) and if the customer is a public limited company then they will publish information on both their website and via their financial statements. This will be vital to the overall assessment of the business and will include detailed strategic information as well as information about management. We will cover non-financial information in more detail in Chapters 4 and 5.

> **Financial information** Information about a business that is purely based on the financial performance.
>
> **Non-financial information** Any information about a business that excludes financial information (this can be from a variety of sources including media reports).

Chapter summary

In this chapter we have explored:

- the use of annual accounts, management information and projections to assess the performance of a business;
- the Accounting Standard FRS 102 and the differences it has made to accounting terminology;
- the three critical financial groups of ratios: liquidity, profitability and financial strength;
- all the financial ratios that are necessary for a bank to analyse the performance of a commercial business;
- the use of these ratios to identify trends in a commercial business; and
- the difference between financial and non-financial information.

Objective check

1 List two ratios from each of the above categories (liquidity, profitability and financial strength) and explain how they are used to assess the financial performance of a business.

2 Why do we group financial ratios under the headings of liquidity, profitability and financial strength?

3 What are the key differences between the annual accounts for a business and its management information?

4 Why is it important to assess the financial trends in a commercial business?

5 Under the Accounting Standard FRS 102, what are debtors, stocks and creditors now known as?

6 Why is there a distinction between financial and non-financial performance in a business?

Further reading

Davis, E, Bannock, G and Baxter, R (2003) *Penguin Dictionary of Economics* (7th ed), Penguin, London

Icaew.com [accessed 13 June 2018] *FRS 102 The Financial Reporting Standard | Financial Reporting | ICAEW* [Online] https://www.icaew.com/en/technical/financial-reporting/new-uk-gaap/frs-102-the-financial-reporting-standard

The Institute of Chartered Accountants of Scotland: https://www.icas.com/

The Institute of Chartered Accountants in England and Wales: https://www.icaew.com/

References

Lee, T (2002) 'The contributions of Alexander Thomas Niven and John Ballantine Niven to the international history of modern public accountancy', *Accounting & Business Research*, **32** (2), pp 79–92

Qhotels.co.uk [accessed 13 June 2018] *Investment Across All Our Hotels | QHotels* [Online] https://www.qhotels.co.uk/qhotels-investment/

Telegraph.co.uk [accessed 13 June 2018] *Woolworths and MFI collapse: Is this the end of the high street?* [Online] http://www.telegraph.co.uk/finance/recession/3527947/Woolworths-and-MFI-collapse-Is-this-the-end-of-the-high-street.html

Suggested answers for activities

Activity 2.1 – Seasonality in different sectors

Seasonality impacts on different types of businesses in different ways:

1 A seaside hotel – the busiest time for this type of business is likely to be the summer, and the much quieter times are likely to be November, February and March with a much greater pressure on the cash flow in these periods.

2 A retailer of luxury goods (based on Oxford Street) – such a retailer will benefit from tourists in the capital but usually the Christmas period is likely to be very busy, which means that the business needs to build up its stock to a much higher level and this will impact on the cash position leading up to Christmas.

3 A care home for elderly people – this type of business is not subject to as much seasonality as the other two businesses. It is dependent on the income from its residents which is relatively stable. Sadly however, if there is a very severe cold weather period, then this can cause a higher than usual mortality rate amongst the residents.

Activity 2.2 – Inventory turnover in different sectors

The inventory in a supermarket, on the whole, will turn over relatively quickly, and this is logical as they sell perishable goods (food). The larger supermarket chains also sell goods such as electrical goods (TVs etc) that will turn over more slowly. Inventory days should be quite low.

The inventory in a luxury car dealership, on the other hand, due to the significantly higher value of the items sold is likely to turn over their inventory much more slowly than the supermarket and therefore will have inventory days that are much higher than those of the supermarket.

The cash implications in each business are that the supermarket is likely to be able to generate cash more easily than the luxury car maker due to the speed with which it is able to sell its stock.

Activity 2.3 – Ratio analysis

Table 2.6 shows the calculation of the key ratios. The commentary about these ratios is in the main text of the chapter.

Activity 2.4 – Capital expenditure

A commercial printer is likely to have several printing machines which will need to be replaced on a regular basis. Depending on the size of the business, they may also have vehicles used to distribute their products and also vehicles used for directors, sales personnel etc.

Table 2.6 The Hotel Company Limited – calculation of ratios

Profitability ratios

	2016	2017
Gross profit margin	28%	29%
Operating profit margin	6%	8%
Profit after tax margin	2.4%	3%

Liquidity ratios

	2016	2017
Trade receivable days	53 days	49 days
Trade payable days	38 days	35 days
Inventory turnover	68 days	66 days

	2016	2017
Current asset ratio	1.08:1	1.41:1
Liquid ratio (acid test)	0.65:1	1.31:1

Financial strength ratios

	2016	2017
Gearing ratio	254%	151%
Debt interest cover ratio	2.65 times	3.76 times

03

Cash analysis

INTRODUCTION

Cash is the 'lifeblood' of any commercial business and the management of the cash position is vital for its survival. As we will demonstrate in Chapter 9, the consequences of a lack of cash or liquidity will often be fatal and in many cases will lead to the demise of the business. Bankers are often concerned about the profits within a business, which is important, but profit is not the same as cash, and many profitable businesses can be 'cash poor'.

In this chapter we will be exploring not only how important cash is to a business but the various ways that bankers will analyse the cash within a business. Some of the techniques we will explore are forward looking, such as cash flow projections, whereas others will be more backward looking such as the cash flow available for debt service calculation, which takes into account the profits generated by a business, and then considers how this cash has been utilized between two accounting periods. The movements of the key working capital elements will be discussed as it is important for you to understand the dynamics of working capital movements and the overall impact on the cash position.

LEARNING OBJECTIVES

By the end of this chapter, you will be able to:

- explain the importance of focusing on cash in a commercial business;

- evaluate how the movements of trade receivables, trade payables and inventory impact on the cash position in a commercial business;

- analyse a cash flow forecast and demonstrate the ability to sensitize one;

- define earnings before interest, tax, depreciation and amortization (EBITDA) and explain its relevance to the bank;

- assess cash flow available for debt service (CFADS) and explain how it can be used in lending decisions by the bank; and

- explain the problem of overtrading and the potential remedies by a business to tackle it.

Working capital, historical movements and the impact on cash

In Chapter 2, we discussed the importance of working capital and the management of this cycle. The end and start point for this cycle is always cash (as shown in Figure 3.1), which you will recall is a current asset. It is important for bankers to understand in an accounting period (usually 12 months), how the movement of current assets and current liabilities impacts on the cash position of a business they are lending to.

We will now explore how the fluctuations in the individual components of the working capital cycle impact on how cash is used in a business. It is critical for bankers to understand where a business is getting its cash from and, just as importantly, how it is utilizing that cash in any accounting period. Look at Figure 3.1 to remind yourself of the cycle.

It is useful to understand what has happened to the assets in a business in an accounting period and we will examine individual current assets and current liabilities first before exploring the cumulative impact of the changes.

Figure 3.1 The working capital cycle

Trade receivables

Trade receivables are monies that are owed *to* the business. As you will recall from the last chapter, trade receivables arise when goods or services have been sold on credit terms and will be paid at an agreed point in the future. We have also examined the calculation of how long it takes for a business to be paid. As bankers, you should also be concerned with how the movement of an asset impacts on the cash position of the business.

The see-saw effect

You may find it useful to consider how the movement of a current asset impacts on cash by thinking about a child's see-saw. By using a straightforward example, we can explore a change between two accounting periods and the see-saw effect.

You will see in Example 1 (Table 3.1) that trade receivables has increased between the two accounting periods by £125,000. An *increase* means that there would have to have been a corresponding *decrease* in the amount of cash in the business. Why is this? Thinking this through logically, and using the see-saw effect, if trade receivables has increased then this must mean that cash has been used in order to finance this increase and therefore cash will need to have decreased in the same accounting period. As you will see from the see-saw in Figure 3.2, there is an opposite movement in cash which is directly correlated with the increase in trade receivables; this is known as the see-saw effect.

Table 3.1 Example 1 – increase in trade receivables

Example 1	£000 *31/12/xx01*	£000 *31/12/xx02*	Movement
Trade receivables	225	350	125

Figure 3.2 Increase in trade receivables

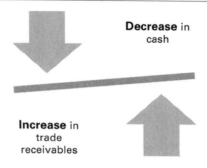

Table 3.2 Example 2 – Decrease in trade receivables

Example 2	£000 *31/12/xx01*	£000 *31/12/xx02*	Movement
Trade receivables	350	225	125

We will now consider how cash is impacted if the movement of trade receivables is in the opposite direction and *decreases*.

In our second example, Example 2 (Table 3.2), you will see that trade receivables has decreased between the two accounting periods by £125,000. Using the same logic as we have applied earlier, a *decrease* means there would have been a corresponding *increase* in the amount of cash in the business. Cash has been released into the business due to the collection, or reduction in trade receivables at the end of the accounting period. Again, as you will see illustrated in the see-saw, in Figure 3.3 (Decrease in trade

Figure 3.3 Decrease in trade receivables

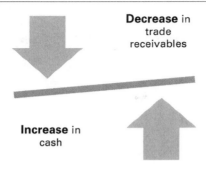

Decrease in
trade
receivables

Increase in
cash

receivables), there is a corresponding increase in the level of cash held, as trade receivables reduce.

Inventory

The principles applied to trade receivables are identical for the inventory (stock) within the business. Managing inventory effectively in any business is important, and retail businesses in particular, which rely on the sales of their stocks to make a profit, have a challenging balancing act between having sufficient levels of stock to sell and the utilization of their cash.

In a similar way to the figures shown above for trade receivables, Table 3.3 shows two different examples for the movement of inventory in an accounting period. As this is a current asset, the implications for cash are the same as trade receivables.

An *increase* in inventory translates into a corresponding *decrease* in cash in that period. A *decrease* in inventory means there will be an equal *increase* in cash in that period. Figures 3.4 and 3.5 (Inventory increase and Inventory decrease), again using the see-saw effect, illustrate this principle.

Trade payables

Trade payables are monies that are owed *by* the business. They arise due to payments that are owed to suppliers, where goods or services have been purchased on credit. Trade payables, as you will recall, are a current liability and therefore any changes which take place in an accounting period, will have a completely different impact on cash.

Under Example 1 (Table 3.4), you will see that trade payables has increased between the two accounting periods by £40,000. An *increase*

Table 3.3 Increase/decrease in inventory

Example 1	£000 *31/12/xx01*	£000 *31/12/xx02*	Movement
Inventory	315	400	85

Example 2	£000 *31/12/xx01*	£000 *31/12/xx02*	Movement
Inventory	400	315	85

Figure 3.4 Inventory increase

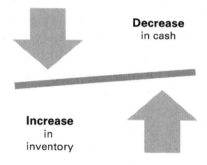

Decrease
in cash

Increase
in
inventory

Figure 3.5 Inventory decrease

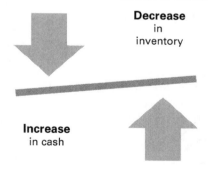

Decrease
in
inventory

Increase
in cash

Table 3.4 Example 1 – trade payables increase

Example 1	£000 *31/12/xx01*	£000 *31/12/xx02*	Movement
Trade payables	195	235	40

means that there would have to have been a corresponding *increase* in the amount of cash in the business. Why is this? If the amount of money owed by the business increases, then cash will increase in direct proportion to the increase in monies owed. This is illustrated in Figure 3.6.

Having looked at an increase, what now happens if trade payables decrease as they have in Example 2 (Table 3.5)?

A *decrease* in trade payables means there would have to be a *decrease* in the amount of cash in the business. This is due to more of the trade payables being paid, with the knock-on impact being that more cash resources will need to be utilized to achieve this. This is illustrated in Figure 3.7 (Trade payables decrease).

Figure 3.6 Trade payables increase

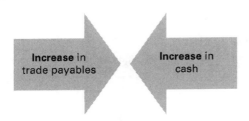

Table 3.5 Example 2 – decrease in trade payables

Example 2	£000 *31/12/xx01*	£000 *31/12/xx02*	Movement
Trade payables	235	195	40

Figure 3.7 Trade payables decrease

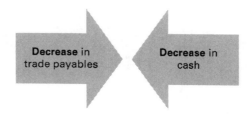

Combining movements in current assets and current liabilities

Having examined what can happen to the individual components of the working capital cycle, we now need to combine all the movements to show what the overall impact of the changes are on cash.

You can see in the combined example (Table 3.6) that, when all of the changes are considered together, even though each asset or liability increases, there is a decrease in cash overall.

> **LEARNING TIP**
>
> The easiest way to approach this type of calculation is to deal with each asset or liability in turn, considering whether there is an increase or a decrease, and then considering whether this will have a negative or a positive impact on cash. The results for each asset and liability then need to be combined as shown in the combined example.

The financial trends in a particular business are important as they show the banker where the pressure points are likely to be over a period of time and, combined with the ratio calculations, give a clearer picture of any areas of concern.

The impact on bank facilities

There is a potential assumption when we examine the movement of current assets and current liabilities, calculating as we have above whether a business needs more or less cash, that we are only concerned with businesses that

Table 3.6 Combined example

Combined example	£000 31/12/xx01	£000 31/12/xx02	Movement	Cash impact
Current assets				
Trade receivables	225	350	125	Decrease
Inventory	315	400	85	Decrease
			210	
Current liabilities				
Trade payables	195	235	40	Increase
			−170	

are running in credit. The reality is much more likely to be that a business will be utilizing its overdraft facilities where there is a higher level of cash needed, and partly repaying overdraft facilities when cash is less needed.

This is why the examination of the movement in the assets and liabilities above is so crucial, as it gives the banker more visibility on how overdraft facilities may be used. Using the combined example above (Table 3.6), we can see that there was a negative movement of cash available of £170,000, which would either use available cash, or use any overdraft facility. Making these calculations over a period of two or three years will show the trends of the business.

Cash flow projections

In the section above, we are primarily concerned with the impact on the cash position from a historical perspective. This analysis comes via information from the past, and, by definition, has already taken place. You will recall from Chapter 2 that we explored what projections were and that cash flow forecasts are a key element of these. A forecast is essentially a prediction of the future, and like any prediction, it may be right or it may be wrong!

The skill for any business, when preparing projections which are credible, is using **assumptions** which are realistic. This is harder than it may sound, and a business does not want to appear either overly optimistic or pessimistic about its future. Producing financial predictions which are wildly optimistic is likely to lead the bank to question the financial acumen of the directors or owners.

A business which has been trading for more than two or three years has arguably more historical information it is able to draw from, on which to base its views of the future. It will be able to factor in issues such as seasonality (discussed in Chapter 2 and below) and is likely to have a better idea of where the 'spikes' (again discussed below) are likely to occur.

> **Assumptions**   The factors that have been used to build a set of projections or forecasts.
>
> **Spikes**   The points in a cash flow cycle when there is a greater requirement for cash due to payment of items such as wages/salaries, rent, tax and loan payments.

New businesses versus existing businesses

A business that 'replicates' the same activity as it is currently engaged in, such as a care home business opening a new care home, will be in a comparatively good position to accurately forecast its future cash needs. However, and continuing with the care home example, this does not mean that the business will not find other areas more challenging to forecast, such as how quickly there will be a take-up of places in the home.

Does this mean that bankers cannot rely on projections prepared by new businesses that are not replicating a previous experience? Not at all, but you may need to dig a little deeper. As a banker you will probably have the advantage of already working with businesses in the same sector, so you will be able to compare the performance of similar businesses to the projections of the new business.

Profit versus cash – timing differences

As discussed in Chapter 2, the starting point for any projections is the preparation of a projected statement of comprehensive income showing the forecast profit or loss in a forecast period. This will be based both on the previous performance of the business and what the owners think can be achieved in the future.

The vital point when considering profit forecasts and cash forecasts is that due to timing differences, a business will not have cash that is directly correlated to its profits. A business that sells on a business-to-business (B2B) basis, where all its sales are on credit, will not see the cash from those sales straight away; however, it will need to pay other obligations such as wages, salaries or finance payments on a monthly basis.

Once profit and loss accounts are prepared, this provides the starting point for **cash flow forecasts**.

> **Cash flow forecast** A prediction of the forward requirements for cash.

Spikes

'Spikes' in the cash flow of a business are points in the month, quarter or year when there is a greater requirement for cash than usual, albeit that these may be short-term requirements, and payments due in will reduce these spikes, or peaks, relatively quickly.

A common error when preparing cash flow forecasts is to not take into account these spikes in usual pattern for the receipt and payment of funds. If forecasts are produced on a monthly basis, then these potentially ignore inter-month peaks in the cash requirements; for example, salaries for staff may be usually paid on the last Friday of every month, whereas trade receivables may be due at the end of the month, and this can then mean there may be a week between the payment of salaries (which is likely to be one of the bigger costs in the month).

The most common areas for larger requirements of cash are:

- HMRC payments (corporation tax/VAT);
- salaries/wages;
- rent; and
- finance payments.

It is quite likely that at some points during the year, a business will experience a point (or points) when some or all of these payments will coincide with requirements to pay suppliers (trade payables) creating short-term spikes which will not always coincide neatly with a month end.

Limited companies have a certain period by which they need to pay their corporation tax based on profits made in the last accounting year. This is usually nine months after the year end, and many businesses leave making this payment as long as they can, particularly if it is a large payment. If it is not paid on time, however, HMRC may levy penalties. The payment will often use significant amounts of cash or overdraft facilities, and even if it is left as late as possible, is likely to coincide with other cash requirements for the business.

Seasonality

As we discussed in Chapter 2, many businesses experience seasonal fluctuations in their trading patterns and these fluctuations will have a direct impact on the cash requirements of the business. For businesses in certain sectors, this will mean that a cash flow projection over a 12-month period will not show an equal requirement and will highlight the periods in the year when cash requirements or overdraft usage is likely to be higher.

CASE STUDY

Retail: trends and financing implications

Retail businesses in the UK have traditionally relied on the Christmas period, which is where they make a significant proportion of their sales and profits. The seasonal cash flow impacts start much earlier in the year as the build-up of inventory (stock) will commence many months before the consumers start their festive shopping in earnest. This may be as early as the summer, especially if goods need to be manufactured in other parts of the world (there can often be a three- or four-month lead time for importing, particularly if goods are transported by sea).

The UK retail trade has also been impacted by other trends such as 'Black Friday', in November, which has been imported from the United States, and is usually the Friday after the US celebration of Thanksgiving. This has necessitated the discounting of products for a limited period, well in advance of the busy December shopping period. The following Monday is often known as 'Cyber Monday' where online deals are also available.

Question

1 What are the cash implications for Black Friday and Cyber Monday?

2 What are the implications for the structuring of financing structures?

3 What are the implications for different sectors?

Consider your answer and look at the answers at the end of the chapter.

Base case scenario and assumptions

When cash flows are prepared, there should be underlying assumptions that have been used. A **base case scenario** is prepared, which the business uses in its initial forecasts. This is normally when one of the key drivers of the business, sales, is forecast. Alongside this forecast, the business should build in considerations of how it is performing at the present time in order to produce a credible 'base case' cash flow. This will include current cost of sales, salary costs, and then factor in prevailing interest rates (base in the UK), current exchange rates (if the business imports or exports), how long it takes the business to be paid (trade receivables), how long it takes it to pay its suppliers (trade payables) and how quickly it turns over its inventory (stock).

You will recall that in Chapter 2 we considered the key ratios for liquidity: trade receivable days, trade payable days and inventory days. The base case needs to reflect the current trading experience of the business for all these components of working capital: if trade receivable days in a business, for example, are normally 37, then this is the figure that should be used as an assumption in the base case. It may be that 'normal' terms of trade for customers are 30 days (as issued on invoices), and it is acknowledged by the customer that 37 days needs to be improved on; however, if 30 days is used as an assumption in the base case it will be unrealistic, producing a more optimistic cash flow than is the reality the business is operating in.

> **Base case scenario** The initial model for business projections, which usually contains the most conservative figures.

Sensitivities

Once the base case is established, sensitizing can take place. Sensitizing is the process of applying 'what if' scenarios to a cash flow. This is also known as 'stress-testing' the projections, to discover where the weaknesses in the ability of a business to generate cash may be.

Businesses (often in conjunction with their accountants) will provide a copy of the cash flows on an Excel spreadsheet to the bank. This will include all the assumptions that were used to prepare it. The bank will then need to consider the different scenarios it considers prudent to apply to the cash flow.

There are two important points to note here. First, if lending is to be agreed based on the projections, the bank will need to be comfortable that the figures provided are realistic as there will be an internal credit process and agreement will usually be subject to adhering to the stated cash flow. The bank cannot therefore simply take initial cash flows without question or due diligence. Secondly, there is a real danger that the bank will apply too many **sensitivities** to the figures, and whilst there needs to be a level of prudency and realism, if the sensitivities are overly pessimistic, it is unlikely the lending will be agreed at all! We will now go on to consider some of the 'what if' scenarios that might be applied.

> **Sensitivities**   The changes that have been applied to a set of projections or forecasts to reflect risks that the business may face in the future.

Sales

Businesses can sometimes produce forecasts, where there is a rapid rise in sales, and at a much faster rate than the business has experienced previously. If the business has been growing at, say, 8–10 per cent for the last two years, and the base case forecast shows 17.5 per cent, due to a new product or service, reducing sales back to 10 per cent growth would not be an unrealistic scenario.

Cost of sales

A rise of raw material costs can be used as a scenario, particularly where a business is using high levels of energy in manufacturing processes. In a case like this, a rise in the price of oil might be a sensible scenario to explore.

Trade receivables/trade payables

You will recall the principles behind the changes in current assets and liabilities from the earlier section. The bank will look to adjust trade receivable days, and either lengthen them (this will *worsen* cash flow) or shorten them (this will *improve* cash flow) to explore the impact on the future cash position. Trade payable days can be adjusted in a similar way, and these changes will have the *opposite* impact: lengthening will *improve* cash flow and shortening will *worsen* cash flow.

Interest rates/exchange rates

The increase in bank borrowing rates can have a huge impact and will therefore be a major concern that a banker will have when considering cash flow projections. Any upward movements in base rate (sometimes also known as bank rate), applied by the Bank of England, will have an immediate and negative impact on cash. Banks usually apply interest charges on a quarterly basis to overdrafts, and often interest is calculated on a daily basis, based on the overdrawn balance at the end of each day. The higher the utilization of an overdraft, the more negative will be the impact of any interest rate rise.

The business may also have base-related loans and these will also be subject to an immediate rise in interest rates, which will impact by the next application of interest at the end of the next quarter. This may necessitate the bank raising the loan repayments to ensure that full repayment is made in the agreed term of the loan (loans that only have a few years left to run, and where the capital amount has been significantly reduced will not be as impacted, by virtue of the fact that a lower capital balance will obviously attract lower levels of extra interest and therefore payments may not need to be increased).

Bankers will therefore build in interest rate rises as a potential scenario, taking into account the prevailing economic conditions at the time.

The impact of the fluctuation in exchange rates will depend on the international trading activities of the business. If it imports goods or exports goods (and it may do both) then the impact of a change in exchange rates will need to be considered. The UK's decision to leave the European Union (EU) weakened sterling, and businesses that were importing from Europe or the United States had to then bear an immediate higher cost of goods (there was also an increase in the cost of goods from China and South East-Asia where payment is usually in US dollars). Conversely the value of sales generally increased for exporters to these countries.

Timescales

Businesses may produce cash flow projections that cover more than one year, but the challenge with this is that, the further away from the present projections are, the less reliable they are likely to be. If a business is in financial difficulties (which we explore in Chapter 9), it is normal to have cash flows which cover the immediate weekly requirements of the business, over the next 12 to 13 weeks, with monthly figures for the rest of the year.

Sometimes, larger commercial businesses prepare 'rolling' cash flows which always look 12 months into the future and are not just linked to the financial year end. If, for example, the financial year starts in January, and a 12-month cash flow forecast is produced, to run until December, a rolling cash flow would be refreshed in February to run through until the end of January, with this process being carried out every month. An important point to note, however, from the bank's point of view is that if rolling cash flow is carried out, then there will need to be a monthly comparison to the original version and any divergences or differences explained in a monthly management report produced by the business.

'What-if' scenarios becoming a reality/unexpected shocks

We have explored how 'what if' scenarios can be used to gauge how cash flow might be impacted. As soon as any of these scenarios become a reality, then cash flows need to be revisited to ensure that the business will not breach any lending agreements and that any remedial action is taken by the business to deal with the issue.

If, for example, base rate is currently 2 per cent, and there is a rise of 0.5 per cent, and sensitivities have been run at 2.5 per cent and 3 per cent, all showing that the business can operate within the requested cash flows, then there will be no further action necessary by the bank. If the interest rate rises are higher than anticipated, and above the sensitivities run, then further discussions will need to take place with the business.

Businesses can be faced with any number of shocks, some which may have been anticipated, as above. Others, however, may not be, such as the failure of a major customer or supplier. The failure of a major customer will have short- and medium-term cash flow implications, and if the business is too reliant on this customer, may even jeopardize the existence of the business. A failure of a key supplier is likely to mean that an alternative supplier has to be found where credit terms may not be as advantageous, and this will have an immediate and negative impact on cash flow.

Improvement in the economy

It is not unreasonable for a banker to assume that proof of an improvement in the economy will result in improved business performance, including cash flow. Ironically, as the external environment improves, this can be exactly the time when cash flow is negatively impacted, as businesses may need to acquire more stock, or take on new customers, where credit is extended beyond existing terms of trade. A period of expansion may also mean having to find more staff and to pay them at a higher rate than existing staff, in order to attract them.

Accuracy of cash flows

We highlighted earlier that a cash flow forecast is a prediction of the future. A banker does not expect the owners of businesses to be clairvoyants and it would be totally unrealistic for the bank to expect that cash flows produced by businesses it lends to will be 100 per cent accurate. Where the business is changing strategic direction, or launching a new product or service, it will be much more difficult to predict future cash flows accurately. There is also a degree of luck that businesses experience (sometimes good and sometimes bad!).

Ultimately, how accurate a cash flow or series of cash flows are, will be judged by what actually happens during the forecast period, and this information will be used by the business and the bank to determine further cash flow predictions in the future.

Building a cash flow forecast

In its purest sense, a cash flow forecast, on a monthly basis, is concerned with four basic elements:

1 opening cash balance;

2 cash in;

3 cash out;

4 closing cash balance.

An existing business will find it marginally easier to produce a cash flow than a new business. This is not because it is easier to forecast if the business is established, but it does have the advantage of having a clearer view of expenses that need to be paid on a regular basis.

It is easy to overcomplicate the principles behind a business cash flow, which are really no different to the budgeting that a private individual would carry out:

Income – wages/salary.

Expenses – mortgage/rent, car lease, food, utilities, insurance etc.

The key issue behind preparing a cash flow forecast is that it needs to capture the monthly *cash* position of the business and, whilst profit is important, the focus in a cash flow statement is to reflect what is happening to cash on a monthly basis. Remember also the 'spikes' we discussed earlier, which will feed into a robust cash flow forecast.

Sales – these will be generated from the normal activity of the business.

Costs – suppliers need to be paid on a regular basis (depending on credit terms) and a cash flow is concerned with what payments need to be made in a particular month. Businesses will of course have fixed costs to pay every month, such as salaries, rent (for the premises), business rates, utilities (gas and electric), telephone, insurance, finance payments, etc. There will also be regular payments that may not be monthly, such as HMRC payments (VAT or PAYE) and finance payments or lease payments, which may be quarterly and not monthly.

Fixed payments, such as business rates, utilities, lease payments, etc need to be paid whatever the cash position of the business is. The owners can't practically argue they are waiting for monies to come in from sales (which may be on credit) before they pay them. The business would very quickly face potential action from bodies like the local council or the utilities companies, and this could ultimately cause the failure of the business.

A cash flow example

Amore Restaurants is an independently owned chain of Italian restaurants. The cash flow (shown as Table 3.7) has been prepared to reflect some of the potential seasonal changes such as a drop in sales in January following the busy December period, an increase for February (Valentine's Day, etc), a steady build-up over the next few months, then a dip in August to reflect when many customers may be away for summer holidays, and then a final peak in December for the festive period. The suppliers are paid within 30 days and therefore are always paid in the following month in the cash flow (January cash flow reflects December suppliers being paid in that month).

You can see that due to the seasonality factors, the business requires overdraft facilities until at least May, after which point it becomes cash positive until the end of the year, apart from August, which is a quieter month.

Sensitivities

We have already discussed sensitivities for cash flows and one of the tasks the banker needs to undertake is to compare the cash flows presented with those from previous years, and also to consider some sensitivities. An obvious sensitivity is to reduce turnover by, say, 10 per cent and see what the impact of this is.

Table 3.8 is a stark reminder of how a relatively small change in turnover (a reduction of 10 per cent) can have a severe impact on cash flow. In

Table 3.7 Amore Restaurants – Cash flow forecast

	January	February	March	April	May	June	July	August	September	October	November	December	Totals
Sales													
Food	30,000	50,000	70,000	70,000	70,000	70,000	70,000	50,000	70,000	70,000	70,000	105,000	795,000
Drink	20,000	60,000	80,000	80,000	80,000	80,000	80,000	60,000	80,000	80,000	80,000	120,000	900,000
Total	50,000	110,000	150,000	150,000	150,000	150,000	150,000	110,000	150,000	150,000	150,000	225,000	**1,695,000**
Expenses													
Suppliers	100,000	25,000	55,000	75,000	75,000	75,000	75,000	75,000	55,000	75,000	75,000	75,000	835,000
Wages	40,000	40,000	40,000	40,000	40,000	40,000	40,000	40,000	40,000	40,000	40,000	60,000	500,000
Business rates	5,000	5,000	5,000	5,000	5,000	5,000	5,000	5,000	5,000	5,000	5,000	5,000	60,000
Utilities	1,500	1,500	1,500	1,500	1,500	1,500	1,500	1,500	1,500	1,500	1,500	1,500	18,000
Telephone	400	400	400	400	400	400	400	400	400	400	400	400	4,800
Travel	750	750	750	750	750	750	750	750	750	750	750	750	9,000
Insurance	600	600	600	600	600	600	600	600	600	600	600	600	7,200
Cleaning	500	500	500	500	500	500	500	500	500	500	500	500	6,000
Rent	10,000	0	0	10,000	0	0	10,000	0	0	10,000	0	0	40,000
Lease payments	2,500	2,500	2,500	2,500	2,500	2,500	2,500	2,500	2,500	2,500	2,500	2,500	30,000
Bank charges	200	200	200	200	200	200	200	200	200	200	200	200	2,400
Drawings	10,000	10,000	10,000	10,000	10,000	10,000	10,000	10,000	10,000	10,000	10,000	10,000	120,000
Total	171,450	86,450	116,450	146,450	136,450	136,450	146,450	136,450	116,450	146,450	136,450	156,450	**1,632,400**

(Continued)

Table 3.7 (Continued)

Net cash in the month	−121,450	23,550	33,550	3,550	13,550	3,550	−26,450	33,550	3,550	13,550	68,550
Opening cash balance	45,000	−76,450	−52,900	−19,350	−15,800	11,300	14,850	−11,600	21,950	25,500	39,050
Net cash in the month	−121,450	23,550	33,550	3,550	13,550	3,550	−26,450	33,550	3,550	13,550	68,550
Closing cash balance	−76,450	−52,900	−19,350	−15,800	−2,250	14,850	−11,600	21,950	25,500	39,050	107,600

Table 3.8 Amore Restaurants – Cash flow forecast (10% reduction in turnover)

	January	February	March	April	May	June	July	August	September	October	November	December	Totals
Sales													
Food	27,000	45,000	63,000	63,000	63,000	63,000	63,000	50,000	63,000	63,000	63,000	94,500	720,500
Drink	18,000	54,000	72,000	72,000	72,000	72,000	72,000	54,000	72,000	72,000	72,000	108,000	810,000
Total	45,000	99,000	135,000	135,000	135,000	135,000	135,000	104,000	135,000	135,000	135,000	202,500	**1,530,500**
Expenses													
Suppliers	100,000	22,500	49,500	67,500	67,500	67,500	67,500	67,500	52,000	67,500	67,500	67,500	764,000
Wages	40,000	40,000	40,000	40,000	40,000	40,000	40,000	40,000	40,000	40,000	40,000	60,000	500,000
Business rates	5,000	5,000	5,000	5,000	5,000	5,000	5,000	5,000	5,000	5,000	5,000	5,000	60,000
Utilities	1,500	1,500	1,500	1,500	1,500	1,500	1,500	1,500	1,500	1,500	1,500	1,500	18,000
Telephone	400	400	400	400	400	400	400	400	400	400	400	400	4,800
Travel	750	750	750	750	750	750	750	750	750	750	750	750	9,000
Insurance	600	600	600	600	600	600	600	600	600	600	600	600	7,200
Cleaning	500	500	500	500	500	500	500	500	500	500	500	500	6,000
Rent	10,000	0	0	10,000	0	0	10,000	0	0	10,000	0	0	40,000
Lease payments	2,500	2,500	2,500	2,500	2,500	2,500	2,500	2,500	2,500	2,500	2,500	2,500	30,000
Bank charges	200	200	200	200	200	200	200	200	200	200	200	200	2,400
Drawings	10,000	10,000	10,000	10,000	10,000	10,000	10,000	10,000	10,000	10,000	10,000	10,000	120,000
Total	171,450	83,950	110,950	138,950	128,950	128,950	138,950	128,950	113,450	138,950	128,950	148,950	**1,561,400**

(Continued)

Table 3.8 (*Continued*)

Net cash in the month	−126,450	15,050	24,050	−3,950	6,050	6,050	−3,950	−24,950	21,550	−3,950	6,050	53,550
Opening cash balance	45,000	−81,450	−66,400	−42,350	−46,300	−40,250	−34,200	−38,150	−63,100	−41,550	−45,500	−39,450
Net cash in the month	−126,450	15,050	24,050	−3,950	6,050	6,050	−3,950	−24,950	21,550	−3,950	6,050	53,550
Closing cash balance	−81,450	−66,400	−42,350	−46,300	−40,250	−34,200	−38,150	−63,100	−41,550	−45,500	−39,450	14,100

SENSITIVITY – 10% REDUCTION IN SALES

reality, it is likely that staff costs would be reduced and there would also be a discussion with the directors about drawings.

ACTIVITY 3.1
Cash flow sensitivities

The following activity requires you to use an Excel spreadsheet and build a cash flow statement based on the initial figures for Amore in Table 3.7.

Once you have built the model, experiment with the sales figures, both increasing and reducing them to see the overall impact on the cash position in this business. Compare your results to the second set of figures which shows a 10 per cent reduction in sales (Table 3.8).

The use of earnings before interest, tax, depreciation and amortization

Earnings before interest, tax, depreciation and amortization (EBITDA) has traditionally been the primary measure that banks have used to assess if businesses can repay their borrowing. We often use the measures of EBITDA as a way of determining the ongoing performance of a business, over a two- or three-year period.

Earnings before interest, tax, depreciation and amortization (EBITDA)
The profits for a business before further items including interest, tax, depreciation and amortization are deducted.

The concept behind comparing calculations of EBITDA are very similar to those of ratio analysis in Chapter 2. By examining these calculations, the banker is trying to analyse the ability of a business to cover its liabilities on an ongoing basis. We will now consider each element of EBITDA in turn.

Interest

This is the total amount of interest that the business has had to pay in the accounting period in question. This figure is the interest derived from all the interest-bearing liabilities the business has (including any overdrafts, invoice discount facilities, commercial loans, leasing or hire purchase facilities and any loans from directors that are interest-bearing).

Taxation

Tax paid shown in a business's accounts is based on the profits in the accounting period that is under consideration. It is impacted significantly by the accounting policies in the business, and particularly by depreciation policies (which are in turn impacted by the tax regimes that are in place for that accounting period). Taxation is a specialist subject and whilst bankers need to be aware of current rates, it is not necessary to be an expert in tax affairs.

Depreciation

We've already looked at depreciation in Chapter 2. You will recall that items such as depreciation are non-cash accounting items only. If there is a high level of depreciation in one year compared to another then this will distort the picture of profitability in that accounting period, and without this readjustment, the business, on the face of it, will not have performed so well. This could negatively influence a banker's view of the business.

We can illustrate this point in a simple example by adjusting the depreciation in the same accounting period to show the impact on overall profits.

In Example A (Table 3.9) you will see that the business has depreciation of £100,000 in the year, and in Example B (Table 3.9), depreciation has been adjusted to £200,000 in the year. Example A has operating profit of £350,000, compared to Example B, with operating profit of £250,000.

The profits in one particular year will be impacted by depreciation and the processing of adding back depreciation in each year gives a consistent picture of the profitability of the business. We can see that once we add back depreciation then the readjusted figure is the same in Example C and Example D (Table 3.10).

Amortization

Amortization is often used to describe the repayment of loans and other long-term financial liabilities, and where funds are lent to commercial businesses, these liabilities need to be fully repaid during the agreed term so that there is no refinance risk.

Amortization, when discussed in profit and loss terms however, means the 'writing-off' of intangible assets that a business might own over a period

Table 3.9 Example A and Example B – changes in depreciation

Example A

Turnover	2,500,000
Cost of sales	−1,750,000
Gross profit	**750,000**
Admin expenses	−300,000
Depreciation	−100,000
Operating profit	**350,000**

Example B

Turnover	2,500,000
Cost of sales	−1,750,000
Gross profit	**750,000**
Admin expenses	−300,000
Depreciation	−200,000
Operating profit	**250,000**

of time. It is important to note that not all businesses have intangible assets. Intangible assets can be anything the business owns and are often intellectual property such as licences and patents which have a finite life span, and may be worth less each year. In the same way that a tangible asset such as a machine is depreciated, a non-tangible asset is written down and this cost is deducted from the profits. This is a non-cash item.

ACTIVITY 3.2
Intangible assets

What kinds of businesses will have significant intangible assets?

In the same way as we have treated depreciation, we also add back amortization in order to have a more consistent view of the business.

When profit and loss statements are produced, the EBITDA figure will not feature in the calculations and therefore the bank will need to calculate this by restating the figures. Using the figures shown in the previous chapter

Table 3.10 Example C and Example D – depreciation readjustment

Example C

Turnover	2,500,000
Cost of sales	−1,750,000
Gross profit	**750,000**
Admin expenses	−300,000
Depreciation	−100,000
Operating profit	**350,000**
Add back depreciation	100,000
Earnings before depreciation	**450,000**

Example D

Turnover	2,500,000
Cost of sales	−1,750,000
Gross profit	**750,000**
Admin expenses	−300,000
Depreciation	−200,000
Operating profit	**250,000**
Add back depreciation	200,000
Earnings before depreciation	**450,000**

for The Hotel Company Limited, the depreciation figures (shown in Table 3.11) have been split out in the profit and loss figures (these were absorbed in the admin expenses previously).

We then need to restate the profit figures (as shown in Table 3.12), by adding back interest, tax, depreciation and amortization (here there are no intangible assets and therefore amortization is not applicable).

Why is EBITDA useful?

EBITDA is useful for bankers as it gives a strong indicator of the ability of the business to generate cash from its *trading activities*. This is before there are adjustments for: 1) non-cash items of depreciation and amortization;

Table 3.11 The Hotel Company

	30-Sep-17
Turnover	**1,841,150**
Cost of sales	−1,302,263
Gross profit	**538,887**
Admin expenses	−346,104
Depreciation	−49,554
Other operating income	732
Operating profit	**143,961**
Interest payments	−38,300
Pre-tax profit	**105,661**
Taxation	−50,427
Profit after tax	**55,234**

Table 3.12 The Hotel Company – EBITDA readjustment

	30-Sep-17
Profit after tax	55,234
Add back tax	50,427
Add back interest	38,300
Add back depreciation	49,554
EBITDA	**193,515**

2) deduction of interest (which is dependent on the levels of debt in the business); and finally 3) deduction of tax (which is dependent on profit levels *after* the deduction of depreciation and amortization).

It is also a useful way of comparing similar businesses, which may have different depreciation and amortization policies and different circumstances with regards to their gearing (the level of interest).

Acquisitions

Banks can be asked to finance the purchase of one business by another and EBITDA is usually used as a way of valuing the target company, with the purchase price being a multiple of the average of the last three years' EBITDA (eg if average EBITDA in the last three years has been £249,000, then, using a multiplier of three or four times, the price might be anywhere between £747,000 and £996,000).

The EBITDA levels will be used as part of the negotiations, with the purchase price being derived from it. The vendors (sellers) of the business will want the highest possible price, whilst the purchasers will be looking for the lowest possible price. EBITDA gives an indication of whether the newly acquired business would have the ability to repay the new debt that the purchasing company might need to incur in order to buy it.

However, using the measure of EBITDA on its own to measure performance only uses profit and loss figures and this does not allow us to have a fuller picture of how the business has used its other forms of funding to pay its liabilities.

Cash flow available for debt service

Cash flow available for debt service (CFADS) is a calculation that banks use to ensure that a business is generating sufficient cash to enable it to repay its borrowing. This is a hybrid of the EBITDA calculation, with further enhancements to reflect items such as changes in working capital movements.

> **Cash flow available for debt service (CFADS)** The starting point for the CFADS approach is to use EBITDA, on the basis that we need to readjust the profit figures for the year to reflect items that are non-cash. Using the following example from a company, Able Ltd, we can build up a picture of the cash performance for this business.

Table 3.13 shows figures for three years and the profit and loss figures before any adjustments. We need to add back depreciation and Table 3.14 shows the position of the business when this has been done.

The next step is to look at the balance sheet position of the business for the three years in question and Table 3.15 shows the position of the assets and liabilities of the business over that period.

Table 3.13 CFADS 1 – Able Ltd

	£000 Dec-16	£000 Dec-17	£000 Dec-18
Sales	12,450	12,990	13,870
Cost of goods sold	−10,458	−10,860	−11,526
Gross profit	**1,992**	**2,130**	**2,344**
Depreciation	−150	−200	−220
Overheads	−1,250	−1,344	−1,485
Earnings before interest and tax	**592**	**586**	**639**
Interest	−50	−55	−55
Tax	−107	−105	−115
Net profit AFTER tax and interest	**435**	**426**	**469**
Dividends	−200	−300	−400
Net profit after dividends	**235**	**126**	**69**

Table 3.14 CFADS 2 – Able Ltd

	£000 Dec-16	£000 Dec-17	£000 Dec-18
Sales	12,450	12,990	13,870
Cost of goods sold	−10,458	−10,860	−11,526
Gross profit	**1,992**	**2,130**	**2,344**
Depreciation	−150	−200	−220
Overheads	−1,250	−1,344	−1,485
Earnings before interest and tax	**592**	**586**	**639**
Add back depreciation	150	200	220
Earnings before interest, tax and depreciation	**742**	**786**	**859**

CFADS is only concerned with the movement of assets and liabilities that have an impact on the ability of business to cover its debts. Without the figures for the period to December 2015, we cannot ascertain the cash movements for the period to December 2016. We will therefore concentrate on the following two years.

Table 3.15 CFADS 3 – Able Ltd

	£000 Dec-16	£000 Dec-17	£000 Dec-18
Land and buildings	250	250	250
Plant and machinery	1250	1350	1350
Total fixed assets	**1500**	**1600**	**1600**
Inventory	75	75	60
Trade receivables	1500	1725	1888
Cash	250	325	558
Total current assets	**1825**	**2125**	**2506**
Tax	110	145	160
Trade payables	1640	1653	1750
Lease purchase agreements	200	200	200
Total current liabilities	**1950**	**1998**	**2110**
Total assets less current liabilities	**1375**	**1727**	**1996**
Lease purchase agreements	800	900	900
Directors loan account	100	225	425
Creditors due after more than 1 year	**900**	**1125**	**1325**
Net assets	**475**	**602**	**671**
Share capital	50	50	50
Profit and loss account	425	552	621
Total shareholder funds	**475**	**602**	**671**

Table 3.16 shows key movements of:

- working capital;
- tax;
- capital expenditure (Capex); and
- dividends.

Table 3.16 CFADS 4 – Able Ltd

	2017 £000	
EBITDA	**786**	
Working capital movements (net) – (note 1)	–212	
Tax (note 2)	–70	
Net capex (note 3)	–300	
Dividends	–300	
CFADS	**–96**	

Note 1 – working capital

(Increase)/decrease in inventory	0	[no movement]
(Increase)/decrease in trade receivables	–225	[1500 to 1725, a movement of 225]
Increase/(decrease) in trade payables	13	[1640 to 1653, a movement of 13]
Working capital movement reconciliation	**–212**	[a netting of these movements]

Note 2 – tax

Closing tax balance/December 2016	110
Tax from profits to December 2017	105
Sub total	**215**
Tax creditor in balance sheet December 2017	145
Cash paid in the period	70

Note 3 – net capex

Plant and machinery at December 2017	1350
Depreciation for period to December 2017	200
Value of P&M BEFORE depreciation – December 2017	**1550**
Plant and machinery at December 2016	1250
Capex movement in the year	300

Working capital – earlier we discussed the principles of the 'movement' of assets and liabilities and the potential impacts on cash in the business and we can see very clearly how these principles operate in Note 1 to Table 3.16. Note 1 shows how each element of working capital has moved, and overall there has been a negative movement in cash of £212,000.

Tax – the payments of tax will be impacted by the year end for the accounts and there will normally be timing differences between when the tax liability is first incurred by profits earned and when it is actually paid by the business. Note 2 shows how this is calculated.

Net capital expenditure (Capex) – Note 3 shows the fixed assets adjusted to show the impact of depreciation in the period and that there must have been cash spent on assets in this period.

Dividends – this is self-explanatory (see below for a further discussion of dividends).

We can see that the overall impact of all the movements creates a negative CFADS of £96,000 when we take all the movements into consideration. Without examining the other impacts of how working capital movements or capital expenditure has impacted on available cash flow, we do not get a full picture of how much the business has to cover its lending liabilities.

Let us now consider the final year in these figures and using the principles we have already employed, Table 3.17 sets out the CFADS position. You will see from the table that there is a positive CFADS of £88,000 when all cash movements are taken into consideration. Able Ltd, as you will already have noticed, pays its directors large dividends. This, in itself, is not an issue if the business can afford to pay them. Dividends are part of the way that directors pay themselves, and, particularly where large sums are involved may be partly discretionary.

The issue of dividends becomes a concern for the bank when the business is struggling financially or where there is a further borrowing request, and CFADS would be adversely impacted by the dividend payments. There needs to be an understanding from the bank's perspective, in terms of what overall remuneration the directors have (including salaries, etc), what they need to fund their lifestyles and what is discretionary.

Using Able Ltd again, we can see that if dividend payments only needed to be £200,000 per annum, this significantly improves the CFADS position for 2017 and 2018, as shown in Table 3.18. We can see that in both years, this increases CFADS, particularly in 2018, where this increases from £88,000 to £288,000.

Table 3.17 CFADS 5 – Able Ltd

	2018 £000
EBITDA	**859**
Working capital movements (net) – (note 1)	–51
Tax (note 2)	–100
Net capex (note 3)	–220
Dividends	–400
CFADS	**88**

Note 1 – working capital

(Increase)/decrease in inventory	15	[75 to 60]
(Increase)/decrease in trade receivables	–163	[1725 to 1888, a movement of 163]
Increase/(decrease) in trade payables	97	[1653 to 1750, a movement of 97]
Working capital movement reconciliation	**–51**	[a netting of these movements]

Note 2 – tax

Opening tax balance/December 2017	145
Tax from profits to December 2018	115
Sub total	**260**
Tax creditor in balance sheet December 2018	160
Cash paid in the period	100

Note 3 – net capex

Plant and machinery at December 2018	1350
Depreciation for period to December 2018	220
Value of P&M BEFORE depreciation – December 2017	**1570**
Plant and machinery at December 2016	1350
Capex movement in the year	220

Table 3.18 CFADS 6 – Able Ltd

	2017 £000
EBITDA	**786**
Working capital movements (net) – (note 1)	−212
Tax (note 2)	−70
Net capex (note 3)	−300
Dividends	−300
CFADS	−96
Add back part of dividends	100
Adjusted CFADS	4

	2018
EBITDA	**859**
Working capital movements (net) – (note 1)	−51
Tax (note 2)	−100
Net capex (note 3)	−220
Dividends	−400
CFADS	88
Add back part of dividends	200
Adjusted CFADS	288

Using CFADS

Once we have calculated CFADS for a business, this allows us to consider the existing borrowing.

Review of existing borrowing for Able Ltd

Using the figures for 2018, before we make any adjustments for dividends, we can see that there is CFADS of £88,000. This is against total finance costs of £255,000 per annum (£200,000 for lease payments and £55,000 for interest payments). The business is not generating sufficient cash from its normal trading activities to cover finance costs.

A bank would normally look for CFADS cover of 1.25 times. Using the table earlier, where we added back part of the dividend payments, we can see that using our adjusted figure of £288,000, CFADS cover would be 1.13 times. This isn't quite within the parameters that we need but is a significant improvement. CFADS would need to be in excess of £319,000 in order to be in excess of the 1.25 times ratio. The fundamental issue with this business is that the level of dividends needs to be on a more reasonable basis going forwards!

ASSIGNMENT/EXAM TIP

You may not have to calculate CFADS and it may be given to you for each year; however, you need to understand the constituent parts of the calculation.

You may also be presented with forecast CFADS figures where you need to assess a new borrowing request. The 'sense' check in this case would be to compare the forecast growth against the performance over the last three years, to ensure that the projections make sense and are realistic. A good starting point for any analysis of further borrowing is to benchmark it against the last actual figures that you have been presented with.

Overtrading

The control of cash in a business is critical and in 'Cash flow projections' (above) we discussed the considerations when forecasting the cash position of a business. As part of that exploration we looked at the external events that might impact on the cash flow position. This is all linked to the working capital management of the business.

In Chapter 2 we discussed how to establish the financial strength (or otherwise!) of a business. If we think of a business as a building, then the building needs to have strong foundations if it is to survive in the future. If the foundations are weak, then the building may fall down when subject to adverse conditions. There are parallels which can be drawn from this analogy when a business is facing a period of growth, and, ironically, when growth is seen in the business which exceeds the expectations of the owners, problems are likely to occur. This is known as **overtrading**.

> **Overtrading** The rapid growth in turnover where there is a weak financial base in the business.

Overtrading can arise from different circumstances:

- Growth at any cost – this is where a business is deliberately chasing sales (turnover) without any regard for the consequences for gross and net margins. The 'top line' looks good but this doesn't translate into profits and ultimately cash. This often occurs in competitive sectors, where the end customer is very powerful. There is an old saying: 'Turnover is vanity, profit is sanity and cash is reality,' and often business owners will focus on sales as being the main indicator of success. Turnover is of course important, but it must be at margins and on debtor payment terms which are acceptable.
- Growth due to a new product or service – sometimes a new product or service launched by a business completely exceeds expectations in terms of sales, and the business does not have the ability to internally generate sufficient cash from its own working capital management and its bank facilities to cope with the demand via sales.

At its most extreme, overtrading can lead to the ultimate failure of the business into insolvency, as it runs out of cash.

Solutions to overtrading

A banker needs to be alive to this situation and provide support where necessary. Steps that can be taken include:

- Control of the working capital position – depending on the type of business, all components of the working capital cycle need very close attention. Trade receivables (debtors) need to be reviewed, to ensure that any outstanding monies that are outside the agreed credit terms are chased urgently. There may also need to be 'tough' discussions with some customers, who are slow payers and could be contributing to the overall cash pressures. Inventory (stock) needs to be reviewed and items that are obsolete, or items that are not selling, need to be critically examined. The ordering of inventory needs to be urgently reviewed to ensure that items that are less essential could be delayed.

The last element to be reviewed is the trade payables. The supplier base needs to be reviewed and more favourable credit terms might need to be negotiated. There is a delicate balance here because the business cannot afford to alienate its supplier base at what is a critical time.

An obvious source of support for the business is from the owners or managers who may be in a position to inject funds into the business, either via an increase in permanent share capital, or through short-term loans. This may also be a time to consider outside equity investment.

- Salaries/drawings/dividends – the owners of a business need to support themselves, but some of their remuneration may be discretionary, and therefore could be delayed whilst the business is in a critical growth phase.

- Funding options – in Chapter 7 we will explore the options that are open to businesses, and an obvious solution to explore, when a business is in a high growth phase, is to consider invoice discounting which releases funds from the trade receivables book. This could ease short-term cash flow pressures, particularly where the bank may be uncomfortable increasing the overdraft facilities.

Chapter summary

In this chapter we have explored:

- the reasons that cash is vital for the day-to-day trading activities of commercial businesses;

- the inter-relationship between the key components of the working capital cycle (trade receivables, trade payables and inventory) and how they can vary the cash available for trading operations;

- the concept of forecasting the future cash requirements of a business using a cash flow forecast;

- the importance of the earnings before interest, tax, depreciation and amortization (EBITDA) calculation and its use in assessing commercial businesses;

- the use of the cash flow available for debt service calculation; and

- how overtrading can impact on the viability of a commercial business.

Objective check

1 Why is it so important that commercial businesses manage their cash efficiently?

2 How does an increase in the holding of inventory in an accounting period impact on the cash holding of the business?

3 What are the key sensitivities that can be applied to cash flow forecasts and why are these used?

4 Under what circumstances is it useful to use the EBITDA calculation?

5 How is the CFADS calculation used to calculate the ability of a business to repay its borrowing?

6 What are the potential reasons for a business overtrading and what might a business do to tackle the problem?

Suggested answers for activities

Activity 3.2

What kinds of businesses will have significant intangible assets? Software businesses, for example, will have a large proportion of their assets as intangible assets, and this will include the proprietary software they sell (Consider Sage who sell accounting software – www.sage.com).

Learners should devise their own answer for Activity 3.1. No model answer is supplied.

Suggested answers for case study questions

Case study – Retail: trends and financing implications

1 Cash implications for Black Friday/Cyber Monday? The cash implications for these earlier events will be similar to those for Christmas inventory purchases and also mean that if Black Friday and Cyber Monday are successful, cash will be generated slightly earlier than the busiest month of December (albeit at reduced profit margins due to the discounting).

2 What are the implications for the structuring of financing structures? One of the implications for bankers to consider is the provision of more flexible financing structures. For overdraft facilities, the limits could reflect the seasonal requirements, with peaks, for example, from June through to December, reducing to lower levels in early January, once the inventory has hopefully sold and cash generated from the sales. Bankers can also consider structuring loan payments to match the seasonal cash flow.

3 The theme from the case study – *Retail: Trends/Financing Implications* may be continued and applied to other sectors. The UK hotel sector, for example, will usually see more positive cash flow in the summer months, as seaside locations will often attract UK domestic holidaymakers and urban areas (for example, London or Edinburgh) will often benefit from both domestic and foreign tourism (despite the unpredictable UK weather!). It can therefore suit the business and the bank to have larger payments in the summer months, with lower payments over some of the winter months.

Agriculture is another sector which is seasonal in the truest sense of the word, and overdrafts for arable farmers (who grow crops) will be best structured to accommodate the timing of when particular crops are sold.

04

How to structure a lending proposition

INTRODUCTION

Every business a bank lends money to is different and even businesses in the same sector do not operate in the same way. Banks therefore need a robust process of assessing every lending proposition to ensure consistency of approach, fairness to customers and that the bank adequately addresses all the risks that face the business and in turn the bank. Lending is a holistic process and no one element is more important than another.

LEARNING OBJECTIVES

By the end of this chapter, you will be able to:

- apply the principle of credit risk to commercial businesses as part of the lending process and as a key component of bank credit policy;
- apply risk mitigation techniques in the lending process;
- identify and apply the separate elements that are required to successfully create a lending proposition;
- identify the main sources of information required to assess commercial lending propositions;

- explain the importance of face-to-face customer meetings (internal and external); and
- identify and apply covenant setting in bank/customer lending agreements.

Credit risk

Credit risk is one of the main risks facing banks when they lend money. It is the risk that customers who have been lent money fail to repay some or all of the funds they have borrowed. This may ultimately leave the bank with impairments and bad debts and will mean that the bank may have to write off monies they have lent.

> **Credit risk** The risk that a customer (sometimes also defined as a counterparty) will default and not pay back their borrowing.

All credit processes that a bank engages in are an attempt to reduce the losses that might be incurred without these processes being in place. All commercial businesses face risks which can then translate into risks for the bank.

This does not mean that the bank will not incur losses in its lending portfolios as that would be an unrealistic expectation.

ACTIVITY 4.1
Review of credit risk

Take the opportunity to look at either your own bank's annual accounts or another bank's accounts and see what is said about credit risk. These can easily be accessed by typing the bank name and 'investor relations' into an internet search engine. Usually you will be given the option to download a pdf of the accounts which you can then search via your pdf reader.

Consider the key areas that the bank focuses on and particularly where there are new risks, such as a change in market conditions due to an event (eg Brexit).

There are some sources in 'Further Reading' at the end of this chapter which may also help you with this activity.

Credit policy

Any bank, as an integral part of its lending processes, will have a **credit policy** which will cover all lending to the commercial counterparties it normally deals with. Depending on its lending focus this may include many businesses we have already explored in Chapter 1, that is, sole traders, partnerships, micro-businesses, small- or medium-sized enterprises (SMEs), mid-sized businesses and corporates (including public limited companies).

Different banks may use different terminology to describe their stance; for example, Barclays Bank uses the phraseology 'credit risk management' (Barclays, 2018).

The purpose of a credit policy is to set out the appetite a bank has towards credit risk, how it may be mitigated (for example, **security** to be taken and the discount factors to be used) and will also focus on particular sectors and industries (see below). One of the principal purposes is to give staff who are actively engaged with lending to commercial customers specific guidelines to allow them to lend effectively.

> **Credit policy**　A formal set of rules adopted by a bank or financial institution which set out the circumstances under which it should lend to businesses.
>
> **Security**　The assets taken by a bank, which are owned by the business. These are used to repay borrowing if the business defaults (sometimes also referred to as collateral).

Sector appetite

Banks will face lending requests from a variety of sectors (we explore a number of key commercial sectors in Chapter 5) and it is important that a bank can articulate its specific appetite to a sector at any time; this is known as the **sector appetite**. **Real estate (property)**, for example, is an important part of a bank's commercial lending book and the bank needs to be clear about the types of customer it will support and under what circumstances.

For investment real estate the bank may only wish to lend up to 60 per cent loan to value, for a maximum of five years, with a concentration risk of less than 30 per cent to any one counterparty (for example, no one tenant is to be more than 30 per cent of the overall annual rental income). Any proposition put forward that is outside those parameters will need very solid justifications as to why it should be supported including mitigants that might be used (for example, extra security offered by the directors, including **personal guarantees**).

Sector appetite   The level of willingness that a bank has to lend to a specific industrial sector.

Real estate   Land and buildings. This can be domestic (private residences – houses/flats etc) or commercial (offices/factories/industrial units).

Property   Another phrase for real estate.

Personal guarantee   A guarantee given by an individual in favour of another individual or a limited company.

Pricing for risk

The overall principle when a bank lends money to any commercial business is that it should charge that business a rate for interest and fees based on the level of perceived risk. In Chapter 6, we discuss in detail the types of security available and the potential value of that security. A fully secured commercial business (on a written down basis) is likely to attract a lower rate of interest on any of its borrowing than a business that has a potentially unsecured element.

Banks will also charge fees based on the complexity of a **lending proposition,** and where higher levels of monitoring are required (eg during the build phase of a new factory), appropriate fees are likely to be charged.

Lending proposition   A proposal prepared by a bank containing all of the information and analysis on a business that requires borrowing facilities. This is prepared using specific headings to ensure that all key risks are considered and discussed.

Sanctioning process

All banks operate a **sanctioning process** which requires a relationship manager to put together a lending proposal that encompasses all the elements that we are exploring in this chapter. The lending proposal includes a recommendation to lend the monies and on what terms. This will then be submitted to a credit department who will agree (or decline) the proposal. The proposition may not be agreed on the exact terms that have been proposed and there may be a number of discussions that take place between the credit department and the relationship manager before the final agreement. This may entail further discussions with the customer and may require the customer to inject further cash into the deal, or provide further security. Terms may also be amended from the original proposal (for example, the **term** of a loan could be reduced).

Once a deal is agreed, the relationship manager will be responsible for issuing **facility** documentation that reflects the agreed terms and will also be responsible for ensuring that any security which is part of the deal has been taken prior to the lending of the monies. Regular monitoring reports will also be required to the credit department to ensure that all agreed terms and conditions are being complied with (for example, covenants).

> **Sanctioning process**   The internal processes a bank goes through when agreeing to lend money, particularly to a commercial business. This will usually involve having a separate credit department as part of this process.
>
> **Term**   The length of time funds are being borrowed.
>
> **Facility**   A specific line of credit provided to commercial customers (eg overdraft/loan, etc).

All banks have lending systems which capture all the details of each individual customer that they lend to. This should incorporate everything that the bank knows about the customer at the current time and it is obviously important that any changes in the business (such as expanding the number of outlets a retail business has) are recorded as soon as possible. Whilst each bank will have a unique system, they will all have similarities, and we will explore these later in this chapter.

The initial information that a banker will be interested in on a day-to-day basis is what 'facilities' a customer has and what the current **exposure** is for each facility. This is likely to be on the front page of any customer's details.

> **Exposure**   The level of lending to a business.

A facility is a type of borrowing that the customer has and can be an overdraft, loan, invoice discount line or a foreign business facility (letters of credit etc). All these different banking services will be examined in more detail later in the book. The exposure is the actual amount of a particular facility that a customer is using at a particular time, for example, if we return to the example of *Amanda's Country Kitchen* in Chapter 1, the business has a loan of £15,000 (which has reduced from the initial borrowing of £20,000), and as this is a reducing loan, the limit has reduced in line with the scheduled **repayments**. The exposure and the limit will therefore be the same. If the business also has an overdraft, then the exposure is likely to fluctuate in line with the working capital cycle within the business. At the month end, for example, when the business needs to pay Amanda's salary then it will be much higher than at any other time in the month.

> **Repayment**   The ability of a business to repay the monies it is borrowing.

When a banker looks at the opening position of a customer in the morning, what they have is the closing position of the customer from the day before. See Table 4.1 for the example for *Amanda's Country Kitchen* at the end of March.

Table 4.1 Amanda's Country Kitchen – as at 31 March

Facility	Limit (£s)	Exposure (£s)
Overdraft	1,000	870
Loan	15,000	14,875
Balance	16,000	15,745

Dominoes and jigsaws

Putting together a comprehensive lending appraisal is a little like considering what the impact may be of a particular risk – in other words what the 'domino effect' might be of something happening and can this risk be isolated and mitigated? Mitigation is the process of reducing a risk to a level that is acceptable to the organization. It does not mean that the risk will be removed completely.

> **Domino effect**   The effect that occurs when one event happens, which usually has ramifications on the ability of a business to repay its borrowing.

The discussion as to whether lending is an art or a science is developed further by the concept of thinking of it as a jigsaw puzzle, where the key pieces need to be placed together in such a way for the whole picture to make sense.

The risk cycle and dealing with credit risk

The major issue that any bank needs to address when lending money is whether the money being lent is likely to be repaid. No banker can predict the future (however experienced they are!) and part of the process of assessing the creditworthiness of a business is to consider the **risk cycle**:

1 identify all the risks that might occur during the life of the lending (and for a commercial loan for a property this might be more than 10 years);

2 assess each risk individually;

3 mitigate against the risks; and

4 monitor the risks on a regular basis.

The key consideration here is that many risks will be experienced by the customer and the role of the banker is to assess how each risk, if and when it manifests itself, will impact on the business and whether this will then impact ultimately on the **ability** of the business to repay the borrowing. The case study below is an illustration of the kind of risks affecting businesses in the creative arts industry, such as graphic design agencies.

Risk cycle   The process of identifying, assessing and considering mitigants and finally monitoring risks.

Ability   The specific capabilities of a business to carry out its core activities and therefore be able to repay its borrowing.

CASE STUDY
Protecting the customer... and the bank

The Big Yellow Design Agency (BYDA) is a partnership which was set up by two university friends, Becky Worth and Sundira Jazinda, who both studied graphic design at university. They left three years ago and decided to set up a business on their own as they didn't want to work for the larger agencies. They are based in Shoreditch, London and have rented office and studio space.

They have slowly built up their business, initially using contacts from university. They now have a good customer base and share the work between them. BYDA focus on providing their clients with a visual identity, through logos, branding and other visual devices for businesses. They are involved with everything a business does, including shop frontages, logos, brochures, leaflets, stationery, and websites. The 'value' within BYDA is based on the creative abilities of Becky and Sundira that run the business, not on more tangible assets such as the computers, and the premises they use.

One year ago, they took out a loan of £30,000 (on a five-year term) to spend on new computer equipment and to refurbish the office space, adding a small area for client presentations.

Consider the following scenario: Becky is knocked off her bike one morning coming into work and dies in hospital later that day. Sundira, her friend and business partner, now has to deal with not only the grief of losing Becky, but also running the business on her own.

The relationship manager at the bank insisted when the new loan was taken out that Becky and Sundira take out an insurance policy called a **key person protection policy** for the full amount of the loan (£30,000). This is a business life policy, and in this case would be on the lives of Becky and Sundira, paying out against the death of one of the partners. The bank took an assignment over the policy.

Question

Consider the issues that Sundira will now be faced with and how this will impact on the bank. Why will the key person protection policy be useful for Sundira and the bank?

Check your answers at the end of this chapter.

Key person protection policy   A life policy that a limited company will take out on the life of a key employee.

Key components of a lending proposition

There are several **lending mnemonics** that can be used to analyse and assess a lending request. These include PPARTSI and CAMPARI. There is no one mnemonic which is better than another and they are, in essence, a way of ensuring that all of the key elements are considered and assessed when analysing a lending proposition.

Lending mnemonic   A set of initials that set out the key headings with which a business should be analysed when it is borrowing money.

PPARTSI

- person
- purpose
- amount
- repayment
- term
- security
- income

CAMPARI

- character
- ability
- margin
- purpose
- amount
- repayment
- insurance (security)

Person The entity that is being lent to.

Purpose The reason the lending is needed.

Amount The total funds that are being lent.

Income The profits generated by a business, which can be used to repay borrowing.

Character The trustworthiness of the principals behind a business.

Margin The rate of interest charged above either base rate or London Interbank Offered Rate (LIBOR).

ACTIVITY 4.2
Hat Enterprises Ltd – assessing a lending proposition

Hat Enterprises Ltd (HE) case study was introduced in Chapter 1. This activity is a continuation of that case study and examines how a bank might decide how much it should lend.

The business was set up 10 years ago, has banked with you all that time, and has always honoured all of its banking facilities. The initial scenario was a request from the directors to borrow £2.25 million towards the cost of a new building of £3 million near Peterborough. The business has built up cash reserves of £750,000 which it is prepared to put towards the purchase.

Further information: the business currently rents its existing premises but has outgrown them. The present five-year lease is due for renewal in 12 months' time (lease payments are £125,000 per annum). The new premises are purpose-built.

The directors have calculated they will need to make repayments of £150,000 per annum on the new loan.

Required: using the information you have, consider this lending proposition, using the lending structure PPARTSI. Concentrating on the non-financial elements of the structure, detail your answer and then compare this to the suggested answer at the end of the chapter. What other questions will the bank want to ask the customer about this transaction?

The above mnemonics can be extremely helpful in building an overall picture of a lending proposition. We will now go on to look at what your key considerations should be when constructing a lending package which meets the needs of both the customer and bank.

Borrowing – what does the customer want (and, what do they need)?

This may seem like a very straightforward question but the answer to it is very important and getting it right will ensure the job of the banker is made significantly easier as they construct a lending package which suits the needs of the customer *and* meets the risk appetite of the bank.

It's a misconception amongst bankers that lending decisions are clear cut and that the only option when considering lending money is to lend the exact amount of funds that the customer has requested, or, if the request does not match set lending criteria, to decline the request and not lend the money at all!

Customers often don't know exactly how much they need (particularly new businesses) and many customers are nervous about asking the bank for too much in case they (the bank) decline the request. A good example of this is lending to customers who are developers of residential property (ie they are building property for private occupation).

THE RESIDENTIAL DEVELOPER

The usual prudent 'rule of thumb' is to add a 10 per cent contingency to the overall costings that are provided by the developer. Residential developments (houses or flats) will typically be over a relatively long period, certainly more than a year (depending on how many properties are being constructed) and will be subject to a number of issues that will be outside the control of the customer (and the bank!). This will include the weather (a harsh winter will mean that work will slow down or stop for a period), the increase in raw material costs, the insolvency of a key contractor (a new contractor will need to be found and this again will slow down the work) or discovering issues when the foundations are being prepared for the development (often this is where many of the 'hidden' costs are in a development).

All of these potential issues will slow down the particular development and will create higher costs for the development. If the developer does not have the funds for contingencies, then inevitably there will be an approach to the bank to lend more money.

The major credit risk for the bank, related to this type of customer, is that once work has commenced, the *only* source of repayment is from the sale of completed houses. If the developer doesn't complete the houses then the only course of action will be for the bank to lend further funds to ensure the houses are completed, or, in more extreme circumstances, to take control of the development, and pay for another developer to finish the work. In both instances, the lending exposure of the bank increases beyond the limit of what was initially agreed and there will potentially be a much narrower gap between the sale prices of the new properties and the funds borrowed. The smaller the gap, the bigger the risk that the bank will not be fully repaid from the sale of the completed properties.

Bankers need to use their expertise and experience (the latter obviously only comes in time!) to guide customers when dealing with new lending requests. This involves assessing the proposition very carefully to ensure that the customer is borrowing enough for their short and medium-term requirements.

What seems obvious to an experienced banker when lending is usually not obvious to the customer. A lack of experience (on the customer's behalf) doesn't mean that a customer will be a 'bad' customer and not repay but it does mean that the banker needs to compensate for this by thinking for the customer and challenge the business proposition in a constructive manner.

The challenge, particularly in lending to new customers, is that if the customer requires further funds in a relatively short period of time, following the initial lend, this can suggest that the customer hasn't thought through their plans and financial projections in enough detail (although this may also be because the business is much more successful than originally antici-pated and requires more day-to-day working capital!).

It can also throw into question the original lending assessment process and even the credibility of the banker who has recommended it. Unexpected things happen of course (and the increase of severe weather events globally is testament to that), and the question that will always be asked is how likely is it that the 'unexpected' event was actually unexpected.

Why do customers borrow?

The reasons customers borrow are as varied as the different types of customer a bank has but can often be sub-divided into different categories:

- Working capital – this is to finance the day-to-day requirements of the business, including the financing of inventory, trade receivables and trade payables (as discussed in Chapter 2).
- New business premises, eg:
  - offices;
  - factory buildings;
  - shops.
- Fixed assets, eg:
  - machinery;
  - vehicles – cars, vans, fork-lift trucks, articulated trucks (etc).
- Property finance (often called **real estate finance**) and this can include:
  - residential developers;
  - residential property investment;
  - commercial property investment.
- The purchase of a new business (which allows a business to grow more quickly than could be achieved organically).
- The purchase of a business from the existing owners/directors by the next level of management (sometimes known as a management buy-out).
- Restructuring of existing borrowing facilities.

Real estate finance The lending of money to businesses that deal in property (residential or commercial).

Assessing the business

This is a very wide-ranging topic and with the extensive range of businesses and sectors that a banker is likely to deal with on a regular basis, it is very important that there is a framework that can be used to analyse some of the internal and external factors. It is important to split this into external and internal considerations.

External considerations

What are the external impacts on a particular business, industry or sector? Even businesses within the same sector will not operate in the same way, albeit that there are often similarities which the banker can use to compare performance.

PESTLE

This strategic tool is discussed in greater detail in Chapter 5. It is a tool used to examine the external factors that can impact on the environment a business operates in. It groups all the external factors together under a number of key headings:

- political;
- economic;
- social;
- technological;
- legal; and
- environmental.

The boxed example below on the Care Home Sector explores how PESTLE could be used to think about external considerations.

THE CARE HOME SECTOR

It is not always necessary to comment on every part of PESTLE, although in a lending proposal you would need to say why you had not commented on it. In this example, we are less concerned with the Political, Technological and Environmental elements, and have concentrated on the other elements.

Economic

The sector was adversely impacted in several ways following the financial crisis of 2007/08. Residential property prices dropped significantly across the UK, with particular parts of the country, such as the North-East of England, experiencing much more pronounced drops in value. The impact of this, particularly for older people wanting to sell their homes and move into a care home, was it meant that they were unable to do so, with a resultant slow-down in new residents taking up care home places.

Social

The UK has an ageing population, with current forecasts for people to live longer than they ever have. As at 2016, those aged 65 and over made up 18 per cent, or 11.8 million people out of the overall population (65.7 million). In the next 20 years, those aged over 65 are projected to increase by another 4.75 million.

This, in turn, provides both a huge challenge for how older people are looked after in the UK and also a huge opportunity for those private businesses that operate in the sector.

Legal

Current figures indicate that the private sector provides 200,200 beds in the UK. The sector is regulated by the Care Quality Commission (CQC) which also regulates hospitals, general practitioners and dentists. Care homes have elderly, vulnerable people in them and this is the reason for the high level of external scrutiny and regulation to ensure stringent safety and other standards are adhered to.

Changes in the legal requirements for care home owners over the past 20 years (particularly the change in room sizes to larger rooms, the move to single occupancy and having en-suite facilities for every resident) has meant that the owners of the older care homes, which are often converted residential properties, have incurred extra costs as they have had to convert properties to meet changing statutory requirements.

(www.cqc.org.uk, 2017)

A business's place in its own marketplace – the importance of a unique selling point

Businesses need to be different and often in very crowded and competitive marketplaces, businesses need a unique selling point (USP) to set themselves apart. Take, for example, crisps and coffee, which are everyday household foods. The humble crisp has had a makeover. There are now a number of independent companies which are challenging the established manufacturers (many of which are household names). Pipers Crisps, established in 2004, is a good example of how a business can differentiate itself. Based in Brigg, Lincolnshire, they provide crisps in a variety of flavours (including Atlas Mountains Wild Thyme and Rosemary, Kirkby Malham Chorizo, and Biggleswade Sweet Chilli), have packaging which focuses on the strong brand and strap-line of 'Made by Farmers' and distribute their products via a diverse number of outlets such as UK delicatessens, farm shops and pubs. They have also responded to changing consumer requirements by having the full range as gluten-free. This approach also means that the company, by moving away from just producing a commodity, can charge a higher price for its products (www.piperscrisps.com, 2017).

In the UK, consumers drink a staggering 55 million cups of coffee every day! The large chains such as Starbucks, Costa, Prèt-A-Manger and Greggs take a large part of this retail trade and one of the largest pub chains, Wetherspoons, has in recent years moved towards coffee (including takeaway options) to complement its other products.

Having a huge marketplace allows smaller businesses to also find profitable niches. Rounton Coffee Roasters is a small business based in the small village of East Rounton in North Yorkshire. They focus on sourcing coffee from around the world (Sumatra, South East Asia was where their coffee was first sourced). They provide wholesale products to a variety of customers including coffee shops, farm shops, delicatessens, restaurants, pubs and hotels. They also provide coffee machines (which can be leased from Rountons) and give barista training as and when required. They also provide products to the individual consumer by post.

Their USP is bespoke products (they produce limited runs of particular blends of coffee throughout the year), focus on the way they deal with their overseas suppliers ethically and provide a personal service to their wholesale customers with dedicated support (barista training etc as mentioned above) (www.rountoncoffee.co.uk, 2017).

ACTIVITY 4.3
Review of a business's unique selling points (USPs)

Pipers Crisps and Rounton Coffee are two examples of commercial businesses that have distinctive unique selling points and ways of operating.
Think about independent businesses that are local to you.

> *What differentiates them from other businesses in the same sector (it might be the product or service, the branding, or perhaps the staff)?*
> *What do they do well?*
> *What do they not do very well?*
> *Write down your answers before continuing.*

Internal considerations – people and products

The entrepreneurial qualities of business owners are so often critical to the success of the business and will carry businesses a long way. People who run businesses need energy, enthusiasm and resilience.

Management

> 'Do what's right, not what is easy' Sir Paul Smith (owner of the global fashion business). (Paul Smith Ltd, 2017)

Running a business is never easy and the quote by the famous entrepreneur, Sir Paul Smith, illustrates this very succinctly. This often requires making decisions which will ensure the business travels in the right direction, even if this means that they are not necessarily easy to implement.

Businesses need to have the right directors and managers who can run the business both now and in the future. There are a number of issues, with attendant risks, that bankers need to consider:

- Ages of owners and succession planning – how old are owners and when do they want to leave the business? If the owners or directors are all nearing retirement age then the bank needs to know what is planned for the next 5–10 years in order to properly assess the risk. If it is a family business, then the bank needs to see that the younger generation (if there is one) has the skills and also the desire to want to take over the business in the future. This may not be an immediate risk but is one where the bank needs to see that consideration has been given to the risk of succession planning.

- Skills of management team – the bank must also feel satisfied that there is a wide enough set of skills covering all the main roles within the business. The finance function must be strong enough to support a rapidly growing business. This is something to look out for even if the business is growing more slowly, and the bank must feel satisfied that there are members of the management team who can cope with the increasing demands of the financial function. The potential risks to the bank include:

- Delays in the production of vital management information – the bank needs to know how a business it is lending to is performing at all times.

- Trade receivables (funds owed *to* the business) are not chased if they are outside the usual terms set by the business and as trade receivable days increase, this can have a negative impact on the cash flow for the business.

- Rapid growth (overtrading) – a banker who is close to their customer will be able to spot these and other pertinent issues (particularly if management information is either not being produced or is regularly delayed, or if trade receivables do not appear to be under control). A way of helping the customer to deal with this issue and to mitigate it for the bank is to have a dialogue with the customer and their accountant, where the accountant may either be able to produce the information necessary or help the customer source a good bookkeeper (and perhaps even, if the business has grown to an appropriate size, a financial director).

    You will probably find that businesses are often highly skilled at the core operations of the business (eg running a small independent chain of restaurants) but may not be as skilled at marketing, particularly using new media such as Instagram, Facebook, YouTube etc. Jamie Oliver is an example of an established personality who has used traditional channels such as cookbooks to build his brand but has also embraced the digital world using his channel called FoodTube, and many brands now engage actively with online 'vloggers' (YouTube, 2017). However, the risk for the bank is that not all managers will have the necessary range and mix of skills to utilize all the marketing channels that are now available in order to build a sustainable and successful business.

- Dynamics within a team – this is only applicable to larger commercial businesses. It is often difficult for a bank to gauge how well a management team works together and often only time spent with the business will allow a banker to judge how the different parts of the business operate as a whole and where potential tensions might exist.

    - For smaller businesses, such as *Amanda's Country Kitchen* (from Chapter 1), the skill of the banker would be in helping and advising the customer as to when they need to expand the management team to help support the growth of the business. Often small business owners try to cover all the roles themselves. For the original café, it might be manageable for Amanda to make all the cakes herself and run the business. If she expands the business and opens another café locally, however, she may struggle to do everything herself and may either need to have someone make the cakes she sells or find someone to run the new café for her.

Staff

A perennial issue with many businesses is the shortage of skilled workers. Certain sectors, such as engineering in the UK are seeing an acute shortage of staff with the right skills (Wallace, 2017). Businesses need to be not only able to attract the right staff but to also retain them. They also need to be able to support staff who need to balance other personal priorities such as caring for an elderly relative or picking children up from school.

A challenge that many businesses also have is that of managing capacity as they need to be able to deal with very busy periods but will not need the same level of staff in quieter periods.

ACTIVITY 4.4
Staff capacity

Consider the following businesses:

- an independent restaurant chain (10 outlets); and
- a regional retail clothes shop chain (10 outlets).

When are the busy and quieter times likely to be and how might this impact on staffing?
Can you think of any other sectors or types of business that will need to manage peaks in demand for staff?
Write down your answers before continuing and check the answers at the end of the chapter.

As a banker you will need to mitigate the risk by ensuring you have a concrete understanding of how the business expects to be able to manage these capacity issues. If it does have shortages, how does it plan to deal with them? Businesses such as care homes (discussed earlier) have legal requirements to have a certain ratio of qualified staff per resident (this requirement is 365 days per year). This can subsequently mean that when there are staff shortages, the home must employ staff from an agency where the costs to the business are much higher. This kind of strategy would obviously have an impact on profit margins, which would need to be taken into consideration.

The product

The product or service a business creates is critical to its success. Listening to customers, being responsive to the market, and adapting to changes are all part of what a business needs to do in order to grow and prosper. The risks facing a business very much depend on the type of business the bank is lending to. For example, as we discussed earlier, if your customer was planning to enter a competitive marketplace, you'd need to be satisfied that their USP was enough to differentiate them from their competitors.

The reasons businesses get into financial difficulties will be explored more fully in Chapter 9.

Ability to repay

This is a critical part of the lending process and where much of the bank's risk analysis will be concentrated.

For a commercial bank, all borrowing should fully amortize over the life of the loan. This means that at the end of the term all the borrowing is fully repaid and the bank is not faced with refinance risk, which is the risk that any residual borrowing is not able to be refinanced at the end of the original term.

The ability of a business to repay its borrowing is based on the profits it can generate, both now and in the future. The initial analysis will revolve around current performance (usually the full accounts from the past 12 months) and current performance using up-to-date management information and trading or cash flow forecasts. If the lending proposition is for an increase in borrowing, then the prudent approach by the bank is usually to calculate if the business can afford to pay the increased borrowings back from *current* profitability rather than *projected* profitability. If it can, then there is a strong argument for supporting the new borrowing.

If the business can't, the projections need to be examined very carefully, and if they show a significant increase in both turnover and profitability, they need to have sensitivities applied to them to show an increase in turnover and profitability which is more reflective of performance in the last few years. This can then be used to assess the request for the new borrowing.

> ## A NOTE ON EXISTING BUSINESSES
>
> It is not necessarily more straightforward to lend to an existing business than a new business but the one advantage the bank does have with an existing customer is that of a 'track record'. The bank knows if the customer has honoured earlier and existing borrowing commitments, it has full details about the operation of bank accounts and also has experience of dealing with the owners or directors on a regular basis.

Interest rates

A major risk to both customers and their bankers, which impacts on the ability to repay and also links directly to credit risk, is that of rising interest rates. At the time of writing the Bank of England has signalled that it is likely that base rates may start to go up.

Many commercial customers often borrow at 'floating rates', which means that the agreement between the customer and the bank will be worded in such a way that the customer will borrow at a rate (or margin) *above* base rate. This margin will be for the term of the loan or overdraft and will remain at the same rate throughout the life of the loan. For example, at a margin of 3 per cent above base and a base rate of 0.5 per cent, the full rate paid by the customer is 3.5 per cent. However, what remains a variable is that base rate can alter, up or down, through the life of the loan. If the Bank of England decides to raise interest rates (to control inflation, for example) then the customer has no option but to pay the increased costs on their loan. This could be for the rest of the term of the loan. Banks will therefore often model serviceability against a predetermined 'default rate' to give a through the cycle view of serviceability.

A small rise in base rate may not appear on the face of it to be too onerous; however, it needs to be put in context with each customer. For every £1 million borrowed by a commercial customer, a rise in base rate of 0.5 per cent creates an extra £5,000 per annum in interest costs. The immediate impact of any rise in interest rates is a reduction in profits and also an impact on the cash position of the business. Most loans have interest applied on a quarterly basis and therefore it is likely that the bank will very quickly increase the monthly or quarterly repayments following an increase in base rate to ensure that the loan is repaid within the original term.

Interest 'roll-up'

Interest roll-up is a technique that the bank can employ when it is lending to customers who require a period of time to undertake the development of a new project. For example:

- residential property development;
- building of a new factory; or
- building of a new care home.

Funds for this type of venture will be lent on a phased basis against agreed milestones (and usually with the involvement of other professionals such as monitoring surveyors). Repayments will not start until the development has completed and is in a position to start generating profits. The logic behind having interest 'rolling up' is that there is no income being generated during the development phase to cover it. Such a lending strategy will be subject to an agreed exit event, often linked to an asset disposal. It is therefore essential that there is sufficient headroom in the value to cover both the capital and accruing interest.

This strategy of interest roll-up may also be applied for businesses in financial distress where repayment is reliant upon a desired trading performance being attained or realization of assets being achieved.

> **Interest roll-up** The process of adding interest to a loan as it is being drawn down over a period of time (often to fund property development).

Security

This should always come towards the end of any lending proposition analysis. This is because the lending proposition should be one the bank wants to support *before* it considers what security it can take. All the risks facing the business, both internal and external, need to have been identified, considered and analysed before security is considered.

Commercial lending is usually undertaken on the basis that the bank has sufficient security to cover it if the customer cannot repay the borrowing. The security can be liquidated (turned into cash) and the borrowing repaid. There is often a widely held belief by bankers that if they are 'fully secured' on a 'written-down' basis that they will not lose money if a business fails. This is simply not true, although if security is held there is a much better chance that the bank will get its money back if the business runs into severe financial difficulties.

The concept of 'written-down' security, as already discussed earlier in the book, is to take any asset that the bank might hold and apply a process of 'writing-down' against it. The guiding principle is that banks should not lend 100 per cent against any asset value that it has as security. There are a number of reasons for this and the main arguments against lending fully against an asset include:

- time – it takes time to sell an asset;
- costs – there will usually be professional costs such as valuations, agents' fees and solicitor fees;
- interest costs – these will continue to be incurred during the period it takes to sell an asset; and
- potential deterioration in the value of the asset.

COMMERCIAL PROPERTY

The sale of any asset held as security by the bank will take time to sell if the best price is to be obtained for it. A light industrial unit (comprising warehouse, office space and a good workshop area) in the outskirts of a major city worth £750,000, depending on the prevailing economic conditions, will need possibly 6 to 12 months to sell. The price may need to be dropped to sell it and there will be the usual costs incurred for marketing the property by professional agents, legal fees for conveyancing etc. This is based on the customer selling the property where there is no sign of 'distress' to the business to those who are interested in buying it.

Working on the basis that £35,000 is taken off the selling price to accommodate a small drop in asking price and to cover the professional fees, the final funds available to repay bank borrowing will be £715,000. If the bank is relying on the full value of £750,000, then when the asset is sold, the bank will be more reliant on other security it holds, or may find itself in a position where part of its borrowing is unsecured.

Holding security gives the bank the ability to have a degree of control over assets a company has. This is particularly true for fixed assets such as machinery, as it means the business cannot dispose of assets that the bank may be either lending directly against or relying on as part of the overall security that it holds.

The use of security to repay the bank when the customer is facing financial distress will be explored in much greater detail in Chapter 9.

Pricing for risk – interest and charges

The bank needs to set a level for fees and interest which reflects the risk that it faces and it will also be impacted by the level and quality of security that it holds. This is called **pricing for risk**. In Chapter 1, the concept of treating customers fairly was introduced, with six key concepts, and whilst these concepts are very much aimed at retail consumers, the principles can also be applied to commercial customers.

Pricing for risk   The adjustment of the price charged by a bank when it lends based on the level of risk that the bank is exposed to.

Banks need to make a profit when they are dealing with their commercial customers. What is charged, however, needs to be commensurate with both risk and time spent by the bank managing the lending.

Interest rates will usually be at a rate above base rate (eg 4 per cent above base rate) and fees for a new loan facility are likely to be based on a percentage of the amount borrowed. New loans may incur rates of, say, 1–2 per cent, whilst the renewal of existing lending facilities may be lower at, say, 0.5 per cent. The bank may also deem it necessary to charge a monitoring fee, particularly during the period of a new development (during the building phase).

The rate of interest charged will be linked also to the level and type of security held, and where the bank feels that security is of stronger quality, then it may improve the rates accordingly. Banks also have the option, if they are lending outside of where they are comfortable, to potentially have a portion of the borrowing on a higher interest rate. An example of this would be using the *Hat Enterprises* example above, where the bank decided to lend the funds despite having £100,000 of borrowing which was outside of the bank's normal lending criteria. There is a strong justification for having this portion of the borrowing on a higher rate than the rest of the borrowing. If the main loan was agreed at 3 per cent above base rate, then the £100,000 might attract a rate of 5 per cent above base rate to reflect the higher risk.

Covenants

Within its lending documentation the bank is likely to have certain terms and conditions often known as **covenants**. Sometimes the terms and conditions are ones which the bank wants to have in place *before* the borrowing takes place, and these are known as **conditions precedent**.

Conditions precedent are often very straightforward terms such as:

- all security being in place before the funds are lent; or

- professional valuations conducted (and addressed to the bank) before the funds are lent.

The reasoning for this is simple in that it is much harder to ensure these things happen after the lending has been made.

> **Covenants** Specific clauses built into loan agreements that provide the ability of the bank to monitor the performance of a business after monies have been lent.
>
> **Conditions precedent** Specific conditions a business must comply with before funds are lent to them.

Monitoring of ongoing risks

Once funds are lent the main concern for the bank is that the scheduled loan repayments are all made on time, in order to repay the borrowing within the agreed period of time. The most basic indicator of all is that a business misses a loan payment. This can be for a variety of reasons, including an underperformance of the business and cash flow issues; however, a prudent banker would prefer not to get to this point before having spotted the potential warning signs of impending problems.

Basic level covenants will include:

- Loan to value (LTV) – as discussed earlier this measures the ratio between the loan and the value of the security (and is normally based on the *gross* value of the security). Using the industrial unit above with, say, a 65 per cent loan to value covenant, based on the gross value of £750,000 the bank would not normally lend more than £422,500. If there is a drop in the value of the security then this would potentially trigger a breach of this particular covenant.

- Annual accounts to be provided within 270 days of the year end.

- Management accounts to be provided within one month of the month end.

- Valuation of key assets (such as key premises – factories/warehouses etc) every three years (or whenever the bank deems it necessary).

More detailed covenants will include:

- Gearing – as explained in Chapter 2, this is the ratio of the borrowing in the business divided by the total capital employed. When new or increased borrowing is agreed this will inevitably increase the level of gearing. The bank will normally set a maximum level of gearing, for example 75 per cent, that must not be exceeded throughout the life of the loan. If repayments are made as scheduled, and the borrowing gradually reduces, then it is likely that the gearing level won't be breached; however, as this ratio is also linked to total capital employed, if losses are suffered, which erode the capital base, this will adversely impact the gearing ratio.

- Debt interest cover – also explained in Chapter 2, this requires interest to be covered so many times by profits. A ratio may be set at 2.5 times, and if the profits are generated as expected, this ratio is likely to increase over time as interest costs will gradually reduce throughout the life of the loan. However, this ratio ensures that if profits are falling, the ratio will reduce and show as a warning sign to the bank that issues need to be addressed.

- Specialist covenants – these will usually be very industry specific 'key performance indicators', eg occupancy levels in care homes – if a home has the capacity for 50 residents, then the funding requirements may require a minimum of 45 residents at any time (90 per cent occupancy).

Sources of information

The key source of information for any bank is, of course, the customer. The bank will usually ask the customer to produce a business plan, particularly in cases where the customer is a new business, or they are hoping to expand their business.

The business plan

If a customer has never produced a business plan then you, as the banker, might need to guide them so that they produce the information that you need. The key areas needed will be those already discussed in this chapter. To recap, the areas are as follows:

- borrowing – the amount and why customers borrow;
- assessing the business – internally/externally/USPs/strategy;
- management and staff;
- product;
- ability to repay;
- security; and
- covenants.

There is a tendency amongst less experienced customers to feel that the business plan is only for the bank and its only purpose is to get the bank to agree to lend money. This is rather missing the point and you can help customers by asking them to articulate why they feel their business venture will succeed. It is a very positive way of letting them explore all the elements of the business; strategically, operationally and financially.

The business plan should show what the aims and objectives are of the business, the strengths of the management team, and the product or service that the business is producing or providing. It should also cover the key risks faced by the business and how these will be addressed.

The banker will use this as a starting point for a detailed analysis of the new proposition and by using a structure that has already been described, the banker can focus on the key areas and build a strong picture of how the business will achieve its aims, and importantly how it will repay the funds it is requesting from the bank.

Trade receivables/trade payables

The details a customer has on both the customers they sell to and the customers they buy from is an invaluable aid to the bank. It helps to fully understand the customer base against which they are lending. Customers can provide an 'aged' list for both types of customer (see below for more explanation on what is meant by 'aged').

Concentrating on trade receivables, this is a list of all customers who owe money to the customer. It will show:

- the name of the customer;
- the amount outstanding; and
- a split of how 'old' the debt is, usually shown in 30 days, 60 days, 90 days and over 90 days. (This is what we mean by the 'age' of debts.)

This allows the bank to assess the concentration risk its customer faces:

- Is it over-exposed to a particular customer?
- Are there issues with collecting monies due from particular customers?

Desk-top research

The business plan is a good starting point for the bank and it should be supplemented with other research such as **desk-top research**. Most customers have websites and these provide a good source of information about the company and its products. Brochures and catalogues are always useful, especially if the customer produces a range of technical products.

> **Desk-top research**   Research carried out on a business using publicly available information.

Reviewing websites and other material not only gives further information to the banker, but it also gives an objective view of how a customer might engage with the business. If the business is in the leisure sector (for example, a hotel or restaurant) then Trip Advisor or similar sites are useful for a view of what the customer thinks. Social media (eg Twitter, Instagram or Facebook) may also be appropriate for the customer's marketing and show how they interact with their customers.

As a banker you need to understand who the competitors are to your customer's business and a review of the competitors' websites will be a useful way of comparing the products and services in the marketplace. For example, if we once again consider the care home sector, you would be able to review your customer's operations and those of the local competition by looking at reports on the Care Quality Commission's website (www.cqc.org. uk). They also produce regular reports on the overall sector which include important information on trends and risks.

Other good sources of information are local magazines, local newspaper articles or business newspaper websites. These often have articles about how a business is bringing out a new product or how it is engaging with the local community.

As a banker you won't be expected to know every detail about every sector; however, bankers are consumers themselves and if, for example, your customer runs a hotel, you could ask yourself how you would view it if you were to use it as a consumer. For example, think about whether or not you would stay there yourself. Does it offer good value for money? Is it in a good location? Whilst not always possible, if your customer owned a number of outlets, you could try to visit a site privately to see what your experience was like, which would give you some subjective information apart from what the customer was telling you. We consider these issues further in Chapter 5.

Customer visits

Desktop research on a business is always very valuable and any customer expects a banker to have done their 'homework' and know about the sector that the customer operates in. However, there is no substitute for spending time with a customer at their premises. Going to visit a business without the customer is much easier if the business is in retail or leisure but much less easy if the customer is a manufacturer. However, if you can arrange visits to factories or industrial sites they can offer you invaluable insight into how a customer operates. By walking around a site you would gain a clear view of what it looks like as well as be able to assess the upkeep and maintenance of buildings and machines.

To give another example, if your customer were building new residential houses it would be important to visit the site on a monthly basis, and use the regular Monitoring Surveyor's report to keep track of the construction progress.

Banks do face an additional risk when they lend to customers hundreds of miles away as it is very difficult to really understand the day-to-day operations on a practical basis. Some banks, such as Handelsbanken, actively promote a local relationship management ethos, and strongly discourage 'distance-banking' where the customer operates many miles from where their relationship manager is (www.handelsbanken.co.uk, 2017).

Making decisions!

So, when you've taken all of the above into consideration, you need to decide: does the deal make sense?

This is not an easy question to answer and requires a detailed analysis of the business and the management using the techniques discussed above. Is there a market for the product or service? If the business is heading in a new direction, do they have the skills within the management team to achieve their new goals?

Part of the decision may involve a level of 'gut-feel' decision making. You will need to trust the customer (and in turn the customer will need to trust you). This is not something that will be in a business plan!

After all the information that a banker has they have to make a decision about whether or not they want to lend to the customer. They need to make a recommendation to their credit department and put forward the specific terms they wish to lend on.

It is often very easy for a banker to defer decisions by asking for more and more information but at some point a decision has to be made as to whether the customer will be supported or not.

Having a defined process and structure makes it much easier for both the customer and the bank and ensures that key risks are covered and that lending decisions are fair, consistent and robust.

Chapter summary

In this chapter there has been an exploration of the key components that the banker needs to take into consideration when deciding whether or not to lend to a customer. This may be to a completely new customer, an increase in lending facilities to an existing customer, or simply a renewal of lending. We have explored:

- the importance of credit risk in lending propositions;
- the significance of risk mitigation techniques when constructing a lending proposal;
- the ability to identify and apply the key principles and practical elements in constructing a lending proposal;
- the key sources of information available to a lending banker when assessing a lending proposal;

- the importance and use of customer meetings and visits to a customer premises; and
- the importance and significance of covenant setting in customer lending agreements.

Objective check

- What is credit risk and why is it important when assessing commercial lending propositions?
- List some key risk mitigation techniques that bankers can employ when assessing credit propositions.
- What are the key components of a lending proposition?
- What are the sources of information that a bank might use when assessing a lending proposition?
- Why is it important to meet a customer when considering lending them money and why is it useful to visit them at their premises?
- Why does a bank insist on having covenants as part of the process?

Further reading

Legal & General – Key Person Insurance [accessed 19 June 2018] [Online] https://www.legalandgeneral.com/life-cover/microsites/businessprotection/business-protection-products/key-person-protection/

Writing your business plan | NatWest [accessed 19 June 2018] [Online] https://www.business.natwest.com/business/Boost/business-matters/starting-a-business/business-planning/business-plans.html

For more information on credit risk (Barclays accounts):

https://www.home.barclays/barclays-investor-relations.html

https://www.home.barclays/content/dam/barclayspublic/docs/InvestorRelations/AnnualReports/AR2016/Barclays per cent20PLC per cent20Annual per cent20Report per cent202016.pdf

For more information on business plans:

https://www.princes-trust.org.uk/help-for-young-people/tools-resources/business-tools/business-plans

For more information on key person protection policies:

https://www.legalandgeneral.com/life-cover/microsites/businessprotection/business-protection-products/key-person-protection/how-it-works/

References

Barclays [accessed 19 June 2018] [Online] https://www.home.barclays/content/
  dam/barclayspublic/docs/InvestorRelations/AnnualReports/AR2017/
  Barclays%20Bank%20PLC%202017%20AR%20-%20FINAL.pdf
Care homes | Care Quality Commission [accessed 19 June 2018] [Online] http://
  www.cqc.org.uk/what-we-do/services-we-regulate/care-homes
Company History – Paul Smith Ltd [accessed 19 June 2018] [Online] https://www.
  paulsmith.com/uk/information/company-history.html
Handelsbanken [accessed 19 June 2018] [Online] https://www.handelsbanken.
  co.uk/shb/inet/IStartRb.nsf/FrameSet?OpenView&iddef=&navid=
  HandelsbankenRB_AbouttheGroup&sa=/Shb/Inet/ICentRB.nsf/Default/
  qF5D7D0EC8FA6784F80257623002D9974
Jamie Oliver [accessed 19 June 2018] [Online] https://www.youtube.com/user/
  JamieOliver
Pipers Crisps [accessed 19 June 2018] [Online] http://www.piperscrisps.com/
Wallace, T [accessed 19 June 2018] Skills shortage bites as fall
  in unemployment leaves Britain short of engineers to fill new
  jobs [Online] http://www.telegraph.co.uk/business/2017/05/08/
  skills-shortage-bites-fall-unemployment-leaves-britain-short/

Suggested answers for activities

Activity 4.1 – Review of credit risk

Review of your own bank's audited accounts regarding credit risk. See 'Further Reading' above for links to Barclays Bank accounts.

Activity 4.2 – Hat Enterprises Ltd – assessing a lending proposition

Using the information provided, you were asked to consider lending to HE using the lending mnemonic PPARTSI

The initial scenario was a request from the directors to borrow £2.25 million towards the cost of a new building of £3 million near Peterborough. The business has built up cash reserves of £750,000 which it is prepared to put towards the purchase.

The PPARTSI lending structure is:

- person;
- purpose;

- amount;

- repayment;

- term;

- security; and

- income.

The logical approach is to use each of the headings, covering the key points in turn:

Person – the customer has been with the bank for 10 years, has a good track record with the bank and has demonstrated the ability to put a significant sum towards the new warehouse. In other words, a customer that the bank will want to support if it can.

Purpose – the directors wish to borrow money to buy new premises in Peterborough. This seems reasonable, considering the position with the lease for the existing premises.

Amount – the initial scenario was a request from the directors to borrow £2.25 million towards the cost of a new building of £3 million near Peterborough. The business has built up cash reserves of £750,000 which it is prepared to put towards the purchase. The request to the bank is therefore for new borrowing of £2.25 million.

Repayment – figures are not provided to analyse for this proposition and it would be necessary to have a full set of historical figures and projections to ensure that repayment could be made. Current lease payments are £125,000 vs new loan payments of £150,000.

Term – commercial loans would normally be agreed over 10–15 years.

Security – using a loan to value (LTV) percentage of 70 per cent, the bank will take the value of the property, and therefore subtract 30 per cent from the gross value of £3 million, giving a figure of £2.1 million. This is the level that the bank will prefer not to lend above. The requested level of £2.25 million would actually give an LTV of 75 per cent. If a lower LTV figure is used this will increase the requirement for further cash from the directors.

This is the area that would require further discussion and negotiation with the directors. See comments in 'Lending Decision' below.

Income – the bank will need to earn money on the transaction and is likely to charge between 0.5–1.0 per cent for a fee to arrange the loan and an interest margin of circa 3–4 per cent above either base rate or the London Inter-Bank Offered Rate (LIBOR).

The Lending Decision – at this point the bank has a number of choices and these are fairly straightforward:

- decline the lending proposition – it is unlikely to make this decision for a long-standing customer without further detailed discussions;

- ask the directors to put a further £150,000 towards the purchase price (the difference between £2.25 million and £2.1 million); or

- seek additional security to move the deal to within acceptable risk bounds.

At this point, the bank decides that it does in principle want to support the business, and the financial performance of the business both in the last few years and current projections suggest that this is feasible (especially if the lease payments are similar to the projected loan payments). However, it is looking for more cash to be put towards the new purchase, preferably, £150,000, to take the bank to an LTV that fits with its current risk profiles when lending for this type of commercial property.

Following further discussions with the customer, the directors have said they are prepared to put £50,000 out of their own funds towards the new lending; however, they wish to be able to withdraw these funds once the bank is within the 70 per cent LTV.

At this point, the bank must make a choice as to whether or not it wants to proceed with a new proposal of financing the new purchase at £3 million, with an overall cash contribution of £800,000, giving a starting LTV of 73 per cent against a new loan of £2.2 million.

It decides it will proceed with a new 15-year loan of £2.2 million, taking the cash contribution of £750,000 from the business and £50,000 from the directors. The directors decide to put their funds in as a director's loan and they 'subordinate' this loan to the bank. What this means in practice is the directors will sign a legal agreement that they will not take their funds out from the company until the new lending has fallen below £2.05 million, allowing the directors to take out their full £50,000 if they wish, and this would bring the borrowing to £2.1 million (70 per cent LTV).

The bank will also need to consider other issues when analysing the request for these new funds:

- What will the impact be on working capital? Will the business need more inventory and will this entail a new (or increased) overdraft facility?

- Will new storage facilities be required in the new building (racking etc)?

- Will there be a further requirement for capital expenditure such as fork-lift trucks etc?

Activity 4.3 – Review of a business's USP

This is an individual exercise focusing on businesses that the learner knows locally.

Consider what makes them different.

Activity 4.4 – Staff capacity

You were asked to consider the following businesses:

- an independent restaurant chain (10 outlets) – all in city centres; and
- a regional retail clothes shop chain (10 outlets) – all in city centres.

A restaurant chain will experience peak requirements for staff usually later in the week (from, say, Thursday to Saturday in the evenings) and lunchtimes (and definitely Saturday and Sunday), and will need sufficient part-time staff to deal with this. During the year there will also be peaks in demand on public holidays, the lead-up to Christmas and the New Year, Valentine's Day, Mothers' Day etc.

The clothes shop chain will have peak requirements in a different way. Saturdays and Sundays will be when the main requirements are but also if the shops are located in shopping centres there may be the requirement to open later, and this may mean that staff will need to swap over during the day and are not working days that are too long and without proper breaks.

Suggested answers for case study questions

Case study – Protecting the customer... and the bank

Sundira will be facing a number of issues, not least of which will be the grief of losing her friend and business partner. She will have some big decisions to make, which will include how she will run the business on her own and how she will continue to make the bank repayments on the loan.

This is where the key person protection policy will be very useful for both Sundira and the bank. This insurance policy is on the lives of the individual partners and will now be paid out due to Becky's death. Whilst the bank has an assignment over the policy, which means it can ensure that the proceeds are sent to the bank, the bank will want to discuss with Sundira the way forward for the business. The funds paid out by the insurance company will allow Sundira to either employ someone else to cover Becky's critical role, pay off some of the bank borrowing or both.

It may seem to be quite cold and calculating on the bank's part, to insist on the key person protection but at a time when Sundira is coming to terms with the loss of a business partner and her friend, this will give her some financial comfort.

05

The strategic analysis of business

INTRODUCTION

The strategic direction that a business travels in is vitally important. In this chapter, we will be exploring how we define strategy, and the practical tools that bankers can use to help them analyse a business including SWOT, PESTLE and Porter's Five Forces. We will also consider the importance of corporate social responsibility and define who the stakeholders are that businesses need to be aware of. We will examine in detail how we use these strategic tools to help highlight the issues a business might be facing and also analyse the potential risks in a business.

We will also discuss some of the key commercial sectors that bankers need to be aware of.

LEARNING OBJECTIVES

By the end of this chapter, you will be able to:

- define strategy;
- differentiate between different key strategic tools to enable an analysis of the external environment;
- apply the appropriate strategic tools to commercial businesses to identify the risks they face;

- define key stakeholders in commercial businesses and explain their importance and impact to commercial businesses;

- explain the strategic importance of corporate social responsibility to commercial businesses;

- differentiate between different commercial sectors; and

- evaluate the importance of sector specialization by commercial banks.

What is strategy?

Strategy, and how businesses use it, is nothing new, as we can see from the boxed example below, *Charles Dickens in the United States*. It is very hard to explain what strategy is. One way to illustrate it is to think about the difference between walking down the street and only being aware of the things close to you, such as your feet, and lifting up your head to see the mountains in the distance. If business owners are to act strategically, they must lift up their heads and see into the distance. They often may not feel as though they have time to do this, but it is vital for the success of organizations.

CHARLES DICKENS IN THE UNITED STATES

The well-known English author, Charles Dickens, faced his own strategic problem over 150 years ago. He was very popular on both sides of the Atlantic; however, the copyright laws in the United States meant that he was not making any money from his books. Instead of fighting the copyright laws in the United States, he decided to organize book tours, in theatres across the country, making money, but in a very different way to his original plan of selling books.

Adapted from an article by Neil Gaiman, 'How I learned to stop worrying and love the duplicator machines' (Gaiman, 2014).

A key attribute that bankers need to develop is the ability to think more widely about the external, strategic influences on a business and an industry sector. First, however, as a banker you will need to have a firm understanding of what strategy actually is. By having a grasp of this, you can then also use it to analyse a business you are lending to, to appreciate what risks this might create and ultimately how this might impact on the ability of the business to repay its borrowing.

> **Strategy**   A long-term view in business that allows the achievement of medium and long-term aims.

Definition of strategy

The Concise Oxford English Dictionary defines strategy as 'a plan designed to achieve a particular long-term aim' (Stevenson and Waite, 2011). Strategy, because it takes a long-term view, can sometimes be dismissed by those who are busy with the day-to-day activities of the business as being too nebulous to be used as a key tool for business purposes. In reality, it is a critical area for owners and directors of businesses that is ignored at their peril.

You will sometimes see strategy discussed in military terms. One of the most famous books on military strategy, *The Art of War* by Sun-Tzu, written in 400 BC, has been adopted by many business strategists, as if the issues in business can somehow be defined in the same ways as those of war (Sun-Tzu and Sawyer, 2003).

There are also many different academic views on how we define strategy and one of the most well-known writers, Michael Porter (a Harvard Business School academic), widened the definition to incorporate the concept of how strategy might also impact on the competitive position of a business: 'Competitive Strategy is about being different. It means deliberately choosing a different set of activities to deliver a unique mix of value' (Porter, 1996).

Strategic choices

When businesses make strategic choices, they often must decide where the 'trade-off' is between:

- quality;
- cost; and
- speed.

This is sometimes known as the triple constraint or the **iron triangle**.

The iron triangle

This describes the principle that when a business decision is made, two of the three constraints have to be chosen but not all three. If, for example, a business wants high quality, and quickly, then it is unlikely to be achieved cheaply. However, undertaking a venture quickly and cheaply is unlikely to achieve a high quality (Burkeman, 2014).

> **The iron triangle** [also known as the triple constraint] The business concept that it is not possible to achieve every aim without having to sacrifice one element in the 'triangle' (eg it is not possible to achieve high quality and quickly without a high cost).

Strategic tools

The ideal way to analyse a business is to use more than one strategic tool or model, as they often have subtle differences. Some of these you may have come across before and we will now consider the most useful tools in turn.

Strengths, Weaknesses, Opportunities and Threats (SWOT)

The **Strengths, Weaknesses, Opportunities and Threats (SWOT)** analysis, as shown in Figure 5.1, is a very useful technique to give an initial impression

Figure 5.1 SWOT diagram

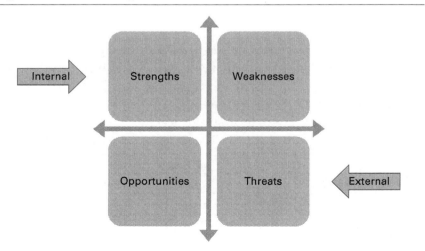

of an organization's capabilities. Generally speaking, it is a tool that can be underestimated in terms of its power.

> **Strengths, Weaknesses, Opportunities and Threats (SWOT)** A strategic analysis tool used by organizations to review their internal position (Strengths/Weaknesses) and their external environment (Opportunities/Threats).

Some strategic tools that we will use in this chapter only focus on the environment that is external to the business. The SWOT tool covers both internal and external issues, as can be seen in Figure 5.1, and often when it is being used there is confusion by users of the tool as to whether to apply the criteria to internal or external issues.

This is usually the way the criteria are applied:

- Strengths/Weaknesses – internal; and
- Opportunities/Threats – external.

Strengths

This is what the business is good at and, in theory, is more likely to have a higher degree of control over than external factors. It can cover many fundamental areas including innovation, products (and the unique selling points they may have), production processes, distribution, staff, management, marketing and financial control.

Strengths are something that can be built on and certainly need to be protected. In this particular model, strengths within the business are likely to be areas that can be strategically linked to future opportunities.

Weaknesses

In a similar way, and covering the key areas that we have discussed above, this part of the analysis covers activities in the business that it doesn't carry out as well as it should.

A very common area that commercial businesses are poor at is the finance function. Businesses can grow too quickly, and the financial controls may not keep up with this growth. The owners or directors often have no financial qualifications and can take time to find a suitable financial controller (or financial director if the business has grown sufficiently).

A weakness is something that needs to be addressed, often urgently. Weaknesses will be an area that link to threats, can cause the business to lose a competitive position and can ultimately lead the business to fail.

Opportunities

Opportunities are impacted by external influences and can be an area where the business can leverage on the strengths it has already. There may be opportunities in new markets – this can be new markets for the same goods, or new products into existing markets (the highest risk would be new products into new markets).

Opportunities may arise very quickly, and the challenge any business has is to be able to respond to that change effectively. For example, if a business has a major competitor that runs into financial difficulties, it gives the business an opportunity to gain new customers.

Threats

These can include any issue that has been identified as something that will impact in the next few years, and this is exactly where strategic analysis reaps the rewards for businesses. It allows businesses to consider how they will deal with any threats and what they may need to do differently. A very live issue is skills shortages and the accountancy firm KPMG carry out an annual survey 'The European Family Business Barometer' which asks businesses about key issues they are facing. The 2017 data shows 43 per cent of UK businesses being concerned about the recruitment of skilled staff, something referred to as the 'war for talent' (www.kpmg.com, 2017).

ACTIVITY 5.1
SWOT – advantages and disadvantages

Consider the advantages and disadvantages of using a SWOT analysis. Write down your answer then look at the end of the chapter for suggested points.

PESTLE

As we have seen above, SWOT looks both internally and externally. **PESTLE,** however, is only concerned with the external environment and should not be used for analysing the internal environment.

Why should businesses care about what is happening externally, especially if they can do nothing to control it? It's a valid question, but if businesses ignore the external environment then they are likely to be adversely impacted by issues they could have adapted to.

The PESTLE model in Figure 5.2 is shown as a cycle, and when an analysis takes place, all elements need to be considered; however, there are also likely to be interdependencies between different elements, which we will discuss as we explore this model.

> **Political, Economic, Social, Technological, Legal, Environmental (PESTLE)** A strategic analysis tool used by organizations to review their external environment.

Political

The political landscape, whether it is in the UK or internationally, will have a direct impact on a business. It is very difficult for businesses to run effectively

Figure 5.2 PESTLE diagram

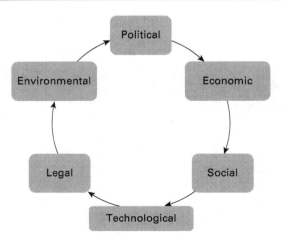

when there is political uncertainty as it makes planning very difficult. In the UK, with a system of having main government elections every four to five years, the period leading up to an election is when businesses often delay larger investment decisions in case a change in government impacts on those decisions (particularly around changes in corporation taxes or capital allowances).

At the time of writing, businesses are being faced with the significant uncertainties of the UK leaving the European Union, which could entail extra costs and administrative burden to export into Europe due to tariffs which could be introduced. Also, at the time of writing, the US Administration is focusing on a US-centric approach to trade, is challenging existing trade agreements such as the North American Free Trade Agreement (NAFTA) (covering trade between North America, Canada and Mexico), and whilst this would not affect trade from the UK, is part of a trend which could see tariffs introduced for goods from the UK, therefore making them more expensive and less competitive.

There is often a link in the PESTLE model between the Political and Legal elements.

Economic

It is a fairly obvious point to make but the overall health of an economy where a business trades will have a direct impact on the fortunes of that business. If there is a diversification of trade into different parts of the world then the health of the economy in those different territories will also have an impact.

If there is a recession in a key economy, the disposable income of consumers will be reduced and, depending on the product(s) or services sold, this is likely to reduce income or profits. It obviously depends on the product or service sold and whilst no business is 'recession-proof' some are less impacted.

Following the financial crisis of 2007/08, certain supermarkets, such as Aldi and Lidl, increased their penetration into the UK market, with a lower cost offering, and consumers who had become much more price-conscious moved to these supermarkets away from the more well-known supermarkets such as Tesco and Sainsbury's.

Social

Businesses operate in a constantly changing environment that is hugely impacted by social changes. These can encompass a multitude of changes and what may have been a 'societal norm', say, 20 years ago, can be very different now.

A good example of this is the demand for housing. More people are choosing to live alone, divorce rates are higher, and the rise in house prices generally means that it is becoming increasingly challenging for people to buy their first property. House-builders therefore need to adapt the type of properties they build to take into account changing consumer demand.

Shopping habits are changing, and with the inexorable rise of consumers using the internet, many sectors such as the travel and retail sectors are having to change to adapt to this fundamental shift in different buying patterns.

Technological

Technology has an impact on every area of business and in every sector. The internet has allowed the rise of what is called disruptive technology. Companies such as Uber and Airbnb are challenging existing suppliers of taxi and leisure accommodation services.

Automation and **artificial intelligence** (AI) are two other significant areas which are having an impact on businesses. Many businesses in all sectors are moving towards significant automation. It is used extensively in manufacturing processes where robots are used instead of humans. Sectors such as retail are being impacted as cashier-less tills are being used instead of tills with human cashiers (see also the case study 'Dark stores' below). Amazon has built warehouses which are staffed by very few employees, and use robots to transport goods across the warehouse.

AI is in its infancy, and is where computers are used for decision-making processes that may have been carried out by people. It is already being seen across the finance industry where investment decisions are being made using AI programmes.

Artificial intelligence   The use of computers and machines that can think for themselves, without human intervention.

Automation   The replacement of humans by robots and other machines, which carry out the tasks that humans used to perform. Used extensively in manufacturing processes.

CASE STUDY
Dark stores

Increasing internet shopping, facilitated by smart phones and other devices, is supporting the rise of what are termed 'dark stores' in the supermarket sector. These are very similar to normal stores but have much wider aisles and the biggest difference is that there are no actual customers. All the 'shopping' that is done there is on behalf of customers who are ordering via the internet. The staff who work there, sometimes known as 'pickers', will have handheld digital devices which help them find the most efficient route across the store (Baraniuk, 2017).

The most obvious impact of technological changes is the impact on human jobs.

Legal

The earlier point about some elements of this strategic tool being linked to each other is particularly pertinent here. Legal changes are often driven by governmental policies.

A good example of this is the drive by governments for better health for its citizens, and the ban on smoking in public places that was introduced in Scotland (2006). Issues such as smoking will always divide the opinion of consumers, politicians and business owners but the immediate impact on pub takings in Scotland was that they initially reduced by 7–10 per cent, as there was not a corresponding increase of business from consumers who didn't smoke (www.news.bbc.co.uk, 2006).

Environmental

The days when anxieties about environmental issues were seen as fringe issues and only the concern of organizations such as Greenpeace are long gone. The environment has an impact on all businesses. Sometimes this may be the weather, causing poor harvests or flooding and, in some extreme cases, hurricanes in all parts of the world.

Businesses have to take the environment seriously, whether this is ensuring that there are no spillages into rivers from manufacturing plants or having greener policies about how they deal with internally generated waste.

The move to cleaner fuel and the embracing of the electric car (and this is linked to the Political and Legal) will all have huge strategic issues for suppliers to the existing car industry.

CASE STUDY
Booths

Booths is a privately-run, family-owned supermarket business based predominantly in the North-West of England, with 28 stores selling a range of products. Many stores are often located in smaller towns (eg Carnforth and Lytham in Lancashire, Keswick and Windermere in Cumbria, and Ilkley and Ripon in Yorkshire), so making them accessible to customers who may not want to travel further afield for their grocery shopping.

They sell well-known brands and also work with independent suppliers to provide foods which are often unique to Booths, giving them the reach of larger competitors whilst at the same time providing products that customers might more naturally find in more specialist delicatessens.

An example would be Pip & Nut, a company that makes nut butters in a natural way avoiding palm oil and started by the entrepreneur Pippa Murray (Booths, 2017), (Pip and Nut, 2017).

Using the Booths case study with the PESTLE model, consider the external impacts on this business.

Porter's Five Forces

Michael Porter, who we introduced earlier, could be described as the academic 'godfather' of modern strategy. He is a Harvard academic and much of the key strategic thinking that businesses use was developed by him. What Porter does very well is make what could be perceived as complicated processes much easier to both understand and apply. **Porter's Five Forces** model is arguably one of the best models to be used for the analysis of the external environment (Porter, 1985).

Porter's Five Forces   A concept developed by Michael E Porter (Porter, 1985) that examines the forces exerted on business: 1) the threat from new entrants/barriers to entry, 2) the power of suppliers, 3) the power of customers/buyers, 4) the threat from substitutes, 5) the marketplace-competition/rivalry.

Figure 5.3 Porter's Five Forces

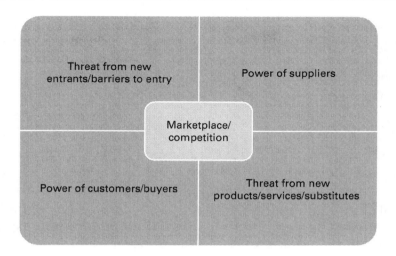

Figure 5.3 shows the different pressures that surround a business and exert pressure on it.

Marketplace – competition/existing rivalry

This part of the analysis is concerned with the marketplace a business operates in. Is it highly competitive? Is it a mature market? How many 'players' are there who are all competing with each other?

The supermarket marketplace, for example, is very competitive and there are large national businesses, smaller independent chains, 'corner shops' and a rising number of specialist food shops and delicatessens. The Booths case study is a useful reference source here.

Threat from new entrants/barriers to entry

This threat analyses how easy it is for new competitors to enter the marketplace and what might be the barriers that might stop new entrants coming in. These threats are normally assessed as:

- high;
- medium; and
- low.

How easy is it for a competitor to set up in competition to existing businesses? Part of the answer to this question depends on the capital required to create a similar business. The minimum requirement for a commercial printer working for retail customers, for example printing display material, will be a factory, machinery, staff, raw materials and working capital. This will require a high level of funds and it will take time to establish the business; therefore, barriers to entry would be said to be *high*.

Power of suppliers

Certain suppliers are driven by market forces, and a good example of this is the cost of energy to businesses. This is impacted by the global price of oil, and there is very little that the energy companies can do to change this. When oil prices are high, the power of energy suppliers is correspondingly high, as even if a business wants to change to a different supplier, market forces (ie the price of oil) will dictate that there is unlikely to be a significant difference in the price paid by the business.

Niche suppliers of goods and services are likely to have a much higher power as they are providing something that a business cannot get elsewhere. Large purchasers of goods (eg supermarkets) on the other hand are able to exert much higher pressure on their suppliers with regards to both prices and also the amount of time it takes for suppliers to be paid. In the latter circumstances the supplier power is *low*.

Power of customers/buyers

There is a link between this force and the power of suppliers and this can create a 'mirror image'. We showed above that supermarkets can create an environment of low power for their suppliers, and they in turn have high power as a customer.

If a business operates in a very 'crowded' marketplace, and cannot particularly differentiate itself, then its customers will have *high* power as they could easily find what they want from another business.

Threat from new products/services/substitutes

Businesses can often face threats from sources that are not immediately obvious. A business aimed at, for example, providing a live music venue for an age demographic of 18–30-year-olds may find that it faces competition from other demands on their potential customers' time. Whilst an obvious source of competition might be other music venues and bars etc, another less obvious source could be computer games, with customers preferring to game at home rather than go out.

CASE STUDY
Golf balls versus two wheels

Golf, traditionally one of the biggest activity sports in the UK, has found itself declining in popularity over the last 10–15 years. Changing social trends, with longer working hours (and less free time), and more households with children where both parents are earners, has meant that spending a whole day on the golf course has become less of an option.

Private golf clubs have sometimes been perceived as rather elitist, with expensive membership fees. There is also a strong argument to say (using one of Porter's other forces above) that previously, barriers to entry were very high, as a good golf club required a large area of high-quality land, with the different holes designed to an exacting standard, and very high levels of maintenance required to keep the quality at what was expected from the members.

The biggest threat to golf seems to be the bicycle. Perhaps inspired by the Tour De Yorkshire and UK successes in the Tour De France and the Olympics, this is one of the fastest-growing sports in the UK.

Consider the power of customers here, and how their spending power has moved from one leisure activity to another. There is always the risk, of course, that this spending power could move to another activity just as easily (BBC, 2017)!

Leisure businesses often can suffer from changing tastes and trends as shown in the case study above, 'Golf balls versus two wheels'.

The state of the economy is also likely to have an impact, and where a product or service is dependent on discretionary spend, in times of a recession, consumers may switch to lower-priced businesses or products. Premium products such as branded coffee may see consumers switching to generic supermarket brands. Restaurants can also be vulnerable to this type of threat, and again the 'substitutes' may not be other restaurants but offers from supermarkets for the 'Dine In' options. The threat for substitutes is therefore *high* in this circumstance.

Product life-cycle

The **product life-cycle** is a model which tracks the life of a product, from its inception right through to its final decline. The four stages are:

- inception;
- growth;
- maturity; and
- decline.

Depending on the success of a new product, sales are likely to rise until the product enters its mature phase. At this point in the life-cycle, sales may plateau and as the product enters the decline phase sales will start to reduce.

The important point to note is that whilst there is a logical progression to the product life-cycle, products can be revitalized by new marketing campaigns, new variations of the same product and in some cases the complete repositioning of a product. Lucozade is a well-known product which was reinvented as a sports-related drink, yet when it was originally sold it was retailed through chemists as a drink to help patients to recover from illness.

> **Product life-cycle**   A model that tracks the life of a product, through its four stages – inception/growth/maturity/decline.

The Boston Consulting Group – growth/share matrix

The Boston Consulting Group (BCG) developed this important matrix in the early 1970s (Henderson, 1970) and it is still a relevant and vital tool, particularly for companies with a number of different products (or services). It splits products into four categories based on: 1) market growth; and 2) market share:

- stars – high market share/high market growth;
- question marks – low market share/high market growth;
- cash cows – high market share/low market growth; and
- dogs – low market growth/low market share.

> **Boston Consulting Group (growth/share matrix)** Sometimes also known as the Boston Star Matrix. A strategic tool which assesses the products/services of a business based on market growth and market share. There are four categories: 1) stars; 2) question marks; 3) cash cows; and 4) dogs.

Stars

These are high-performing products which are producing high levels of profit and may be continuing to grow. They are likely to continue to have potential into the future.

Question marks

These are products which have potential to develop into a product that has high market share; however, they don't at the present time. They are likely to need investment in order to gain the desired market share.

Cash cows

These are products which command a high market share, in what are likely to be mature markets. They will be producing profits which can be used to support other products and will not need as much investment as the other categories. They run the risk of declining and becoming Dogs.

Dogs

These are products which are likely to be in declining markets, will be a drain on resources of the business (time/funds) and strategically will need to be either sold or closed.

There is a link between this model and the product life-cycle model (discussed above). Ideally a business has a mix of different products and services which are at different stages of growth and development; however, the model can be used for a commercial business that has only one product to ascertain where that product sits.

Generic strategies

Using another of Michael Porter's theories, 'Generic Competitive Strategies' (Porter, 1985), Porter puts forward the theory that businesses can gain a competitive advantage by having two distinct approaches: low cost or differentiation. By using these two approaches, he argues that businesses then have three **generic strategies** that they can pursue which he calls:

- cost leadership;
- differentiation; and
- focus.

Focus is then split further, into cost focus and differentiation focus.

> **Generic strategies**   A strategic approach by Michael E Porter that focuses on low cost and differentiation as tools of competitive advantage. The three strategies are cost leadership, differentiation and focus. Focus is then split further, into cost focus and differentiation focus.

Cost leadership

As you would expect, this requires a very keen focus on costs at every level in order to provide goods and services which are cheaper than the competitors in the sector. There are many routes to achieve this and technology is highly likely to be employed. New entrants may use this strategy, particularly if they are not providing all the services or products their competitors are. Low-cost airlines are a good example of this as they offer a 'no-frills' service, where customers need to pay extra for things such as refreshments, or to put their baggage in the hold.

The challenge with this strategy, is that to be the leader requires a constant focus and the worst scenario is that all the competitors, including those who were not previously competing on the basis of price, enter into a price war which can cause long-term damage to the sector or industry by weakening competitors within it.

Differentiation

The key challenge is how a business can set itself apart from its competitors and how it can position itself to be exclusive. If it can do this then it will be able to charge a premium for its products and services. Often with SME businesses, the people dimension of the business is what sets the business apart from its competitors and enables it to win repeat business.

In strategic terms we sometimes also talk about whether a business has a unique selling point (USP). This is the element that sets one business apart from another.

Focus

This requires a business to decide where it wants to position itself in a particular part of the market, and where it should put its much narrower focus. A manufacturer of bathrooms, for example, can concentrate on the luxury end of the marketplace rather than the mass market. This allows a competitive advantage to be created, by having a much narrower scope.

The bathroom manufacturer is an example of differentiation focus, which is one of the two variations of this strategy.

Cost focus is also a strategy that can be pursued at the same time as aiming for a niche market. A power tool manufacturer, for example, could aim to produce low-cost versions of its high-end tools, aimed at the DIY enthusiast rather than the professional user.

Stuck in the middle

Porter talks also about a situation where a business tries to follow all of these strategies at the same time, and ends up with no competitive advantage in any way. This is usually what we might term a 'recipe for disaster' and means that the business is just seen as average by its customers, and any advantage it does have will be exploited by its competitors.

Scenario planning

Many activities which are linked to strategic planning consider what the future might look like. The oil conglomerate, Shell, developed this idea further considering different 'states of the world' that they might face, based on the key commodity they dealt in, which was oil, and particularly the price of oil. On the back of this they developed the concept of **scenario planning** (Shell, 2018).

> **Scenario planning**   A planning technique used particularly by Shell (the oil company), which examines future states of the world and formulates strategic responses to these possible scenarios.

Shell looked at the complex interactions that they had with the world (including major **stakeholders** – customers, suppliers and governments) and instead of trying to predict the future, explored how they, as a large organization, would deal with the different consequences of varying oil prices.

Stakeholders Individuals or organizations that have an interest in a business.

One of the driving forces behind this strategic tool is having the ability, as a large organization, to deal relatively quickly with the changes in a marketplace which is very driven by the price of an underlying commodity. This tool does not predict the future, but low oil prices and high oil prices are two possible scenarios that Shell could plan for. We will examine these below alongside the possible consequences that might occur for each scenario.

Low oil prices

This would necessitate the shelving of further exploration, or the slowing down of exploration. It might necessitate redundancies, impact on the investment in alternative power sources, cause major supplier relationships to be revisited and would most certainly cause the organization to critically examine its cash position.

High oil prices

This would allow a significant expansion of the organization including further employment opportunities and might prompt acquisitions of competitors in the sector. It would allow the investment in higher risk projects and may prompt investment in alternative energy sources.

How do bankers use these strategic tools?

The key consideration is the logical use of one or more of these tools to analyse a business and its surrounding environment. Using Porter's Five Forces and PESTLE together should enable a comprehensive review of the marketplace that a business operates in. Research is key in terms of what is currently happening in a sector, and the application of the reality test (discussed under 'Sectors' below) are all a vital part of using these tools.

When dealing with customers, these tools often provide an excellent basis for asking more probing questions about the business. You might find that sometimes customers may not have considered issues in such a structured manner.

> **ACTIVITY 5.2**
> PESTLE and Porter's Five Forces
>
> Choose any industry that you are familiar with and using these strategic tools review it, considering where there are potential overlaps and where some of the key headings do not apply.

Stakeholders

All businesses have what is known as stakeholders and they need to be taken into account when considering strategy, and strategic change. Broadly speaking these are individuals or organizations that have an interest in a business. Businesses often have to balance the interests of all the stakeholders; however, this is not an easy task as they are not always aligned and sometimes will be diametrically opposed to each other. The main stakeholders in a business are as follows:

- Shareholders and investors – this group is concerned with the financial performance of the business and will want to see a return on their investment.

- Managers – managers will be concerned with the medium- and long-term survival of the business as their careers and also their financial reward will be linked to the business success.

- Staff – the staff will have similar concerns to the managers. From the business's perspective, the key issue will be ensuring it has sufficient skilled staff, who are motivated and correctly awarded. It will also be concerned about retaining staff.

- Customers – the customers are the key driver behind the success of the business and understanding what they want and need will be essential. The business will need to consider the segmentation of customers into different groups (particularly where it is dealing with personal consumers).

- Suppliers – suppliers are a vital component of the success of any business, and relationships will be influenced to some degree by how powerful the supplier is.

- The government – some sectors are very impacted by government policy and regulations.

- The media – this includes the more formal sources, such as newspapers, and increasingly social media driven by consumer comments needs to be managed.

- The community-businesses can have a significant impact on the local community. Pollution, for example, is likely to be reacted to negatively. There is the opportunity for a business to engage with a community positively, especially if the business is a big employer, particularly if the business can influence local social problems.

- Environmental groups – environmental groups can often be linked to the local community, as local residents are becoming increasingly vocal about the impact a business may be having on the local environment.

Corporate social responsibility and sustainability – being different?

Corporate social responsibility (CSR) can cover many broad issues. The 'Key Term' box gives a definition of CSR from the World Business Council for Sustainable Development but interestingly, it does not articulate some key components such as:

- What does behaving ethically mean?
- How is contributing to economic development defined?
- How is quality of life measured?
- How is local community defined?

> **Corporate social responsibility (CSR)**   'The commitment by organizations to behave ethically and contribute to economic development whilst improving the quality of life of the workforce and their families as well as the local community and society at large' (World Business Council for Sustainable Development, 2018).

Corporate social responsibility (CSR) is becoming increasingly important as a strategic choice for businesses, not just the preserve of a 'green minority'. You will recall from earlier in the chapter that Michael Porter talked about being different and that being different is part of a competitive strategy.

As consumers become more concerned about the ethical stances of the businesses they buy from, this in turn influences how businesses themselves behave. CSR becomes an increasingly important commercial decision as it will have very real impacts on the profits for the business if a positive CSR stance is well received by customers and the wider market.

CSR is often encompassed under the term of sustainability and there can be a tendency to perceive this as being concerned with the environment when in fact it covers many areas of business.

There is also very real danger of 'tokenism' by businesses where any ethical or environmental activity is concerned. Some industries run the risk of facing criticism from customers if, on the face of it, they appear to be taking a positive environmental approach, but the reality of their operations tells a different story. Take, for example, a large clothing chain using recycled packaging to demonstrate their environmental concern. If, at the same time, the processes they use to manufacture their clothing use a significant amount of natural resources, they will find themselves open to criticism. The T-shirt, a staple clothing item for millions of people, takes a significant amount of water to make (including the process of growing the cotton).

There is arguably the tendency to think that only large corporations have the power to influence the environment positively, but smaller SMEs, and the ones that you as a banker are likely to deal with, can have a very positive impact, particularly where they can link with their local community. This can give them a real competitive advantage.

ACTIVITY 5.3
Exploring corporate social responsibility – the *Modern Slavery Act 2015*

There has been a concerted effort by governments across the world to deal with workers who are modern slaves. Cases in the news have included nail bars and the fishing industry.

Research this act and consider how this might impact on a bank. There is a very good article by Annie Kelly (*The Guardian*) in the 'References' section at the end of the chapter.

Sectors

Banks create their own strategic advantage by concentrating on particular sectors. They specifically train staff to specialize in certain sectors (such as professionals, healthcare and real estate), and give them portfolios (of customers) which are only comprised of one sector. This has a number of advantages, both from the bank and the customer's point of view. The bank is able to use its wider knowledge of a sector to benchmark the performance of individual businesses (which helps from the bank's risk perspective) and is also able to help these businesses by sharing best practices. Please note that this section of the chapter is not designed to be a definitive guide to every commercial sector but is a starting point for learners to carry out more research themselves.

ACTIVITY 5.4
Sector specialism in banks

Review the strategy of your own organization towards specialist sectors.
    What sectors are focused on and why? Does your bank provide targeted financial support to certain sectors?
    There will often be internal case studies available within your organization based on an actual lending scenario and these are very useful to understand the type of lending structures that can be provided.

The reality test?

It is also very important that bankers think about how, as consumers, they would react to a customer's proposition. As we noted in Chapter 4, we are all consumers, and whilst we all have different tastes, it is important not to lose our own judgement when considering a business, particularly in the 'real world'.

If the customer runs five care homes, you may have a family relative in a care home. Ask yourself how does this business compare to the business where your relative is? What are the size of rooms, facilities etc? Do the residents seem happy? What is the quality of the décor? How do the staff deal with the residents? A business may be a small chain of hotels. What do you look for yourself when you stay in a hotel? What is the quality of the fixtures and fittings (eg carpets, curtains, beds etc)? What is the quality of the décor (eg does the hotel need painting or new wallpaper?)?

It is important also to note that in an exam situation, it would be impractical to expect learners to know in detail about every commercial sector; however, there would be an expectation to be able to approach a question logically and with a reasonable level of knowledge as shown in the above two examples. When faced with a lending proposition from a customer operating in a particular sector, there are key factors that need to be considered.

Professionals

The usual professional firms that you are likely to encounter will be accountants and solicitors. There are of course many other professional firms such as architects, surveyors and creative agencies.

Accountants

As we discussed in Chapter 1, all limited companies, by law, need to produce accounts, which are held at Companies House. It is in the interest of any business to produce annual accounts and there is therefore a steady source of business for accountants. Some firms will focus exclusively on individuals (for example, advising on tax returns) and smaller businesses, whilst others will cater for SMEs. The national and international firms (such as EY or KPMG) will also look after PLCs.

A core service is preparing annual accounts and auditing the financial records of the business. We have also discussed earlier the need for regular management information and accountants will often prepare this on behalf of their clients. Many firms also offer services such as preparing forecasts or cash flows which are used by businesses when they are preparing business plans.

Some firms specialize in providing services to particular sectors, for example, GPs or farmers. Some firms also specialize in services such as insolvency advice (some of the partners will need to be licensed insolvency practitioners – which we discuss in Chapter 9 or corporate financial advice aimed at businesses wishing to dispose of their business or acquire another one.

The key issues for bankers are:

- The underlying assets in the business are in the work-in-progress (effectively the inventory) and the debtor book (trade receivables). Remaining close to the 'make-up' of the debtor book is important to ensure the firm is close to the collection of outstanding monies and doesn't allow funds to take too long to be collected.

- The value of the business is in the partners and staff as services are provided by these individuals.

    If a down-turn is evidenced, partners are often unable to immediately adjust their drawings which can lead to losses and pressure on the cash.

Solicitors

Solicitors will focus on a variety of specialisms such as commercial real estate, personal real estate, litigation, wills and estate planning, matrimonial, criminal, corporate finance, banking and insolvency advice. Not all firms will offer all of these services – some will focus on services aimed at individuals, whereas others will focus on the SME marketplace. It is fairly common to have firms who just focus on one specialism such as criminal cases.

There are many regional firms who have a broad focus in a particular geographic territory, such as the south-west of England or the north-east of England. In a similar way to large accountancy firms who have expertise with PLCs, it is usually the large national and international firms which have expertise in dealing with this type of corporate entity. Scottish law is different to English and Welsh law and this requires firms in Scotland to be able to deal exclusively with Scottish law.

The key issues for bankers (which are very similar to accountancy practices) are:

- Many areas of specialism such as litigation and matrimonial can absorb large amounts of cash and therefore have an impact on the working cash cycle.

- The underlying assets in the business are in the work-in-progress (effectively the inventory) and the debtor book (trade receivables). It is important to understand what percentage of the work-in-progress converts to debtors (eg it might be 30–40 per cent). Remaining close to the 'make-up' of the debtor book is also important to ensure the firm is close to the collection of outstanding monies and doesn't allow funds to take too long to be collected.

- The value of the business is in the partners and staff – services are provided by these individuals.

    If a down-turn is evidenced, partners are often unable to immediately adjust their drawings which can lead to losses and pressure on the cash.

Care homes

This is a very highly regulated industry, because it deals with the provision of care to vulnerable elderly people. There are over 200,000 residential places in the UK.

Many care homes are operated from older residential properties (often Victorian) that have been converted. Economies of scale are important and often operators of a small group of homes are able to achieve cost savings. Homes usually require qualified nursing staff to oversee the care in a home.

The sector in the UK has been dominated in the past by large conglomerates such as Southern Cross (SC), who operated 750 homes, many of which were on a 'sale and leaseback' basis (the freeholds of care home sites were sold to investors, where they were then leased back to SC). The company failed in 2011: 'Southern Cross was hit by a triple whammy: falling property prices put the brakes on what proved to be a reckless expansion programme; tough economic conditions saw local councils freeze or lower fees for residents;... the company was now locked into rising rents at a time when income was being squeezed' (Wachman, 2011). The issues with SC raised concerns about large entities and particularly the sale and leaseback model.

Smaller care homes below 30 residents are finding it much harder to survive. New builds tend to be over 60 beds capacity with rooms not less than 14.5 m².

The key issues for bankers are:

- Care Quality Commission can inspect on an unannounced basis and provide a ratings system with four levels: 'outstanding', 'good', 'requires improvement' and finally 'inadequate'. Inadequate means that there is a finding against the operator and that CQC have taken some form of 'enforcement action' against the operator of the home. The latter category can have very serious impacts on the ability of a home to operate and may mean they cannot take in any further residents until the issues are resolved.

- Occupancy levels are critical to the success of a home and need to be set by the bank at a realistic level that will allow the debt to be serviced.

Real estate

Residential development

Small housebuilders are vital to the continued growth of residential housing in the UK. Many suffered post the financial crisis as they were unable to sell the properties they had built and ended up being in a position of having to rent out properties that they needed to sell.

The key issues for bankers are:

- Sites need to be developed on a phased basis, to create cash flow from sales, rather than building all the units at one time.
- Development of flats is a greater risk to the bank.
- Strict monitoring is required with monthly reports from a monitoring surveyor.
- Cost over-runs are common and a contingency of at least 10 per cent needs to be factored in.
- The financial strength of sub-contractors is important.
- Skilled labour can often be a challenge to source.

Commercial development

In the SME sector, commercial development will usually be on behalf of larger companies, with specific projects (rather than being speculative) and is likely to be on a contractual basis. This creates potential problems for a bank financing this type of customer as the value of the debtor book is concentrated in the end user.

The key issues for bankers are:

- Contractual debtors are poor security for the bank.
- At the end of developments there can often be delays in the final payment of contractual payments.
- Skilled labour can often be a challenge to source.

Residential investment

This type of customer is likely to build up a portfolio of property which is financed by the rental income generated by the different tenants. Some portfolios may focus on certain types of tenant, such as students.

The key issues for bankers are:

- Regular capital expenditure required on the fabric of properties (eg roofs/exterior décor/windows/doors.
- Voids (unoccupied properties) need to be monitored closely.
- Rental income must be monitored on a regular basis to ensure it is all being remitted to the bank.

Commercial investment

Again, this type of customer is likely to build up a portfolio of property which is financed by the rental income generated by the different tenants. Commercial property can comprise many different types of property including shop units, offices and industrial units. For office space, users require a high level of technology infrastructure and there is a move towards shorter lets, with more flexible leases.

The key issues for bankers are:

- It is important to understand the different types of commercial tenant and to understand the concentration risk (for example, to certain sectors, companies or both).

- Location of commercial property is important.

- Regular capital expenditure required on the fabric of properties.

- Voids (unoccupied properties) need to be monitored closely.

- Rental income must be monitored on a regular basis to ensure it is all being remitted to the bank.

Agriculture

Farming is a key industry in the UK and an important contributor to GDP. The sector is facing many challenges, including how it will operate after the UK has left the European Union. There are a number of factors that are common to the different types of farming in the UK:

- Environmental pressures – farmers are under continued pressure not to pollute the surrounding environment and the local watercourses. For livestock particularly, this means controlling animal slurry and ensuring that there is the correct roofing on buildings housing animals. Animal welfare is also a key concern of many consumers and other stakeholders (RSPCA etc). There has been the introduction of nitrogen vulnerable zones limiting the amount of nitrogen fertilizer (inorganic and organic) that can be applied, restricting the timing of application and creating minimum storage requirements for organic manure.

- Succession planning is a continual issue as the average age of many farmers is late 50s and unless farms are passed to family members this may cause problems in the future.

- Many businesses in this sector are highly leveraged, where debt has built up over many years.

- Health concerns and changing tastes can have an impact.
- Subsidies – the risk to many farmers is that subsidies which are linked to European support will diminish and disappear as the UK exits the European Union.

Arable farming

Famers grow crops (eg, wheat, vegetables and salad products) and some businesses focus exclusively on certain crops such as potatoes. For obvious reasons, the weather has a significant impact on arable farmers, and as weather patterns change both in the UK and globally, this will continue to be a concern. The long cycle for production means that farmers are susceptible to the changes in input costs.

Certain producers use specialist technology such as hydroponics (a technique of growing plants using water-based technology, sometimes without the use of soil) which can be conducted in industrial type units and don't require the same amount of land as more conventional farming techniques.

The key issues for bankers are:

- Long 'production' cycles.
- There is significant pressure from supermarket chains who can control prices.
- Commodity prices can fluctuate significantly including both input and output prices.
- Regular capital expenditure required for buildings and machinery.

Dairy farming

Under this type of farming, focus is on the production of milk, cheese, eggs and other dairy produce. Focusing on milk production, in global terms, the UK is relatively small, producing around 13.5 billion litres of milk per annum. The UK market itself is unusual as 50 per cent of production is used to supply the fresh liquid milk market.

There has been significant rationalization and the average size of farms has increased. The bulk of trade of dairy commodities is within the country boundaries where the milk is produced. Only around 5 per cent of production is traded globally, with small movements in production of the main global producers (New Zealand, the United States, Australasia) having a significant effect on trading prices.

The key issues for bankers are:

- There is significant pressure from supermarket chains who can control prices.

- Diseases such as foot and mouth will have a huge impact.

- Commodity prices can fluctuate significantly including both input and output prices, for example, fodder, milk prices, livestock prices.

- Regular capital expenditure is required for buildings, and mechanization (including automated milking machinery).

Beef and sheep farming

This involves the rearing of livestock for both meat and wool. There are of course other types of livestock rearing, such as pork; however, we have just considered beef and sheep here. The welfare of animals continues to be of importance (including the distance between the farm and where they are slaughtered). There are also increasing health concerns as antibiotics continue to be used on animals, despite there being moves to limit their use unless the animals actually need them.

The key issues for bankers are:

- There is a move towards selling directly to producers (away from traditional livestock markets). This in turn carries cash flow implications, from same-day payments to extended credit terms (30–60 days).

- The farm supply base is potentially decreasing, and there is therefore more pressure on buyers, which will increase 'farm gate' prices.

- Changing eating habits may move consumers away from 'red-meat' to other meats such as pork and chicken.

- Diseases such as foot and mouth will have a huge impact.

Manufacturing

This is a broad sector in the UK, and we only have room to give an overview here. Universities can sometimes be a source of new businesses, with the 'spinning-out' of research and development projects. Geographically, there are often concentrations of smaller manufacturers, for example, those supporting car manufacturers in the north-east of England such as Nissan. Other manufacturers may have a specific focus on certain industries, such as the oil and gas sector.

Common themes in the industry include:

- Offshoring – the movement of manufacturing to another part of the world and out of the UK has been a common strategy for many manufacturers. This has been due to more beneficial costs, including much lower wage costs. This has required businesses to lose manufacturing capability in the UK, along with the loss of skilled labour jobs. It has also necessitated funding in different ways, with the use of letter of credit facilities, and an increasing exposure to the risk of foreign currency price fluctuations. The downside to this method of sourcing products globally is that there is a much longer 'lead time', as goods are often transported by sea. Quality, particularly for high specification components, can sometimes be an issue and there are increasing concerns about the pay and working conditions of workers in countries such as China and India.

  The negative aspects of offshoring have brought about some reversals of this strategy, and some manufacturers are bringing back manufacturing to the UK, or in other words, onshoring.

- Supply chain management – and that the smaller manufacturing businesses do not have large amounts of capital tied up in inventory (stock).

- LEAN – this is vital to ensure that processes are as efficient as they can be, and particularly that waste in the whole manufacturing process is kept to a minimum.

The key issues for bankers are:

- Skills shortages – this is exacerbated by a perception of manufacturing being boring and low paid.

- Automation – this is a constant within the industry and requires significant capital expenditure.

- Environmental pressures – to ensure that there is no damaging pollution by the business.

Retail sector

This is another very wide sector in the UK, and covers small independent retailers through to the large multiple chains. There are many types of retail business selling a wide variety of goods, including clothes, food, books, and electrical goods. Retailers sell from physical shops and also online.

Consumer spending is impacted by a number of factors including the rate of inflation and the level of interest rates, and a reduction in disposable income will have a knock-on impact on the consumer's spending power.

The death of the high street is often discussed, driven by a continuing trend of online consumer spending. Shopping is often seen as a leisure activity, and the continuing trend to browse in the high street and then purchase online at home is continuing to challenge retailers who have a physical presence on the high street. Interestingly, certain brands, such as Apple, are using their stores for customers to visit and get help with the technology.

Supermarket shopping is also changing with many consumers preferring to have their shopping delivered to their house rather than visiting the shop.

The key issues for bankers are:

- High street retail sites (particularly in new centres) attract high rental payments.
- The impact of the living wage.

Chapter summary

In this chapter we have explored:

- the definition of strategy;
- the explanation of strategic tools and how these can be used to analyse commercial businesses – SWOT/PESTLE/Porter's Five Forces/product life-cycle/Boston Consulting Group Matrix and Porter's Generic Strategies;
- key stakeholder analysis;
- the importance and relevance of corporate social responsibility to commercial businesses; and
- different commercial sectors and the relevance of specialist knowledge to the bank when lending – sectors discussed are care homes, professionals, real estate, agriculture, manufacturing and retail.

Objective check

1 What is the definition of strategy?
2 Identify one strategic tool that enables an analysis of the external environment.

3 Explain the importance of this tool when applied to a commercial business.

4 Identify three internal and external stakeholders and assess their importance in a commercial business.

5 Define corporate social responsibility and explain its importance to commercial businesses.

6 Identify one commercial sector that banks may focus on.

7 How important is it to have a sector focus approach when lending?

Further reading

Klein, N (1999) *No Logo*, Fourth Estate, London – the Canadian author and social activist is a very influential writer, and No Logo, published in 1999 is her seminal book about globalization.

Epstein-Reeves, J and Weinreb, E *Michael Porter: coining vital business strategies for sustainability* [accessed 21 June 2018] [Online] https://www.theguardian.com/sustainable-business/michael-porter-coined-competitive-advantage – further research on Michael Porter.

References

Baraniuk, C [accessed 21 June 2018] Shop, but don't enter: The strange world of dark stores [Online] http://www.bbc.com/future/story/20150804-shop-but-dont-enter-the-strange-world-of-dark-stores

BBC News [accessed 21 June 2018] Smoke ban 'has hit pub takings' [Online] http://news.bbc.co.uk/1/hi/scotland/5276680.stm

BBC Radio 4 [accessed 21 June 2018] In the Rough: Golf's Uncertain Future [Online] http://www.bbc.co.uk/programmes/b08wn9mj

Booths Supermarkets | The UK's Food, Wine and Grocery Store [accessed 21 June 2018] [Online] https://www.booths.co.uk/

Burkeman, O [accessed 21 June 2018] This column will change your life: triple constraints [Online] https://www.theguardian.com/lifeandstyle/2014/jan/11/this-column-change-life-triple-constraints

European Family Business Barometer [accessed 21 June 2018] [Online] https://assets.kpmg.com/content/dam/kpmg/uk/pdf/2017/11/efb-barometer-sixth-edition-uk-results.pdf

Gaiman, N [accessed 21 June 2018] How I learned to stop worrying and love the duplicator machines [Online] https://boingboing.net/2014/11/06/neil-gaiman-how-i-learned-to.html

Henderson, B [accessed 21 June 2018] The Product Portfolio [Online] https://www.bcg.com/publications/1970/strategy-the-product-portfolio.aspx

Kelly, A [accessed 21 June 2018] The UK's new slavery laws explained: what do they mean for business? [Online] https://

www.theguardian.com/sustainable-business/2015/dec/14/
modern-slavery-act-explained-business-responsibility-supply-chain

Pip & Nut [accessed 21 June 2018] [Online] http://www.pipandnut.com/

Porter, M E (1985) *Competitive Advantage: Creating and sustaining superior performance*, The Free Press, New York

Porter, M E (1996) What is Strategy? *Harvard Business Review* (November–December), p 60

Shell [accessed 21 June 2018] Shell Scenarios [Online] https://www.shell.com/energy-and-innovation/the-energy-future/scenarios.html

Stevenson, A and Waite, M (2011) *Concise Oxford English Dictionary*, Oxford University Press, Oxford

Sun-Tzu and Sawyer, R (trans) (2003) *Art of war*, Running Press, Philadelphia, Pa

Wachman, R [accessed 21 June 2018] Southern Cross's incurably flawed business model let down the vulnerable [Online] https://www.theguardian.com/business/2011/jul/16/southern-cross-incurable-sick-business-model

World Business Council for Sustainable Development [accessed 21 June 2018] [Online] http://www.wbcsd.org/

Suggested answers for activities

Activity 5.1 – SWOT – advantages and disadvantages

You were asked to consider the advantages and disadvantages of using a SWOT analysis.

Advantages are:

- It is a very easy to use tool – issues can be separated into different categories.

- SWOT can be completed in a relatively short timescale.

- It does not require a great deal of technical knowledge to use.

- SWOT is a good starting point for strategic analysis.

Disadvantages are:

- The four headings are quite basic and do not give any guidance on identifying areas within the business that should be concentrated on.

- It is easy to overemphasize what a business thinks it's good at (strengths) and be less aware of what it is not so good at (weaknesses).

- Opportunities and threats are not always obvious.

There may be other valid points you have made.

Activity 5.3 – Exploring corporate social responsibility

You were asked to research The Modern Slavery Act 2015 and how this might impact on banks. Newspaper and other media articles have unearthed a number of cases where workers in small businesses such as nail bars were actually slaves.

Bankers have a responsibility to ensure that they are not financing illegal activities (eg drugs/prostitution) and the Modern Slavery Act is certainly something bankers should consider when questioning customers about their workforce.

Learners should devise their own answers for Activities 5.2 and 5.4. No model answers are supplied.

Suggested answers for case study questions

Case study – Booths

The PESTLE model needs to be detailed. It stands for: political/economic/social/technological/legal/environmental. It is important to note that PESTLE is a strategic tool which is used to analyse the external environment (and would not be used to analyse internal issues of the business).

- Political – there is a potential link to environmental/legal issues such as the introduction of the legislation charging for plastic carrier bags. There is a great deal of concern by consumers generally about the level of packaging in food and if there is the political will to address this then it may result in legislation that could mean that supermarkets may need to take a more responsible attitude towards packaging of food (particularly where they have own label brands). This could have an impact on Booths' costs in the future.

- Social – this is a regional supermarket and will be impacted by the local economies in the areas it serves. The overall economy in the UK will also have an impact. It offers many bespoke products that might be found in delicatessens and this will appeal to customers who want more individual products.

- Technological – it offers a high-quality service in its 28 stores, rather than focus on an internet delivery of its products. It has a good web presence to support the local stores.

- Legal – supermarkets, like many employers, will be subject to legislation on equal pay, the living wage and health and safety legislation.

- Environmental – this has been touched on under the 'Political' heading and issues such as sustainability will be important.

06

Securities for lending

INTRODUCTION

When banks lend money to commercial customers they assess whether the customer can repay the monies they are borrowing. The bank will then often take security to cover this lending and this is where the phrase 'secured lending' originates (in the case of sole traders or partnerships, the bank may take personal security from the individuals involved in the business). Security is only usually used by the bank when the customer has defaulted and is unable to repay the borrowing. The bank then uses the security as an alternative source of repayment. Banks should not, under normal circumstances, lend money just because they have security.

It is important for you as the banker to understand what security may be available, both from personal customers and commercial entities, and how this security is taken. You also need to understand the types of charge that can be taken by the bank, the rights this gives the bank and how the bank can exercise these rights.

If you want to read more widely around banking law, you will encounter a bewildering range of technical terms and a language that is quite different to other aspects of banking. In this chapter we hope to demystify some of the intricacies of the law that relate to taking of security when lending.

LEARNING OBJECTIVES

By the end of this chapter, you will be able to:

- evaluate the importance of security and explain why banks take security from personal and commercial customers;
- assess the ideal characteristics of security from a banker's perspective;
- distinguish between the various types of personal and commercial security available;
- differentiate between the different types of charge a bank can take;
- assess the values banks assign to different categories of security; and
- evaluate the importance of discount factors when taking security.

The importance of security

When banks are lending to commercial customers they will often take security (if it is available). Security is important to the banker because if the customer is unable to repay the borrowing then the security can be turned into cash and these liquid funds can be used to repay the borrowing. Security is effectively the back-up plan, the contingency plan, the Plan B if you will. It is the way that a banker will endeavour to get the funds they have lent back.

One of the key concepts which is really important for you to grasp is that, in most circumstances, the asset that the bank takes as security (and this could, for example, be a factory owned by a company) does not change ownership when it is used as security. By this we mean that the owner of the asset can continue to use it, and the ownership does not move to a third party (in this case the bank). The bank does, however, have control over the disposal of the asset. This means, in practice, that the business cannot sell the asset without accounting to the lender for the sale proceeds (which would be used to repay borrowing) or obtaining the lender's prior agreement.

When a banker considers a lending proposal from either an existing customer or a new customer (which we covered in significant detail in Chapter 4), the banker should carefully consider the proposition, making a decision as to whether or not they wish to lend *before* they consider what security is available to be taken.

It is poor banking practice to lend to a commercial customer just because you have security. Any security taken will never make a bad lending decision a good one and whilst the bank might be repaid using the security, it may often be through good luck rather than through good judgement! Bankers live in the real world however, and there may be times that monies are lent where the decision may be 'marginal' and the security given may be the deciding factor in whether or not to lend.

It is very easy for a banker to think that if they have taken assets of a company or an individual and used it as security for the borrowing that they are not going to lose money in the future. That is a very dangerous position to take and the experience of all banks in the UK, post the financial crisis, showed how the value of assets they had as security could fall to such an extent that they were forced to write off lending and faced significant bad debts because of this. In any event, the cost associated with pursuing recovery should not be underestimated and can significantly reduce the ultimate sums realized under the security.

What makes good security?

Is there such a thing as 'good' security and if so, what do we mean by this? Ideally, any security which is taken should have all of the following; however, it is unlikely that any piece of security taken by a banker will have all these attributes, and often the banker has to compromise. A good example would be property (real estate) and under the 4S structure below we consider the difference between security that is simple to take and security that is simple to realize.

The 4S of security structure is as follows:

1 simple to take;

2 simple to value;

3 stable in value; and

4 simple to realize.

Simple to take

Banks have standard documentation, usually produced by their internal credit documentation department which they use to 'perfect' security. This ensures a standardized approach and simplifies what could otherwise be a complicated process. Often the 'title' to an asset will have an impact on how easy it is for a bank to take a particular asset as security. We will explore later how the true title to property (residential property for example) can be established by using the **Land Registry**. Certain types of security, such as personal guarantees, are relatively easy to take; however, if they are to be effective in the event of default then they need to go through a legal process which involves using external solicitors to impartially explain the legal impact of signing the **guarantee** document. Property (also known as real estate), whether residential or commercial, is not particularly easy to take as security (and for residential property there are a number of other considerations such as whether there are other occupants).

Land Registry A central government department covering all registered land in England and Wales (see also below).

Guarantee The promise by one party to repay part or all of the liabilities of a third party, if the third party fails to repay the borrowing they are contractually obliged to.

Registered land Any land or buildings (domestic or commercial) in England and Wales that is registered at the Land Registry. Title is evidenced by a land certificate.

Unregistered land Any land or buildings (domestic or commercial) in England and Wales that is not recorded at Land Registry. Title is evidenced by a set of deeds.

Simple to value

Some types of security such as **life policies** (with a surrender value) or shares in PLCs (quoted on the Stock Exchange and with prices that are readily available) are easy to value and do not require any professional expertise. However, there are other types of security, such as real estate, which require professional advice. With the greatest respect to bankers, they are not professional valuers and whilst it is quite possible for bankers to have a reasonable view as to the value of, for example, a residential property in a particular area (values can be easily compared on the internet), this is only a view and shouldn't be taken as a reliable value when using property as security. The more specialized a property becomes (particularly for specialist use, such as a purpose-built care home), the more the banker has the need for an external view. Assets such as plant and machinery and inventory (stock) will usually always need specialist valuations.

> **Life policies**   A product issued by an insurance company on the life/lives of an individual/s. The policy will pay out on the death of the life insured.

Stable in value

When a banker lends money, they will often do this on a term basis which means that the borrowing will reduce over the term of the borrowing until it is fully repaid. The ideal situation for any security held is for that security to stay at the same value throughout the life of the loan (or even increase!). This is unrealistic for some assets as they will depreciate (ie be worth less each year), such as machinery or vehicles due to 'wear and tear', and the higher the usage of the asset, the more quickly they will depreciate. There is an argument to say that an asset is only worth what someone may be prepared to pay for it and this is true to a certain extent. Asset values are of course impacted by external circumstances and if the UK is, for example, facing a prolonged recession, then certain types of security will be impacted by this. Real estate may be depressed in value and over the course of the last 40 years in the UK there have been several recessions which have caused property values in both residential property and commercial property to drop and then recover.

Some assets, such as shares, can fluctuate widely in value, due to both the fortunes of the particular company the shares are held in and to the overall performance of the stock exchange.

Simple to realize

What do we mean by realize when it comes to security? We mean turning an asset that the bank holds as security into cash. A particular challenge for banks when they do want to realize security, and this is certainly true for real estate, is that whilst it may be desirable security, the bank may have to wait up to a year, and perhaps even longer to obtain the best price for the asset. If the customer is working with the bank to sell the asset, then this will help the overall sales process and the property will need to be properly and professionally marketed. If it is residential property that is being sold, then due consideration needs to be given as to whether or not the property has tenants or if there are occupants who will have certain rights. There are often external costs incurred when assets are realized, for example, professional fees for solicitors and estate agents.

Different types of charge

It is useful for you as the banker to consider how you can control assets that your customer has, whilst still allowing the customer the ability to use them. Under English and Welsh law, we can categorize security under different types of **charge**.

> **Charge**   Where the bank takes a controlling interest in an asset. It restricts the owner of the security dealing with the asset without the consent of the bank.

TYPES OF CHARGE

Mortgage   This allows a lender to legally take control of an asset (although court action may be also required).

Equitable charge   This is created by the holding of security, and with a Memorandum of Deposit signed by the customer. This creates the intention to create a legal mortgage in the future should the bank wish to enforce its security (due to customer default).

Lien   This is defined as 'a right to keep possession of property belonging to another person until a debt owed by that person is discharged' (Concise Oxford English Dictionary). It is likely to arise when a service is provided involving an asset. A simple example would be where a garage servicing a car may hold a lien over the car until the bill has been paid.

Pledge   This is not a particularly common form of security and is usually seen when the bank finances international trade transactions. Letters of credit (which will be discussed briefly in Chapter 7) are often used to finance international trade and involve transit documents (usually shipping documents) and documents that give title to the goods involved in the transaction. When a bank issues a letter of credit on behalf of a commercial customer, the bank enters into a financial commitment that it must honour. It will then debit its customer. If the customer does not have sufficient funds, then the bank may take possession of the goods in lieu of payment. In reality, goods would be placed in a 'bonded warehouse' at a UK port under the bank's control, and the bank could arrange to sell the goods to discharge the outstanding debt.

When dealing with security, the **mortgagor** is the party giving the security (usually the customer), whereas the **mortgagee** is the party taking the security (usually the bank).

A commercial banker is most likely to see the first two types of charge due to the nature of transactions they will be dealing with.

Mortgage   This is sometimes also known as a 'legal mortgage'. A holder of security signs a document that is an agreement between the bank and the holder of that security, allowing the bank to take control of that security if certain events happen (such as borrower default).

Equitable charge   This is sometimes also known as an 'equitable mortgage'. This is when a holder of security signs a document that is an agreement between the bank and the holder of that security, allowing the bank to take a mortgage over that security if certain events happen (such as customer default).

Lien   This is the right by one party to hold an asset belonging to another party until an outstanding debt has been repaid.

Pledge   An undertaking that an asset may be used as security and potentially disposed of by a bank if funds are not paid out under a transaction (often involving international transactions).

Mortgagor   The entity borrowing the funds and is usually the party *giving* the security (the customer).

Mortgagee   This is what the bank becomes when it lends money and is the party *taking* an interest in the security (the bank).

Limited company security

You will recall from Chapter 1 that the legal precedent *Salomon v A Salomon and Co Ltd [1897]* established the important legal principle of a limited company being a separate legal entity. It is this principle that allows a company to give certain types of security such as **debentures** that an individual cannot. Debentures give the bank a **fixed charge** over fixed assets and a **floating charge** over floating assets, which we will return to later in the chapter.

> **Debenture**   Security given by a limited company to a bank. This gives the bank a fixed charge over fixed assets and a floating charge over floating assets.
>
> **Fixed charge**   A charge given by a limited company, which attaches to certain assets that are classified as fixed (eg machinery, land and buildings etc).
>
> **Floating charge**   A charge given by a limited company, which attaches to certain assets that are classified as floating (eg trade receivables, inventory etc).

Companies House

One of the key issues that bankers need to be aware of when dealing with the security for limited companies is that there are extra steps that must be taken to ensure that any security is completely robust. This involves filing documents at Companies House, which, as we discussed in Chapter 1, is the key entity in the UK maintaining a register of all limited companies. The key information that is available is:

- list of all companies;
- details of directors (including directors who have been disqualified);
- details of all financial information;
- register of all charges (eg debentures) (www.gov.uk, 2017).

Any charges over real estate must be registered at HM Land Registry (which we discuss later in this chapter) and bankers must also ensure that company security is registered at Companies House within 21 calendar days of it being signed by the directors.

Companies House information, as the central register in the UK, is useful for bankers as it provides protection against one bank (or any other lender) attempting to take assets that another bank already has a charge over as security. It is a public record and any further charges would first require consent from the existing lender and secondly would sit behind the original charge.

Debentures

The debenture is an integral part of any lending proposition to a limited company, and as such it is very important for you to understand what a debenture is, what powers it gives the bank and why one should always be taken when lending to a corporate entity. Limited companies can have as their current assets, which we have already touched on, trade receivables (monies owed to the company) and inventory (stock). The banker will want to take these assets as security and the debenture is a method of doing so.

Many bankers struggle with the concept of a debenture and the following part of this section will explain the key principles behind this important piece of security.

The two parties involved are:

1 the **chargor** – in this case the limited company (the customer); and

2 the **chargee** – in this case the bank.

> **Chargor** A party giving a charge over security.
>
> **Chargee** A party taking a charge over security.

The limited company (chargor), by signing a debenture in favour of the bank (chargee), gives the bank control over assets owned by the limited company. The debenture creates something called a charge over the assets that the limited company owns. As already touched on, there are two very different types of charge created by the debenture: a fixed charge and a floating charge.

The concept of creating a charge is that, whilst the asset owned by the limited company doesn't have its ownership altered (ie transferred into the name of the bank), the bank, as the chargee, has a degree of control over the assets. This limits what the chargor (the limited company) can do with the asset, without liaising with the bank.

A fixed charge creates a fixed charge over the fixed assets owned by the business (although in practice the bank will usually take a legal mortgage over assets such as commercial property, which we will discuss further below). Fixed assets are likely to include **freehold** and **leasehold** property, fixed machinery, intellectual property (patents etc), and goodwill.

Freehold The owner of land or property (real estate) who has an absolute right to deal with the property in any way they wish including selling it. Ownership stays with the owner of the property without any time limitations.

Leasehold The owner of the freehold property grants a lease over the property, giving the leaseholder the ability to use the property as if it were their own. The ownership of the property stays with the freehold owner. This will be for a specific period of time and can be up to 999 years. The leaseholder must comply with the terms of the lease including making the lease payments.

A floating charge creates an equitable charge over assets which tend to fluctuate in value on a regular basis, and, where it would be impractical, time-consuming and expensive to have a fixed charge. The assets involved include inventory, work-in-progress (if applicable), furniture, machinery (moveable) and trade receivables. In England and Wales the case *Re Yorkshire Woolcombers Association [1903]* established a number of important principles regarding how a floating charge is established and how it should operate. The following is taken from the summary of this case:

(1) if it is a charge on a class of assets both present and future;

(2) if that class is one which in the ordinary course of the business of the company would be changing from time to time;

(3) if it is contemplated by the charge that, until some future step is taken by or on behalf of the mortgagee, the company may carry on its business in the ordinary way so far as concerns the particular class of assets charged.

The floating charge is therefore created over current assets that the company owns now and in the future, so that an important asset such as inventory, which will be used to sell and make profits, and will fluctuate over the course of a week, a month and a year will still be captured under the floating charge. Importantly, it allows the limited company to use its key current assets, without having to ask permission from the bank every time it sells stock.

Trade receivables – fixed or floating charge

Do debentures give a fixed charge over 'book debts' (trade receivables)? This has been a hotly debated subject and is of particular importance to bankers.

The relevance of this question is important because it links to the order that funds can be used to repay bank borrowing in an insolvency situation. As we have seen in an earlier section, there are different types of charge that a bank can take, and these give the bank different powers. A fixed charge gives the bank more power over the asset that has been charged.

For many years banks considered that if they had a debenture then it gave them a fixed charge over book debts, and this helped the bank when it was using overdraft facilities to support the working capital requirements of a company. It knew that in an insolvency situation it could use the monies owed to the company to go first towards repaying the outstanding overdraft (and other borrowing the bank might have). Banks relied on the case of *Siebe Gorman & Co Ltd v Barclays Bank Ltd [1979]* which stated that banks had a fixed charge over book debts. However, two key cases, *Agnew v The Commissioner of Inland Revenue [2001]* (also known as the *Brumark case*) and *Re Spectrum Plus Limited [2005]* confirmed that the bank through its debenture can only have a floating charge over book debts. The House of Lords confirmed in their judgments that if the customer has full control over the asset (the book debts) and the proceeds (ie the cash) generated then by definition, the best a bank can have is a floating charge.

The only way a bank can have a fixed charge is by controlling the book debts and having funds paid into a specific account (separate to the main trading account) which is controlled by the bank.

Other available assets

Goodwill

This usually arises when one business buys another, is the difference between the value of the assets of the business and the price actually paid and is a way of reflecting the value of the business that has been bought. Businesses being purchased may have brand names and trademarks which can have considerable value. It is usually written off against profits over a number of years.

Patents/intellectual property

These are known as 'intangible assets' as they cannot be seen or felt in the same way as a tangible asset such as a building. A software company is an example of a business which will have significant intellectual property, as it will have developed commercial software which it will be able to sell and licence to their customers.

Plant and machinery

Any business that manufactures will use machinery and this will reduce in value over a period of time due to wear and tear. This is a natural reduction in value (think of how a car reduces in value over time).

Real estate (property)

Real estate lending is a key component of lending by a bank to commercial businesses. This can be by either lending directly to a company for the purchase of business premises (such as offices, factories or warehouses) or by taking personal (residential) property which might be used to support personal guarantees by the directors of the business. Real estate is a relatively new term in the UK (originating in the United States) for what would have previously been called commercial property or residential property in the UK.

Registered land

In England and Wales there is a system of what is called registering land, where a central register is maintained at the HM Land Registry. This central registry has over 25 million individual titles to property and, importantly for a banker, is a place where the interests of banks, such as legal charges or mortgages (and other lending institutions) are also registered. The owner of the registered property has a certificate which confirms ownership. For limited companies, charges must also be registered at Companies House, as discussed earlier.

In the past land was usually unregistered, where title would be evidenced by a set of deeds which showed, by conveyance documents, the transferring of a particular property to different individuals (or companies) over a period of time. Over time there would be a growing set of documents and the HM Land Registry made it compulsory for land and property to be registered when it was sold (and by definition, ownership was transferred).

Property categorization

There are two main types of property in England and Wales, freehold and leasehold. These two ways of owning property were established in the *Law of Property Act [1925]* (for further details see the 'Legislation' feature later in this chapter).

Freehold is where the owner of the property has an absolute right to deal with the property in any way they wish including selling it. The ownership stays with the owner of the property without any time limitations.

Leasehold is where the owner of the freehold property grants a lease over the property, giving the leaseholder the ability to use the property as if it were their own. The ownership of the property stays with the freehold owner. This will be for a specific period of time and can be up to 999 years. The leaseholder must comply with the terms of the lease including making the lease payments.

Overriding interest

When a banker takes real estate as security, the ownership of the property does not transfer to the lender from the borrower. The bank, however, may need to take control of the property in the future if the borrower defaults and it will be very difficult to do this if there are other parties, separate to the borrower, who have an interest in the property. These are likely to be partners (including spouses) of the borrower and children. In the case of *Williams & Glyn's Bank v Boland [1981]*, it was decided that a spouse (in this case a wife), due to them being an occupant of a property, had an interest in the property called an 'overriding interest', which gave the spouse certain rights. In this particular instance, the borrower, the husband, had mortgaged the property to the bank, without his wife's knowledge, and when the bank tried to take possession of the property, they were unable to do so, as the wife's right to occupy the property was deemed by the courts to be more important than the bank's rights.

The concept of overriding interest was therefore established. We will explore the banker's potential remedy to this dilemma below.

> **Overriding interest** When a party (or parties) other than the borrower has an interest in a property (usually a domestic residence). This will usually be a spouse/common law partner and/or dependents (including children) who would lose their home if the bank took control of it. The interests of the other parties are seen to be more important than those of the banks.

Undue influence

Leading on from the principle of overriding interest we will also explore how the concept of **undue influence** can have an impact on the security held by a banker.

Undue influence is the power that one party may have over another when contracts are entered into, with one party being influenced to enter into a contract they may have, without the influence of the personal relationship. The bank needs to be fully satisfied that when legal documents are signed, all parties are entering into the contract of their own free will.

There are a number of possible variations here including:

- husband and wife/cohabitees/common-law partners; and

- parent and minor child (under 18).

One of the key legal precedents was in the case of *Barclays Bank v O'Brien [1994]*, where it was established that husband and wife have a presumed risk of one influencing the other and therefore the bank needs to take steps to ensure that all parties are fully aware of what they are signing. In this case, the husband ran a business and was asked to give a personal guarantee by his bankers, Barclays, which was to be also secured by a second legal charge over the property that he lived in with his wife. Both Mr and Mrs O'Brien then signed a second charge document in favour of Barclays but Mrs O'Brien did not receive independent legal advice when she executed (signed) the second charge document. When Barclays tried to enforce their security, it was deemed by the courts that Mrs O'Brien should have received separate independent legal advice and there was a duty on Barclays to ensure that this was provided.

> **Undue influence** The influence that one party is presumed to have over another, often in a domestic situation (eg a husband over a wife or vice versa).

The remedy – independent legal advice

Bankers can protect their position when security is granted by ensuring that all parties, and particularly those who are not the borrower, obtain impartial, **independent legal advice** given by a qualified solicitor. The solicitor needs to explain the legal implications of the documentation that is being entered into and also explain the consequences of what may happen if loan agreements are not adhered to, and how this will impact on security. The consequences can include the bank taking control of the security and the fact that it may be sold in order for borrowing to be repaid.

The solicitor will need to sign a declaration that they have explained the implications of the documentation and that the parties signing it know what they are signing. In the *Royal Bank of Scotland v Etridge [1998]* case, there were a similar set of circumstances to the *O'Brien* case above, and the courts ruled that even if undue influence was not presumed, banks still had a duty to the party (in this case it was the wife) who was not directly involved in a commercial transaction to ensure that they received independent legal advice when they were signing charges over matrimonial property.

> **Independent legal advice**   Where a solicitor explains the legal implications of documentation that is being entered into and also explains the consequences of what may happen if loan agreements are not adhered to, and how this will impact on security (such as guarantees).

Guarantees

What is a guarantee? It is the promise by one party to repay part or all of the liabilities of a third party, if the third party fails to repay the borrowing they are contractually obliged to.

In commercial banking terms a banker is likely to be involved with two different types of guarantee:

- personal guarantee; and
- corporate guarantee.

> **Corporate guarantee**   A guarantee given by a limited company.

Personal guarantee

This is where an individual gives a guarantee in favour of a corporate entity. The individual will usually be a director or a shareholder (and sometimes both) of the business and it is a way of the bank linking the director to the business financially (we discussed above the *Salomon v Salomon* principle where directors do not have personal liability for the debts of the corporate entity).

Banks will usually take personal guarantees when there is no other security, and particularly for a new company, with no track record and where no assets have been built up in the business, this is a way of the bank having some comfort if the business fails. Banks will also take personal guarantees from directors, when there is not sufficient security in the limited company to cover the commercial lending or to evidence the director's personal commitment to the company.

For personal guarantees, there are certain requirements which must be satisfied in order for them to be valid:

- Limited in amount – they must be for a specific amount. If for example the guarantee is for £100,000 this is the total liability for the director(s).

- In writing.

- Time bound – guarantees do not, however, have to be limited in time (ie have an expiry date) to be valid.

Guarantees will usually be worded on the basis that they cover *all* the liabilities of the company that is being guaranteed; if there are overdrafts and loans these will be aggregated to arrive at a total liability (the individual outstanding balances on different facilities is then irrelevant).

You will recall from Chapter 1, that we discussed the principles of personal liability in a partnership, and we introduced the important concept of 'joint and several' liability. This concept applies in a similar way to personal guarantees. With joint guarantees, all individuals who have signed as guarantors, are individually responsible for the full amount of the guarantee and will be sued jointly. The death or bankruptcy of one of the guarantors is a 'trigger' event (discussed in Chapter 1).

With **joint and several guarantees**, all individuals who have signed as guarantors are again individually responsible, but the difference here is that the bank can pursue individual actions against each party up to the full amount of the guarantee. The monies collected, however, cannot be more than the total guarantee liability. Please see the example of Jones, Mohammed and Hassan below for an illustration of this point.

Joint and several guarantee A joint personal guarantee given by more than two or more guarantors. Each guarantor is individually responsible for the full amount of the guarantee and if the guarantee is called on by the bank, the amount outstanding can be recovered from the guarantors in any ratio acceptable to the bank.

JOINT AND SEVERAL GUARANTEE LIABILITY – JONES, MOHAMMED AND HASSAN

Three directors, Mr Jones, Mr Mohammed and Ms Hassan give a guarantee for £150,000 on a joint and several basis in favour of their residential building company, J, M & H Limited. If the business fails and the bank then subsequently calls on the guarantee, the bank will make demand on all three directors for the full amount of the guarantee, ie £150,000. They will not divide the guarantee and claim £50,000 from each director. The guarantors are likely to have different financial circumstances and as such, the amount recovered from each individual may well not be equal and could, for example be £25,000 from Jones, £50,000 from Mohammed and £75,000 from Hassan.

The bank cannot recover more than the total amount of the guarantee.

You will recall from Chapter 1 that we explored the rights and duties that the customer and the bank have. Guarantors do not have to be customers, but they do have certain rights which are ongoing throughout the life of the guarantee. For example, all guarantors have the right to be informed of their liability whenever they ask for it. Banks have a duty of secrecy, which we explored in Chapter 1, and if the liability is less than the guaranteed amount the bank will quote this amount, and if the borrowing is more than the amount of the guarantee, the bank will inform the guarantor(s) that the guarantee is being fully relied upon. The guarantors do not have the right to know the specific details about the operation of the company's bank account (this point is obviously not relevant where the guarantor is a director of the company as well as they will have full access to bank accounts).

The value of a personal guarantee

A guarantee only has a value if the individual giving it has sufficient assets to repay the guarantee if it is ever called on. Bankers will normally ask new guarantors to complete an asset and liability statement which details the full financial position of the guarantor, including all loans, personal mortgages, credit cards and the value of the assets that may be held which can include real estate (houses, flats etc), **stocks and shares**, cash and life policies (with surrender values).

Guarantees are often classified as being unsupported or supported – by this we mean whether or not the guarantor has given security to the bank which it can then rely on in the future. Often guarantors will give second-charges over personal property, where there will be a **first charge** to another lender (a bank/building society) for the original mortgage.

> **Stocks and shares** Quoted investments in securities that are traded on the Stock Exchange.
>
> **First charge** When a bank takes security, this is when the bank has priority over any other lender.

How can a guarantor be released from their liability? This can happen in three ways:

1 Bank release – if all borrowing to the company is repaid, the bank can release the guarantor from their liability.

2 Bank demand – in the event of the company defaulting and the guarantee being called upon by the bank demanding on it, and once funds have been received to fully cover the guarantee then the guarantee will be released.

3 Determination by the guarantor – a guarantor is fully entitled to pay to the bank the full amount of the guarantee (even if it hasn't been called by the bank) and then ask for the guarantee to be released, which the bank will be obligated to do. In practice the bank will be likely to place any such monies received into a separate account that it has control over, which could be used at some point in the future.

Independent legal advice

This was discussed earlier, but to reiterate, it is vital that independent legal advice is given to all guarantors to avoid any dispute in the future. All guarantors must be fully aware of their liabilities.

Completion of security

The following will need to take place in order for security to be completed:

1 Financial standing of guarantor established – asset/liability statement completed. Proof may also be required of assets held.

2 Standard bank guarantee form used – all banks will have their own documentation which will be used. Banks will not usually, unless there are exceptional circumstances, change any of the clauses in their documentation.

3 Independent legal advice – for the reasons already outlined, banks will normally insist that guarantees are signed at a solicitor's office, and that all guarantors are given independent advice (sometimes more than one partner in the firm may give advice). The solicitor will usually sign a declaration to the bank that the legal implications have been explained to the guarantor. Signatures will also be witnessed by the solicitor.

4 Joint and several guarantees – where there is more than one guarantor, all guarantors must sign the guarantee for it to be valid.

5 Copy guarantee – all guarantors should be given a copy of the guarantee.

6 Annual advice to guarantors – it is good practice for the bank to advise all guarantors of the ongoing validity of the guarantee and the fact that the bank is still reliant on the guarantee.

7 Guarantor standing – the bank may ask for updated asset/liability statements on an annual basis.

8 Guarantor's consent to change the terms of the underlying facilities which may adversely affect the guarantor's liability.

Individual guarantees are one type of guarantee that a banker is likely to see; the other type is a corporate guarantee, which we will go on to consider now.

Corporate guarantees

The most common type of corporate guarantee is where there are guarantees between companies in a 'group' – corporate entities sometimes arrange their affairs where they have separate limited companies for different parts of the business.

A common business structure is therefore likely to be:

- a parent company; and
- subsidiary companies.

Parent companies and subsidiary companies are limited companies in their own right and what links them together is their ownership. Often the parent company will own all the shares in each subsidiary company.

Using The Luxury Hotel Group Limited (Figure 6.1) as an example, we will explore the practical way the bank can do this by:

CASE STUDY

The Luxury Hotel Group Limited

The Luxury Hotel Group Limited (TLHG) is a hotel business that has five individual hotels, in different parts of England and Wales, including sites in London, Manchester, Cardiff and the Cotswolds. Each hotel has been set up as a separate limited company and each limited company owns the hotel it relates to. There is a 'parent' company which owns 100 per cent of the shares in the subsidiary companies. There are three directors.

The bank lends to the business on a group overdraft basis, for working capital, with a total limit of £500,000. There are also loans to the separate subsidiaries totalling £2 million, which have been lent for property improvements, and capital expenditure (new beds, soft furnishings etc).

Each of the individual companies is likely to have different borrowing requirements at different times, and the bank will be comfortable lending on a group basis if it can use all of the assets of all the individual companies to secure all the borrowing.

- taking a fixed charge over the property that each company owns; and
- taking a debenture that takes a charge over all other fixed assets and a floating charge over all current assets.

This will take place for each individual company. The final stage is to be able to link each company together and the bank will do this by taking what is known as a **composite corporate cross-guarantee**. This is a hybrid of the personal guarantee document already discussed and means that each company guarantees the liabilities of the other company. The bank holds security in each company by virtue of the fixed charges and debentures.

For guarantees to be valid there has to be commercial justification for the security to be in place, and the providing of a group overdraft facility that each individual company could use would be considered as sufficient commercial justification.

There are other variations of corporate guarantees where a parent company can guarantee the liabilities of a subsidiary and a subsidiary company will guarantee the liabilities of a parent company. This is known as **down-stream guarantee**, where the parent company gives the guarantee to the subsidiary company and an **up-stream guarantee**, where the subsidiary company gives the guarantee to the parent company.

Figure 6.1 The Luxury Hotel Group Ltd

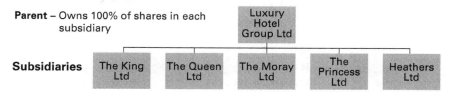

Parent – Owns 100% of shares in each subsidiary

Subsidiaries

The King Ltd | The Queen Ltd | The Moray Ltd | The Princess Ltd | Heathers Ltd

One subsidiary will guarantee the liabilities of all parts of the Group – This is repeated by each company in the Group

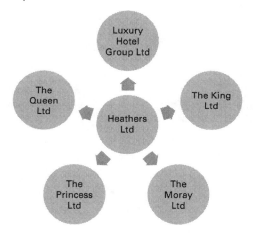

Composite corporate cross-guarantee   Guarantees given between companies in the same group (see also down-stream guarantee).

Down-stream guarantee   A guarantee given by a parent company in favour of a subsidiary company (see also composite corporate cross-guarantee).

Up-stream guarantee   A guarantee by a subsidiary company to a parent company.

ACTIVITY 6.1
The Luxury Hotel Group Ltd

Scenario – The directors have now approached the bank as they have found a hotel in the Lake District, The Consort, which is ideally suited to the image of the hotel. They wish to borrow £3 million on a new loan towards the purchase price of £3.25 million. They have established a new limited company, The Consort Limited, and want to complete the purchase as soon as possible.

The bank is prepared to lend the money but due to the relatively small contribution by the business have said that a condition of lending is that the three directors give a joint and several guarantee of £500,000.
Consider the following issues:

1 What security needs to be taken by the bank in order to fully protect itself for the new loan and to ensure that the new company, The Consort Limited, is supported by the security held already?

2 What issues does the bank need to consider when taking a new personal guarantee by the directors?

3 What else will the bank need to do before it lends the funds?

Personal security

We have touched on different types of security that can be pledged by individuals and there are other assets that are worth us exploring.

Cash

An obvious question is why anyone would use cash as security when they are borrowing money? Why not just use the cash? This is a valid question and the answer is that cash is often taken as security to cover the liability of a third-party guarantor. This will be placed in a bank account controlled by the bank and a charge will be taken over the cash so that it can't be released without the consent of the bank.

Stocks and shares

This a phrase used to describe shares and other tradeable instruments in limited companies. From a bank's perspective, the best type of stock or share is one that is freely traded on the London Stock Exchange. Shares registered on other stock exchanges such as The New York Stock Exchange will not normally be taken as security.

Shares in private limited companies will also not normally be considered as security the bank will wish to take as they are very 'illiquid' and there will normally be restrictions on the granting of them as security (via the company's articles and memorandums of association).

The shares a customer will have to offer as security very much depends on what they already own, and whilst the ideal would be to have a widely spread portfolio of shares, often in reality, the banker has to deal with what is offered, which may be shares in either one or just a few companies.

Gilts

Gilts are issued by the UK Government and are usually issued for a fixed period of time and are redeemable at what is called par (ie at face value), with a fixed interest rate (or coupon) on them. An example would be 5 per cent Treasury Stock 2025. This particular gilt matures in 2025 and pays 5 per cent on each £100 face value of gilt.

The strength of gilts is based on the fact that the issuer is the UK Government.

> **Gilts**   Issued by the UK Government, these are a savings product issued for a fixed period of time and are redeemable at 'par' (ie at face value), with a fixed interest rate (or coupon) on them.

Unit trusts

Unit trusts are a hybrid of investing directly in shares, where an investment company offers shares to individuals in funds which themselves invest in a variety of different shares (and different sectors). This allows investors to invest in the stock market but spreads the risk.

The process for taking of shares as security involves a number of documents. This process can also apply to unit trusts:

- Share certificate – this is evidence of the holding of the shares and needs to be held by the bank.
- Memorandum of deposit – this document is signed by the owner of the shares and allows the bank to hold the shares as security and also creates an equitable charge over the shares (discussed earlier).
- Signed and undated stock transfer form – this is an instruction to the registrar (who maintains a register of all the shareholders) and is held undated, so that if the shares are needed to be sold in the future, the transfer form is simply dated and sent to the registrar.

> **Unit trusts** Investment products that consist of a pool of stocks and shares to spread the risk.

Life policies

Life policies are issued by insurance companies and are written on the life of an individual (known as the 'life assured') with a beneficiary. The beneficiary can be a third party or can be the same as the person who is the life assured:

- Whole of life/reducing term assurance – this type of life policy is usually a life policy that provides a pay-out if the person who is the life assured dies. There is no savings element to the policy. Often this type of life policy is taken out when borrowers have mortgages on personal property and is particularly important where there are two parties to the mortgage, and the death of one party, and the loss of their earnings would impact on the ability to repay the mortgage.

- Whole of life – this provides a fixed amount of life cover throughout the life of the insured.

- Reducing term – this provides a reducing amount of life cover over a fixed period.

> **ACTIVITY 6.2**
> **Whole of life versus reducing term**
>
> You are about to take as security a whole of life insurance policy with a value of £150,000.
>
> *What is the difference between this type of policy and a reducing term policy? Review your answer at the back of this chapter.*

- Endowment policy – an endowment policy is a policy that is used for long-term savings (usually 10 or more years). Often these are taken out to pay for an event in the future (university education/wedding etc) and may have an element of life cover built in but they don't have to. This type of policy will have a value which will usually build up in value assuming all the premiums are paid.

- Key person protection policy – we first discussed this in Chapter 4 in relation to the *Big Yellow Design Agency* case study. This is often taken by bankers as security as it provides life cover on key individuals in a business, and without whom the business might have a problem operating properly.

TAKING LIFE POLICIES AS SECURITY

The following is the process the bank would normally follow:

- Original life policy – this must be held by the bank, who will need to confirm the life assured and the beneficiary.

- Value – the bank will need to be informed of what is known as the 'surrender' value of the policy – ie what the policy is worth now if it is cashed in.

- Assignment – the bank will take a charge over the policy using an assignment and once this is signed by the life assured the bank can then contact the insurance company who has issued the policy.

- Interest in the policy – the bank will register its interest in the policy.

- Premiums – the bank will need to know that these are up to date and that they will continue to be paid as long as the bank has an interest in the policy.

Valuation of security

We have now discussed a number of different types of security that you are likely to come across as a banker, and you will recall that we discussed at the start of the chapter what the attributes of 'good' security for a bank would ideally be. One of the 4Ss was 'Simple to value' and we will now explore how achievable this objective might be.

Some items of security are relatively easy to value and do not require any specialist knowledge; other security needs the view of a professional.

Personal security

We have discussed a number of different types of security that an individual might offer and as we have already identified, the most common form of security that will be offered is property (real estate). This will usually be a residential property and often where the grantor of the security lives.

Real estate

It is easy to use web-based search engines such as Rightmove and Zoopla to confirm what properties are on the market in a certain area and it is also easy to find out how much a particular property was sold for the last time it changed hands. This, however, doesn't particularly help if a property has been owned for a number of years.

This is when independent advice will be most useful and necessary. The following lists what a bank will ideally want to see for any property that it takes a charge on:

- Bank instructed bank addressed valuation – often the main UK clearing banks have 'panels' of valuers which provide the level of expertise and service the banks need and all valuers have to take qualifications set out by the Royal Institution of Chartered Surveyors (RICS). Valuations will be carried out on an **open market value** basis and will include:

  - open market value – ie when a property is on the market in the normal manner through an estate agent; and

  - how long a property is likely to be on the market before it's sold.

The value of the security will not just depend on the value of the property and it is also likely to be impacted by whether or not there is a first charge already on the property (which will usually be to another bank or building society who has lent funds for the original mortgage). The outstanding mortgage needs to be deducted from the value of the property. See the example in the box below to show how this impacts on a bank taking a **second charge**.

Open market value   The value of real estate where a sale might take place under normal market conditions (ie not in a distressed situation).

Second charge   When a bank takes security and there is already another lender in place (eg a personal mortgage).

SECOND CHARGE

When a bank takes a second charge behind another lender, it effectively 'sits behind' the original lender and cannot take action against the borrower without the consent of the original lender. The bank will need to discount the value of the property to reflect the fact that another lender has priority over it.

If we take an example of a customer offering a second charge:

- where the property is worth £250,000;
- there is a first mortgage – £150,000.

Table 6.1 Impact on a property value by a first mortgage

Property	Discount Factor	Mortgages	Value
£250,000	80%		£200,000
First mortgage		£150,000	£50,000

The other issue when banks take second charges is that the first lender often has the right to lend more money to the customer, which would rank before the second charge, reducing the potential value of the security of the second charge holder even further.

An option the holder of the second charge has, if the first mortgage is relatively small, is to pay off the first mortgage, and then become a first mortgage holder, with the increased powers that then gives the bank.

Guarantees

As we have already highlighted, personal guarantees have a value linked to the personal assets of the guarantor. The bank is in a much stronger position if it takes tangible security to support a guarantee. Whatever the tangible security is, the comments under the specific category need to be taken into account when considering value.

Cash

Cash is worth its face value, and as long as the deposit is in an account that the bank has full control over then the bank can fully rely on the full balance at any time. The only potential issue is where cash is offered in a currency other than sterling. If US dollars or euros are offered then the bank faces a potential reduction in the value of the cash if exchange rates change.

Stocks and shares

The value of this type of security is easy to calculate as it is based on the prices of shares as quoted on the London Stock Exchange. These prices are publicly and readily available. Prices vary on a day-to-day basis and will even fluctuate during the day. The fortunes of a particular sector, such as retail, can impact on the values of all shares in that sector. Share prices are published daily in the *Financial Times* (FT).

Gilts

The prices of gilts are impacted by interest rates and, like share prices, gilt prices are published daily in the FT.

Life policies

If there is no savings element to a life policy, as discussed earlier, then there is no value to a policy. If there is a savings element, as long as the premiums are kept up to date, the bank can obtain a current valuation by writing to the insurance company.

Company security

Real estate

A banker is likely to encounter a wide variety of different types of commercial real estate and this will include investment real estate (both residential and commercial), factories, offices, warehouses, hotels, day care nurseries and care homes.

Many of the same considerations apply to commercial real estate as they do to personal real estate. A professional valuation is always needed (**bank instructed bank addressed valuation**) and often the bank will specify how often it will require further valuations in loan documentation (eg every three years).

Bank instructed bank addressed valuation   A valuation that a bank asks to be conducted, where the purpose of the valuation is for security purposes.

The use of a professional valuer needs to also reflect the nature of the property that is offered as security. For commercial property, the bank would look to ascertain:

- value of the property taking into account the business operating from it;
- open market value;
- timescale to sell the property;
- **alternative use** – and the value for this use; and
- **bricks and mortar value.**

Alternative use   This is used to examine how specialist the property is and whether there would be other uses for it. Please see the example below, 'Alternative use/bricks and mortar? – care homes'.

Bricks and mortar value   This is the pure value of a property without the value of the business that operates from it.

ALTERNATIVE USE/BRICKS AND MORTAR? – CARE HOMES

Many care homes in the UK were originally large private houses that have been converted to allow the housing of elderly residents. This often involved full-scale conversions providing bedrooms with en-suite facilities, general areas and kitchen facilities.

Once the care home is operational it then has an income stream based on the number of residents which gives it a value which is substantially above the property without the business.

If the bank ever needed to realize this type of property, it would initially look to sell the property to another care home operator, but if this was unsuccessful would need to know from a valuer what the property's value worth was on a stand-alone basis.

Always bear in mind that many firms of valuers in the UK have specialist knowledge in particular types of property. It would always be wise for the bank to use a firm that has experience in the type of property being given. Christie and Co, for example, have extensive experience in the leisure sector (hotels, pubs, etc), and Knight Frank have wide experience with purpose-built student accommodation (both in the UK and Europe) (www.christie.com, 2017), (www.knightfrank.co.uk, 2018).

Trade receivables

These are funds owed to a business and, via the debenture, they become part of the security the bank can rely on. The value of the 'debtor' book is based on the ability of those customers to pay the funds they owe. Many businesses tend to take out specific insurance on their trade receivables, and the diligence by a specialist insurance company will include specific credit checks on all the customers. The insurance company may exclude certain customers if they are considered to be a poor risk. The bank may insist on credit insurance to mitigate the risk. The total value of the debtor book is based on the total of what is owed to the business.

A bank will normally compare the usual credit terms offered to customers with the trade receivable days calculation.

Inventory

The stock of a business is difficult to value and often will require a specialist valuer, especially if the goods are high quality luxury goods. You will recall from our discussion of seasonality in Chapters 2 and 3 that stock can quickly become obsolete, particularly if they are fashion items or sports goods (consider a football shirt where there is a regular change of sponsor – last season's shirt can very quickly become valueless).

The other potential problem that banks face with stock is that the supplier can have what is known as a 'retention of title' clause, also known as a 'Romalpa' clause. The impact on the bank is that if the stock is not paid for, if the company goes into an insolvency procedure then the supplier will claim the stock is still owned by them. This is based on the legal case, *Aluminium Industrie Vaassen BV v Romalpa Aluminium Ltd [1976]*.

Discounting factors

A bank will not normally lend 100 per cent against most of the assets it takes as security, apart from cash. There are a number of reasons for this:

- It can take time to sell an asset – if in that time period interest on a loan cannot be covered then it will need adding to the loan which will increase the bank's exposure.

- Professional fees – if an agent is involved, then their fees will need to be covered.

- Real estate suffered significant falls after the financial crisis (2007/08).

- Customer contribution – if the customer has to place their own cash into a transaction then they also stand to lose if there are problems in the

Table 6.2 Discounting factors guidelines

Commercial assets	Suggested write-down (of the original value)
Goodwill	100%
Commercial premises	60–65%
Plant and machinery	20–30%
Inventory	20–25%
Trade receivables	50%

future. They are therefore more likely to work with the bank to try to resolve any issues.

- In an insolvency situation.

The **discounting factors** shown in Table 6.2 are a guideline as to how a bank is likely to discount security it has charged.

Discounting factors   The percentage used to write-down an item of security that a bank has.

ACTIVITY 6.3
Discounting factors

Taking into account the suggested write-downs of security, what are the likely values of security held by the bank?

Table 6.3 Asset discount table

	Value	Suggested write-down	Potential value
Goodwill	£100,000		
Commercial premises	£1,500,000		
Plant and machinery	£250,000		
Inventory	£100,000		
Trade receivables	£450,000		
	£2,400,000		

Write your answer in Table 6.3 and review the model answer shown in Table 6.4 at the end of the chapter.

Realizing security

To reiterate what has already been said at the start of this chapter, when we talk about realizing security, from a banker's perspective, we normally mean that the bank will exercise any rights it has over security, and will want to turn that security into cash, in order to repay the borrowing.

The bank has a number of rights which are included in its mortgage documents, where the bank has a legal mortgage. It is an important concept to note that the bank does not *have* to exercise all these rights but has the power to do so if it wishes. In any event, it will only exercise its rights if there has been a default by the customer.

REGULATION
The Law of Property Act [1925]

This law is the main legislation which governs the law relating to property in England and Wales. It gives a number of rights to charge holders:

- Appoint a receiver – this will often happen where there is rental income from the property the bank has a charge over and the bank wants to preserve that income, ensuring the receiver does this on the bank's behalf.

- Enter into possession – this would be where the bank actually transfers ownership into the name of the bank (in reality when this happens the property will be transferred into the name of a nominee company owned by the bank). One of the reasons that banks often do not exercise this right is because if there is contamination on land (linked to a commercial property), by taking possession, the bank then would assume the liabilities for cleaning the land up.

- Sell – this gives the bank the power to sell the property charged to it. Once the borrowing has been repaid, any funds left after costs have been deducted will be given back to the borrower (assuming they are not in any form of insolvency procedure – this is discussed in Chapter 9.

- Foreclosure – this involves not only taking possession of the property but also gives the right of the bank to retain any monies that are surplus, once borrowing is repaid. The courts are unlikely to grant this right to a bank and in reality this power is seldom used. The courts will be more likely to make the bank sell the property.

If the mortgagor (the person who has given the charge) can find a way of repaying the borrowing then the bank will be required to desist in any action it is taking and release its charge. These potential actions are subject to the bank having to obtain permission via a court process.

To source your own updates of this legislation visit: http://www.legislation.gov.uk/ukpga/Geo5/15-16/20

Chapter summary

In this chapter we have explored:

- The reasons why banks take security from personal and commercial customers and how security can be used to protect the bank's position when it is lending by giving the bank an alternative source of repayment if a customer fails to repay their borrowing.

- The key characteristics of what makes ideal or good security using the 4S structure: 1) simple to take, 2) simple to value, 3) stable in value and 4) simple to realize.

- The various types of security available to the lending banker for personal and commercial customers including cash, gilts, life policies (personal), real estate (personal and commercial), guarantees (personal and commercial) and debentures (limited companies).

- The different type of charges that are available for the lending bank including mortgage, equitable charge, lien and pledge.

- How security can be valued and particularly for real estate, why it is important to use professional valuers.

- The use of discount factors that are used to write-down security to ensure that banks do not lend 100 per cent against the original gross values.

Objective check

1 Why do banks take security from commercial and personal customers when it is available?

2 What are four *ideal* characteristics of any security that a bank can take?

3 List three different types of security for both personal and commercial customers.

4 What are the different types of charge a bank can take?

5 What are the different types of values that banks can assign to different categories of security?

6 Detail the discount factors that could be used for three different types of security.

Further reading

Royal Institution of Chartered Surveyors – https://www.rics.org/uk/
UK Debt Management Office [accessed 21 June 2018] [Online] https://www.dmo.gov.uk/about/who-we-are/

References

About us – Companies House [accessed 21 June 2018] [Online] https://www.gov.uk/government/organisations/companies-house/about

Corporate & Independent Services | Commercial Property | Christie & Co [accessed 21 June 2018] [Online] https://www.christie.com/services/

HM Land Registry [accessed 21 June 2018] [Online] https://www.gov.uk/government/organisations/land-registry/about

Law of Property Act 1925 [accessed 21 June 2018] [Online] http://www.legislation.gov.uk/ukpga/Geo5/15-16/20

UK Student Property Investments & Development | Knight Frank [accessed 21 June 2018] [Online] http://www.knightfrank.co.uk/commercial/student-property

Legal case references

Agnew and another v The Commissioner of Inland Revenue and another [2001] UKPC 28

Aluminium Industrie Vaassen BV v Romalpa Aluminium Ltd [1976] 2 All ER 552, [1976] 1 WLR 676

Barclays Bank plc v O'Brien [1994] 1 AC 180, [1993] 4 All ER 417

Re Spectrum Plus Ltd; National Westminster Bank plc v Spectrum Plus Ltd and others [2005] UKHL 41

Royal Bank of Scotland plc v Etridge (No 2) [1998] 4 All ER 705, 76 P & CR D39

Siebe Gorman & Co Ltd v Barclays Bank Ltd [1979] 2 Lloyd's Rep 142, 10 LDAB 94

Williams & Glyn's Bank Ltd v Boland [1981] AC 487, [1980] 2 All ER 408

Yorkshire Woolcombers Association Ltd, Re, Houldsworth v Yorkshire Woolcombers Association Ltd [1903] 2 Ch 284, 72 LJ Ch 635

Suggested answers for activities

Activity 6.1 – The Luxury Hotel Group Ltd

Learners were asked to consider the following issues:

1 What security needs to be taken by the bank in order to fully protect itself for the new loan and to ensure that the new company, The Consort Limited, is supported by the security held already.

2 What issues does the bank need to consider when taking a new personal guarantee by the directors?

3 What else will the bank need to do before it lends the funds?

Answers:

1 The bank will need to take a new composite cross-guarantee, which links all of the companies to each other. It will also need to take a legal charge over the new hotel and will also want to take a debenture from the new limited company.

2 The directors have been asked to give a new joint and several guarantee. The bank will need to ensure that all of the directors give a full asset and liability statement, and that they all receive independent legal advice from a solicitor.

3 The bank will want to ensure that it has a valuation of the hotel and may also need to consider if funds need to be lent for capital expenditure and whether working capital facilities need to be increased.

Activity 6.2 – Whole of life versus reducing term

You are about to take as security a whole of life insurance policy with a value of £150,000.

The question given is what is the difference between a whole of life policy and a reducing term policy?

The whole of life policy provides cover for the life assured of £150,000 until that individual dies. A reducing term policy is usually based on a particular repayment profile on a mortgage and over a period of, say, 25 years, the amount outstanding on the mortgage will reduce and the life cover on the policy will usually reduce to match the repayment profile.

Activity 6.3 – Discounting factors

Taking into account the suggested write-downs of security, what are the likely values of security held by the bank?

The values in Table 6.4 reflect suggested write-down values.

Table 6.4 Suggested write-down values of security

	Value	Suggested write-down	Potential value
Goodwill	£100,000	100%	£0
Commercial premises	£1,500,000	60%	£900,000
Plant and machinery	£250,000	20%	£50,000
Inventory	£100,000	20%	£20,000
Trade receivables	£450,000	50%	£225,000
	£2,400,000		£1,195,000

07

Lending products

INTRODUCTION

In this chapter we will be examining the different types of lending product and service that are available for a banker dealing with commercial customers. An important skill for any banker is the ability to match the products and the services that the bank can provide with the needs of the customer. It is an obvious thing to say but no customer is the same as another, and the needs of each customer can be quite different. Having said that, it is possible to group needs together and whilst a banker should not try to place 'square pegs in round holes', a skilled banker can recommend structures for lending which work for the customer and the bank.

There is an important point to make here in that a banker does not have to provide all the lending services a customer requires and there may be occasions where the bank will look to share the risk to a particular business by allowing another lender to provide part of the lending facilities.

We will discuss the advantages and disadvantages of the different types of product and service and also examine when it would be suitable to use them. We will also explore alternative forms of finance for businesses, including peer-to-peer lenders, and consider how the main UK clearing banks deal with situations when they decline lending requests.

LEARNING OBJECTIVES

By the end of this chapter, you will be able to:

- evaluate key commercial lending products and assess their specific advantages and disadvantages;
- evaluate the importance of asset based lenders as an alternative to banks;
- assess the circumstances when international trade products are used to support commercial customers; and
- analyse the alternative sources of finance available if traditional sources of funding are unavailable.

Lending products

We will first explore the basic products that a banker needs to understand and be able to use.

Overdrafts

This is the most common form of lending product a business is likely to have. It is sometimes known as a 'vanilla' product as it can be quite plain! The business is able to go into a debit position on its main trading account, which will be a current account, up to an agreed limit. We have already discussed the working capital cycle in Chapter 2 and this is the most common way that businesses will use **overdrafts** to 'smooth' out their cash flow. All businesses face cash flow pressures at different times of the month, and regular monthly and quarterly payments to suppliers, staff, landlords and HMRC are likely to trigger the use of the overdraft. Some businesses also have seasonal requirements through the year for extra cash (particularly retail and leisure businesses).

In an ideal world, businesses should operate their current accounts so that they 'swing' from credit to debit (overdrawn) and back again. As we will see in Chapter 9, a business running a current account position where they are overdrawn all the time (often known as 'hardcore') is a possible warning sign that there is a problem.

Overdrafts should not be used for purchase of capital expenditure for the business and the only exception may be where a **loan** has been agreed and the overdraft is used to purchase the asset as the funds are being transferred from the loan account.

The advantages of overdrafts are:

- They are easy to arrange.
- They are flexible.
- The facility can be drawn on and repaid depending on the requirements of the business.
- Interest is only payable on the outstanding balance.
- They are useful for seasonal cash pressures on the business.

The disadvantages of overdrafts are:

- Usually security will be required.
- Fees are payable.
- They are repayable on demand.
- They are usually renewable every year.
- The limit is not flexible.

Loans

This is another basic commercial product that banks provide to their customers and, in the same way as a basic overdraft can be considered a 'vanilla' product, loans are a straightforward lending facility and can be used for any legitimate business purpose. The most common loans are usually for fixed assets such as buying premises, vehicles or machinery. Facilities are provided on a medium- to long-term basis, depending on the asset being financed, and require regular repayments of the initial capital and interest payments over a set term of years. For example, a loan for a new van, with a life of four years, should normally be lent over that period (or shorter).

Many of the advantages and disadvantages are similar to those discussed for the overdraft above.

The advantages of loans are:

- They are easy to arrange.
- Documentation is straightforward.

- Loan payments are agreed at the outset – this allows accurate budgeting by the business.

- They have a simple structure.

- Loans fully amortize (ie all of the initial capital that is borrowed is fully repaid at the end of the agreed term).

The disadvantages of loans are:

- Usually security will be required.

- Amounts repaid cannot be 'redrawn'.

- Rising interest rates may require higher repayments.

- Repayments will need to be made every month/quarter (irrespective of the peaks and troughs in cash flow).

- The term and loan amount are fixed.

- Breaching of loan covenants, including a default on payments, can mean a default on other borrowing facilities.

Revolving credit facility

A **revolving credit facility** (RCF) is an alternative to an overdraft and is usually only offered to larger commercial and corporate businesses. As a lending product it sits somewhere between an overdraft and a loan; it is more flexible than a standard loan facility, and gives rather more certainty than an overdraft would.

Typically, RCFs will be a separate lending facility provided by the bank and are committed facilities by the bank.

The advantages of revolving credit facilities are:

- Amounts drawn can be repaid and then redrawn.

- Facility suitable for seasonal or cyclical payments (such as VAT/HMRC payments).

- No set capital repayments.

- Higher level of commitment from the bank and not repayable on demand.

- Longer term than overdrafts – usually two to five years.

The disadvantages of revolving credit facilities are:

- Fees will be payable.
- Non-utilization fees are payable – due to the 'committed' nature of the facility by the bank these fees will be payable whether or not the facility is used (these are normally a percentage of the facility agreed).
- Covenants will normally be set.

Business credit cards

All businesses are likely to have directors and other employees who will have regular expenditure which will need to be paid for in advance and then will be claimed back. This could be for travel and accommodation costs, including airline tickets, train tickets, hotel costs, meals and entertaining. The easiest solution is to provide a **business credit card** facility, with individual cards issued to named directors and employees. An overall limit will be agreed between the credit card provider (this will often be another division of the bank) and the business and within that limit, credit cards, in the name of the business, will be issued to named directors and employees with limits on each card.

On a monthly basis the business will be debited, usually via a direct debit to the business's current account, for the aggregate of all the expenditure on every card. The business will receive a monthly statement showing a breakdown of the expenditure on each card which can then be reconciled with individual expenses claims by directors and employees.

The advantages of business credit cards are:

- They allow a business to monitor expenditure for expenses.
- An overall credit card limit will be given to the business, which can then be sub-divided into individual limits for specific directors/employees.
- They allow directors/employees to have individual lines of credit for business-related expenses.
- Directors/employees can book travel (airlines/trains) and accommodation (hotels etc) themselves using their business credit card.

The disadvantage of business credit cards is:

- The overall credit limit for the business credit card facility will be part of the lending facilities for the business and may be deducted from an overdraft facility.

Overdraft   An ability to borrow on a current account up to an agreed limit.

Loans   An amount of money lent to a business over a term period (usually a number of years). Interest is charged on the outstanding capital amount and repayments are set at a level that will repay the outstanding borrowing and the interest over the agreed term.

Revolving credit facility   An alternative to an overdraft and is usually only offered to larger commercial and corporate businesses. A lending product, it sits somewhere between an overdraft and a loan. Usually agreed over a two- to five-year period.

Business credit cards   A version of a credit card that is used by a director or employee for business purposes only.

Invoice funding

Invoice funding is a type of financing that is a hybrid of an overdraft facility and usually considered as an alternative to overdrafts. It focuses on using trade receivables (the debtor book), which you will recall are monies owed to the business. As we discussed in Chapter 6, the bank, using the traditional overdraft to fund working capital requirements, doesn't usually allow more than 50 per cent to be borrowed against the outstanding debtors. This is because it doesn't have any control over the monies owed. Particularly with a growing business, the increased sales can have a negative impact on working capital and may lead to new customers being turned away.

Invoice funding [see also **factoring** and **invoice discounting**]   A hybrid type of financing and usually considered as an alternative to overdrafts. A financing option where a bank or other finance institution will use the invoices issued by a business to its customers and discount these, providing upfront (immediate) funds before the invoices are paid by the customers.

To remind you of what is usually involved with business to business trading, the normal process is for an invoice to be issued by a business to its customer once a sale has taken place (this can be for goods or services). As part of this transaction the customer becomes a debtor, where an agreed period of time is given to allow the debtor to pay the monies owed. A business may give a discount to encourage early settlement but usually they will have to wait until the monies owed are paid.

For a business, invoice funding facilities are an alternative method of releasing a greater portion of monies owed and usually much more quickly than by using an overdraft. There are normally two types of invoice funding facility:

- invoice discounting (often called confidential invoice discounting);
- factoring.

> **Invoice discounting** Sometimes also referred to as confidential invoice discounting. A type of invoice funding.
>
> **Factoring** A type of invoice funding. A variation on an invoice discount facility, the major difference being that the funder buys the outstanding debt and effectively steps into the place of the business that has the debtor.

Invoice discounting

This is a financing option where a bank or other finance institution will use the invoices issued by a business to its customers and discount these, providing upfront (immediate) funds before the invoices are paid by the customers. Usually a percentage of around 70–80 per cent is applied and once the bank has proof of the invoice being issued it will immediately lend funds to the business, using the agreed percentage. The rest of the funds (ie 20–30 per cent) are advanced once the invoice is settled.

The fundamental difference between an overdraft facility and an invoice discounting facility is that there is a much higher level of oversight and scrutiny by the invoice discounter.

The invoice discounting company will spend time examining the financial records of the company it wishes to support, including checking on all the customers the business has. It will check the credit record of each customer to ensure their creditworthiness and will also consider 'concentration risk'. If the company has a customer that is a particularly large percentage of monies owed, then the invoice discounter may decide to lend a smaller percentage against that debtor (eg 60 per cent rather than 70 per cent).

Most facilities are confidential which means that the debtors do not know about the funding arrangements.

To summarize, the main differences between an invoice discount (ID) facility and an overdraft are as follows:

- ID facilities require the business to maintain a separate current account which is used to collect the debtor monies when they are paid.

- The invoice discount provider will carry out regular audits of the debtor book.
- An electronic link will be provided to allow for the immediate uploading of new invoices.
- Bad debt insurance is provided against debtors.

The advantages of invoice discounting are:

- Drawdown of funds against new invoices will be immediate – cash flow is therefore significantly improved.
- A higher percentage is allowed against each debtor.
- The debtor is unaware of the funding arrangements.
- This type of facility is very suited to businesses that are growing quickly.
- The debtor book continues to be run by the business.

The disadvantages of invoice discounting are:

- The debtor book can only be used to support the invoice discount facility.
- Interest rates and fees may be higher than a standard overdraft facility.
- Contractual debtors are not usually suitable for discounting (eg a business supplying cleaning services to schools and hospitals).
- Foreign debtors are usually not discountable (due to the difficulties of collecting this type of debtor).
- A high number of small debtors may be less attractive to a lender (higher administrative burden).

A final point that you need to be aware of is that invoice discount facilities rely on a substantial level of trust between the business being funded and the invoice discounter. There is a very real possibility, despite the close relationship between the funder and the business, that false invoices could be issued, allowing drawdown of funds against debtors that don't exist and creating lending that is based on a fictitious asset, and potentially leaving the funder with a bad debt.

CASE STUDY
Invoice discounting and The Cheesy Factory

The Cheesy Factory (TCF) is a small manufacturer of specialty cheeses. It supplies independent retailers (mainly delicatessens) and has recently won a new contract with one of the major supermarkets. The contract is worth £50,000 per month, and the supermarket wants extended credit terms of 65 days rather than the 30 days which are TCF's normal terms. TCF is struggling to finance the new contract through its overdraft as the bank is not prepared to increase the overdraft to fund the contract.

An invoice discount facility is arranged through one of the specialist divisions of TCF's bankers. The new invoice discounting line agreement is to exclusively finance this contract and allows TCF to drawdown 65 per cent of the invoices issued immediately (this is a slightly lower percentage than discussed earlier to cover concentration risk). The final 30 per cent is paid when the final invoice is paid.

In this instance, TCF, using its overdraft, would need to fund £50,000 in month 1, £50,000 in month 2 and would not be paid for month 1 until just into month 3, assuming the supermarket pays on time. By using an invoice discount facility, £32,500 will be released into cash flow each month.

Questions

1 What are the advantages to The Cheesy Factory of having an invoice discounting facility?

2 What are the disadvantages of them having an invoice discounting facility?

3 How might this product help the overall sales strategy for the company?

Factoring

This is a variation on the invoice discount facility and was the initial way that this type of funding was provided, before invoice discounting was developed to the sophisticated level that it is now. The principles behind factoring are similar to invoice discounting, except that the major difference is that the funder buys the outstanding debt and effectively steps into the place of the business that has the debtor. Typically, a factoring facility will allow a higher percentage of the debt to be drawn down immediately, often up to 90 per cent. They will take control of the debtor book including the issuing of statements to debtors and will be responsible for the chasing of any late payments.

Factoring is normally offered as two types of facility:

- With recourse – this means that if a debtor doesn't pay against a valid invoice, then the factoring company has the right to claim back funds it has advanced (this might involve withholding funds on fresh invoices which are due for payment).

- Without recourse – the factoring company has to stand any loss if the debtor fails to pay.

The advantages of factoring are:

- Drawdown of funds against new invoices will be immediate – cash flow is therefore significantly improved.
- A higher percentage allowed against each debtor.
- This type of facility is very suited to businesses that are growing quickly.
- The debtor book is run by the factoring company, reducing the administrative burden on the business.

The disadvantages of factoring are:

- Debtors are aware of the factoring facility and may consider this to be a weakness.
- The factoring company may be aggressive with its debt collection processes, which could in turn damage the relationship between the company having its debts factored and its debtors.
- The debtor book can only be used to support the factoring facility.
- Interest rates and fees may be higher than a standard overdraft facility.
- Contractual debtors are not usually suitable for discounting (eg a business supplying cleaning services to schools and hospitals).
- Foreign debtors are usually not discountable (due to the difficulties of collecting this type of debtor).
- A high number of small debtors may be less attractive to a lender (higher administrative burden).

The bank perspective – cost of capital and risk weighted assets (RWAs)

Since the financial crisis there has been a much greater focus on the costs of capital for banks and the requirements of Basel III have meant that banks have examined much more closely the way they provide working capital facilities to businesses. Banks have what are known as **risk weighted assets**, where they have to allocate capital to different types of assets. Overdrafts would be one type of asset, invoice discount facilities would be another.

Overdrafts require a much higher level of capital to be held against them and due to the fact that they are 'committed' facilities, must have capital put against them for the total amount of the limit; for example, if the limit is £2 million but the customer only tends to use £1 million, the bank still has to put aside capital for the total limit (ie £2 million in this case). Invoice discount and factoring facilities, due to the greater degree of control that a bank has over the debtors, are deemed to require lower levels of capital than overdraft facilities and this encourages banks to lend in this way.

> **Risk weighted assets** Assets held by a bank that require a certain level of capital held against them. Higher risk assets require higher levels of capital.

Fixed asset funding – hire purchase and leasing

We have discussed loan facilities earlier, and an alternative way of financing fixed assets, particularly plant and machinery, is by using **leasing** and **hire purchase** facilities. This type of lending, due to the way the underlying asset is used as security, usually allows a greater amount to be borrowed against the asset and also means that the business wanting to invest in a new asset does not have to pay up front for the total cost of the asset.

The leasing industry in particular has become extremely sophisticated in recent years and assets as diverse as waste disposal plants and aeroplanes can be financed in this way.

Many businesses require intensive and regular investments in capital expenditure. Capital items (eg commercial lorries) tend to depreciate in value over time, and common sense should tell you as the banker that the more intensely an asset is used, the more quickly it is likely to depreciate.

Hire purchase and leasing facilities as alternative financing products for businesses give two very important advantages to businesses:

- They do not have to find the full amount for capital items purchased up front.
- They can renew their capital assets on a regular basis.

There are a number of examples of hire purchase and leasing companies and they can be subsidiaries of UK clearing banks, part of investment (merchant banks), part of industrial conglomerates or independent providers.

> **Leasing** A finance agreement using business assets, with a lessor (the owner of the asset) and the lessee (the party using the asset). The lessee effectively rents the asset throughout the agreement period.

> **Hire purchase** A finance agreement where when a business wants to purchase a capital item it will enter into an agreement with a hire purchase (HP) provider, where the asset is purchased by the HP provider and the business then pays for the asset over a set period. At the end of the agreement period the business that is the hirer will have the option to purchase the asset for a nominal figure from the HP provider.

Hire purchase

Under this type of arrangement, if a business wants to purchase a capital item it will enter into an agreement with a hire purchase (HP) provider, where the asset is purchased by the HP provider and the business then pays for the asset over a set period. These payments will include interest and will usually be fixed during the term of the agreement. At the end of the agreement period (and this will link to the life of the asset) the business that is the hirer will have the option to purchase the asset for a nominal figure from the HP provider.

From an accounting perspective, if a business enters into an HP agreement, even though the HP provider is the owner of the asset, current legislation in the UK allows businesses to class the asset as if they owned it (although technically a final payment is still required for the transfer of the asset to take place). Again, under current legislation, businesses can claim capital allowances for plant, machinery and other fixed assets that are financed under HP agreements.

The advantages of hire purchase are:

- It allows a business to buy new machinery on a regular basis without having to own it.
- It is very beneficial where machines wear out quickly and need to be replaced.
- It often allows assets to be funded by other lenders and not just the main bank.

The disadvantage of hire purchase is:

- The asset is not owned by the business until the end of the term.

Leasing

This type of financing arrangement is similar to an HP agreement. The parties to the agreement are the lessor (the owner of the asset) and the lessee (the party using the asset). The lessee effectively rents the asset throughout the agreement period.

There are two different types of leasing agreement:

- finance lease; and

- operating lease.

A finance lease is the closest to an HP agreement as it is usually for a longer term than an operating lease and will often link to the life of the asset being funded. The asset is normally shown on the balance sheet, although current legislation states that for agreements of less than seven years, the leasing company takes advantage of any capital allowances.

An operating lease tends to be for much shorter periods and the leasing company takes all the risk for owning the asset that is being leased and therefore the asset would not show on the lessee's balance sheet. This type of lease will suit assets that are needed for much shorter periods of time, such as plant and equipment needed for a customer building residential houses. For both types of agreement, the lease payments are able to be deducted from profits of the lessee. The ownership of the asset does not transfer to the lessee at the end of the lease period.

> **Finance lease**   A type of leasing agreement. Usually for a longer term than an operating lease and will often link to the life of the asset being funded. The asset is normally shown on the balance sheet of the business.
>
> **Operating lease**   A type of leasing agreement. It tends to be for much shorter periods than a finance lease (the leasing company takes all the risk for owning the asset that is being leased and therefore the asset would not show on the lessee's balance sheet).

The advantages of leasing are:

- It allows a business to keep changing its assets on a regular basis.
- Responsibility for ownership is that of the leasing company.
- It is very useful where an asset is only needed for a short period.

The disadvantage of leasing is:

- The asset is never owned by the business.

ACTIVITY 7.1
Hire purchase and leasing companies

As discussed earlier, many major banks have subsidiaries that provide this type of finance. Research the services that your bank provides and compare them to those provided by either another bank or another specialist provider.

Asset based lenders

Since the financial crisis in 2007/08, many of the traditional sources of finance to commercial customers have become less available as banks have become much more concerned about risk and cost of capital. See the earlier comment about risk weighted assets leading to banks becoming more stringent with their lending policies. This has seen a rise in other funders.

Asset based lenders (also known as ABLs) is a phrase used to describe a category of lender that, as the term suggests, provides specialist financial services, primarily lending against an asset or assets that a business has. We have discussed in other chapters the principle of the ability to repay and you will recall that with this type of approach to lending, security taken by the bank comes at the end of the lending process.

Asset based lenders A category of lender that provides specialist financial services, primarily lending against an asset or assets that a business has.

There are many reasons why businesses might approach this type of funder. Sometimes it may be because the business is a new business and has no track record. It may be because a bank has no appetite for the sector the customer operates in. The risk may be unacceptable, and the bank may not be comfortable with the proposals put forward by the customer to repay the borrowing. The following are the main points to consider with asset based lenders:

- Security – with an asset based lender, security has a primary importance in the lending decision. The ability to turn an asset into cash with this type of lender will be the primary concern before the rest of the proposition is considered. Personal guarantees are usually required.

- Interest rates – these will tend to be much higher than the rates that a major clearing bank will require and in many cases the customer will need to cover interest on a monthly or quarterly basis. Interest 'roll-up' will sometimes be accepted but only if there is a sufficient margin between the security offered and the borrowing requested. The higher interest rates reflect the fact that this is a different type of financing model to a clearing bank, and that there is a higher risk and reward.

- Capital repayments – these are usually not required throughout the term of the borrowing.

- Term – this is not usually long-term finance and often terms will be up to 12 months.

There are different types of asset based lender, some being divisions of major clearing banks. There are also many niche providers of finance to business and an example of one of these specialist providers is Aldermore Bank, established in 2009, serving their commercial base through nine regional offices (face to face) as well as through a phone and internet service. Their main areas of focus are asset finance, invoice finance, SME commercial mortgages and residential mortgages.

See 'References' at the end of this chapter for details of a regional firm, Reward Finance Group.

What happens when the bank says no?

Many UK banks are acutely aware that they face criticism if they do not support businesses and they now have a duty to provide a referral system that allows businesses that do not fit their lending criteria to find other sources of finance. Customers that have had their requests for finance declined have the right to ask for a referral within 30 days of being refused finance to a 'government designated finance platform'.

The banks involved in this referral system are the major banks in the UK (known as designated banks):

- AIB Group (UK) Plc (t/a First Trust Bank);
- Bank of Ireland (UK) Plc;
- Barclays Bank Plc;
- Clydesdale Bank Plc;
- Northern Bank Ltd (t/a Dankse Bank);
- HSBC Bank Plc;

- Lloyds Banking Group Plc;
- Royal Bank of Scotland Group Plc; and
- Santander UK Plc.

The banks above will provide referrals to four main platforms:

- Alternative Business Funding;
- Business Finance Compared;
- Funding Options; and
- Funding Xchange.

This scheme is aimed at UK businesses of up to £25 million turnover and covers the main types of funding we have already discussed in this chapter, including overdrafts, loans, invoice finance and asset finance (although interestingly excluding operating leases) (www.ukfinance.org.uk, 2017).

CASE STUDY
Santander Bank

Santander UK Plc is part of the Banco Santander SA group. It has an increasing importance in the provision of finance to commercial customers, and through its Specialist Sector Groups, is providing services to customers in certain sectors including real estate, education, healthcare and hotels. They are, however, aware that they cannot always provide finance to businesses:

We want to support your business but it's not always possible for us to offer you lending. In these situations, we'd like to help by giving you some information about other sources of finance and support that may be available to you. (www.santandercb.co.uk, 2017)

Their website gives a number of alternatives for commercial businesses, including all the government-designated finance platforms already discussed. It also provides signposting to Better Business Finance and Mentorsme (a mentoring service for commercial businesses). It also gives details of alternative funding including Crowdfunder Ltd and Funding Circle Limited – these funders are discussed later in the chapter. To learn more about these services follow these weblinks: www.mentorsme.co.uk, www.crowdfunder.co.uk, www.fundingcircle.com

It is worth considering the advantages and disadvantages to providing other resources for businesses that a bank is unable to lend to.

ACTIVITY 7.2
UK Finance

In July 2017, a new organization was established, UK Finance, which is an umbrella trade organization representing 300 different financial services firms and encompassing the activities of the Asset Based Finance Association, the British Bankers' Association, the Council of Mortgage Lenders, Financial Fraud Action UK, Payments UK and the UK Cards Association.

UK Finance have a very useful website. Spend some time exploring the sites for the Asset Based Finance Association and the British Bankers' Association. You may also find the site for Better Business Finance useful: www.ukfinance.org.uk, www.abfa.org.uk, www.bba.org.uk, www. betterbusinessfinance.co.uk

Where else can businesses find funding?

The British Business Bank

Since the financial crisis, the main UK clearing banks have been under significant pressure to continue to support industry. We have discussed the normal processes that banks follow to lend to customers and sometimes businesses need higher risk capital or do not have the security to support their lending requests and growth ambitions. Recognizing the difficulties that businesses have in raising finance, **The British Business Bank** (BBB) was established in 2013, and is owned by HM Government in the UK.

British Business Bank   Owned by the British Government (established in 2013), the British Business Bank supports UK businesses via a combination of finance and guarantees to banks and investors who will then deal directly with the business that is looking for the support.

British Business Bank – aims

"Our aim is to make finance markets work better for small businesses in the UK at all stages of their development: starting up, scaling up and staying ahead." British Business Bank, 2017.

It is important for bankers to understand the vital services offered by BBB and how they can use them to complement the facilities offered by their own bank. The first point is that the BBB is not a bank in the traditional sense of the word and does not provide traditional services such as overdrafts and loans. What it does do is to provide a range of financial solutions which give opportunities to businesses that might not be available through their own banks without the support of BBB. This is predominantly through a strategy of providing a combination of finance and guarantees to banks and investors who will then deal directly with the business that is looking for the support. They provide many different types of support under the different categories of 'starting up', 'scaling up' or 'staying ahead'. Under the last category, one of the extremely important initiatives is the **Enterprise Finance Guarantee scheme**.

Enterprise Finance Guarantee scheme

The Enterprise Finance Guarantee scheme (EFGS) was actually originally launched in 2009 and has become one of the key initiatives supported by the BBB and is a successor to previous initiatives such as the Small Firms Loan Guarantee scheme. The EFGS is supported by over 40 banks which are described as 'accredited lenders', including all the major banks (eg Barclays and HSBC), some of the smaller banks (eg Metro and The Co-operative Bank) and a number of specialist providers (eg County Finance and Ultimate Finance).

> **Enterprise Finance Guarantee scheme**   A UK government-backed scheme providing support to UK businesses via the British Business Bank.

A business would be able to raise funds via this scheme if it were a business that a bank or other lending institution would support, but has found a significant stumbling block in a lack of tangible security. Under these circumstances the business can apply through its lender (who will need to be an accredited lender) to see if support can be provided. EFGS support will be via a guarantee to the lender (and this is important as it is not directly to the borrower) for 75 per cent of the value of the funding line.

- Banking facilities guaranteed can be for:
  - overdrafts;
  - loans;
  - invoice discount facilities; and
  - asset finance facilities.

- Amounts agreed:
  - £1,000 to £1.2 million.
- Term:
  - up to 10 years – term loans and asset finance facilities; or
  - up to three years for revolving facilities (eg overdrafts) and invoice discount facilities.
- Other relevant criteria:
  - business must be UK based and in an eligible industrial sector;
  - turnover no more than £41 million; and
  - have a good business plan and a sensible borrowing proposal.

Mechanics of support

The mechanics of the support to the bank are that once the EFGS support is agreed, The BBB will issue a guarantee in favour of the lending institution. If, for example, £1 million is the agreed facility by the bank, the guarantee will be for £750,000. The borrower will pay a 2 per cent annual fee (based on the value of the guarantee) and this is normally paid on a quarterly basis. Under the terms of the scheme, the directors of the business will not be able to give personal guarantees to the bank for the unsecured portion of the lending – in this case £250,000.

The lending relationship is between the bank and the business is exactly as it would be without the EFGS support, and the business has the obligation to repay the bank according to the terms and conditions of any lending agreements.

Default

If the business fails (and we discuss this in greater detail in Chapter 9), the lending bank will approach the BBB to ask for repayment under the EFGS. The BBB will want comfort that all the usual risk procedures that the bank would have taken if it didn't have the guarantee had been taken, and that all actions had been taken to save the business. Payment will normally be paid to the lending bank and the funds received will be used towards repaying the borrowing.

Peer-to-peer funding

Banks have traditionally had the role of 'financial intermediaries' where they match those with surplus funds (depositors) and those who have a deficit of funds (borrowers). In these circumstances, the depositor and the borrower use the bank as the 'middleman' and each party only has a relationship with the bank. Depositors will receive a deposit rate of return on their investment and their deposits will be protected up to the current level of the Financial Services Compensation Scheme. They do not have any influence in how their money is lent out to commercial businesses.

In the last 10 to 15 years there has been a rise in sources of finance where small businesses can access funds from smaller investors. This is sometimes known as **peer-to-peer funding** or social lending. Individual consumers can borrow funds in this way and increasingly businesses are using this type of funding. Some funders, such as Crowdfunder, provide funds which do not have to be repaid, whereas the Funding Circle provide loans. Both are explored in more detail below.

> **Peer-to-peer funding** An intermediary service that allows the direct investment in businesses (an alternative to more traditional funding by banks).

Crowdfunder

Crowdfunder Limited supports many different types of enterprise including small businesses, charities, community projects and social enterprises. It is not strictly a peer-to-peer lender as funds raised are not lent and the business that is a recipient does not have to repay these monies.

It is often an excellent way for a start-up business with no track record to test its product or service. At the time of writing, there is a current trend for consumers to support businesses local to where they live, particularly in the food and drink sector. Investors can either make a donation or can make a 'pledge' and depending on the size of the pledge will get some form of 'reward' which is linked to the size of the pledge. A new delicatessen, for example, may give future discounts on food or drinks.

The enterprise requesting the funding will start up a campaign which usually lasts for a specific period of time (eg 28 days) and will have a target amount of money that needs to be raised. One of the options is *flexible funding* where even if the target of funds raised is not achieved, the money that is raised in pledges will be passed to the business at the end of the campaign period.

The monies raised are not a loan to the business or enterprise and do not need to be repaid. In some instances, the investors may become shareholders in the business.

Crowdfunder also links with other organizations including banks (Santander) and local councils who have funds to give to projects where the project may be delivering something that impacts on a community more widely, such as social change. This may not be fully applicable to businesses, but there may be some element of what the business is doing that does link to this – a community café for example.

Staying with the food and drink sector there are many examples of businesses that Crowdfunder has supported, some small and some with much larger ambitions. A chocolate business and a family cheese shop are just some of the businesses benefiting from much wider exposure. We explore one business which has benefited from the Crowdfunder approach in the case study below, *Glenwyvis Distillery*.

CASE STUDY

Glenwyvis Distillery, Dingwall, Scotland

Dingwall is a small town in the Scottish Highlands, just north of Inverness. It has a long history of distilling and over the years the area has had mixed economic fortunes.

Large sums were raised for a new distillery, which initially raised over £2.5 million from over 2,200 investors. These investors became shareholders and the funds raised were to be used towards the construction of a new whisky distillery costing an estimated £3.8 million.

This is a great example of success using the Crowdfunder model.

It is an important point to note for bankers that if this level of funds can be raised it is a very positive sign if a lending request is also being considered to help finance the business. It doesn't mean that the bank has to agree the proposition, but it does show that the business has a significant interest in it.

Questions

1 Go on the Glenwyvis website and see an update on the project.

2 Download the Business Plan which shows the level of detail and planning in the project.

3 Why do you feel customers are so keen to support this kind of project?

www.crowdfunder.co.uk, 2017, www.Glenwyvis.com, 2017

Funding Circle

On their website, Funding Circle say they are 'Revolutionizing a broken system' where they feel businesses are not getting access to the funds they deserve through their banks. They have been in existence since 2010 and lend to a range of businesses in the UK, and in Europe. They lend on an unsecured basis (although they are likely to ask for personal guarantees from directors when they are lending to a limited company), on amounts from £5,000 (minimum) to £500,000 (maximum) and for periods from six months to five years. Starting rates are 4.5 per cent which compares very favourably with the main UK clearing banks. There are usually no early repayment fees.

Funding Circle is supported by both private investors and institutional investors (such as Accel Partners, BlackRock and Sands Capital). It also has equity injected from the British Business Bank (via British Business Bank Investments Ltd), which is owned by the UK Government (via the British Business Bank, as discussed above).

The key difference between Funding Circle and Crowdfunder is that Funding Circle is a lender and monies borrowed need to be repaid.

ACTIVITY 7.3
Peer-to-Peer Finance Association

Using the website for the trade association which covers peer-to-peer finance: www.p2pfa.info, research other firms that provide this form of financial service. Compare how they operate with what we have discussed for Funding Circle and Crowdfunder.

Alternative funding

Many of the products we have explored in this chapter are debt related, and even if they are a hybrid, like leasing, have regular repayments over the agreed life of the facility. This is an alternative to debt funding (which has to be repaid and will have interest costs).

Equity funding is only applicable for limited companies and does not suit all businesses. Some directors will not want to give away ownership in the business and a share of the profits in the future.

Equity

You will recall from Chapter 1 that we discussed the ownership of a company and how important share capital is. This is the equity in a business and is the highest risk capital in the business (usually because if the business fails the shareholders will lose all their money). The counterbalance to this is also the fact that with the higher risk should come higher rewards and shareholders are fully entitled to take profits from the business (assuming of course the business can afford it!).

Understandably, many business owners do not want to share the rewards of their business success with those outside the business, and after they have paid staff, covered all their costs (including finance costs) any profits left can be withdrawn through dividends and/or reinvested. There are occasions, however, when businesses need access to capital and funding where the routes we have discussed above are either not enough or are not available to the extent that the business requires. This is usually through the purchase of shares in a business by outside investors.

Depending on the type of equity, the investors may share in the profits (through dividends), although in the early years there may not be profits available. The exit route (the method the investors get their money back) can be a variety of options in the future, including a trade sale (to a third party), and a management buy-out (by the tier of management below the owners).

Private equity

There are a number of regional, national and international **private equity** providers. The larger firms such as the UK firm 3i will invest in businesses where turnover is in excess of £100 million. Private equity firms bring together investors who are looking for higher rates of return and businesses that need investment.

> **Private equity** The investment in a business by the purchasing of part of the share capital of the business by an external investor.

A banker will always want a very clear view as to how they will get their money back. A firm making a private equity investment is usually taking a much longer-term view and its exit may be from the sale of the business. Private equity firms take a much higher risk than a banker, and to mitigate some of the risk are more likely to be involved with the management of the business. As part of their investment, the private equity firm will often stipulate that they want to have a seat on the board (they may have a non-executive director appointed to be their representative) and will have the right to attend board meetings (although they may not have voting rights in terms of decisions within the business). Many businesses see this as a very positive contribution to their businesses, as the non-executive director will often have a great deal of experience in the sector and be able to make practical contributions to the growth of the business.

CASE STUDY
YFM Equity Partners

YFM is a northern-based private equity firm which has offices in Leeds, London, Manchester, Birmingham and Sheffield and can invest up to £10 million. Their approach is to support:

- ambitious management teams;

- an innovative approach to market, strong brand or proprietary technology;

- scope to become a niche market leader;

- capacity to create strategic value growth (www.yfmep.com, 2017).

As you can see from their aims and objectives they look to support businesses that they feel have opportunities to grow and develop. They invest in a variety of businesses and sectors and their investments are for the medium to long term.

Questions

1 What kind of businesses benefit from the investments that YFM can make?

2 Why might business owners approach YFM rather than their bank?

Business angels

Business angels tend to be wealthy private individuals who have funds to invest in businesses. They may be entrepreneurs who have successfully run and sold their own business and want to be involved in a business. Business angels will often invest by buying some of the shares of the business.

Business Growth Fund

Business Growth Fund is an independent organization set up in conjunction with the major UK clearing banks and has investments from Barclays Bank, HSBC, Lloyds Banking Group, Royal Bank of Scotland and Standard Chartered Bank. Its purpose is to make minority equity investments of between £2 million and £10 million in businesses that have turnover of between £5 million and £100 million (BGF, 2017).

Business angels Wealthy private individuals who wish to invest in private businesses. This may be either through loans or via purchasing part of the shares of the business.

Business Growth Fund An independent organization set up in conjunction with the major UK clearing banks. Its purpose is to make minority equity investments of between £2 million and £10 million in businesses that have turnover of between £5 million and £100 million.

International trade finance

International finance, or international trade finance as it is often known, is a specialism in its own right and this section of the chapter is not intended to replace further studies that you may undertake. However, many commercial customers will be involved in international trade and will need to use specialist products to support this. This part of the chapter is intended to be a brief overview of products and services that you, as a banker, may encounter.

Any business customer engaging in international trade is likely to face a number of risks. One of the most serious is that of payment risk, ie for an exporting business, that they will not be paid for the goods they have shipped abroad.

The most common international trade product is the **documentary letter of credit**.

Documentary letter of credit A method of securing an international trade transaction (exporting/importing), where trade documents are used. The banks will often be involved in 'guaranteeing' the finance for the transaction.

Documentary letter of credit

This is a method of guaranteeing payments between customers in different parts of the world where the bank for each customer is also involved in the process. It is often based on one transaction, where the importer wants to buy one consignment of goods. Many UK businesses have moved manufacturing processes to different parts of the world ('offshoring') and often facilitated by third party companies. The third parties will manufacture the goods but will want a guarantee of payment before they ship the goods (and they may want this before they start manufacturing an order).

The importing customer will approach their bank and ask them to issue a documentary letter of credit (L/C) in favour of the exporter. The importer's bank will arrange the L/C through the exporter's bank.

As the product's name suggests, it is based on the documents used in the transaction and often goods are transported on the sea. The documents are likely to include bills of lading (shipping documents), lists of the goods shipped, and bills of exchange.

Important points to note from a banker's perspective are:

- The process is controlled through the banks for the importer and the exporter.

- It is based on the documents that support the underlying transaction and these will usually be the documents of title to the goods, which is why the banks need to control the process.

- Payments will be made if the documents are in order – the importer's account will be debited, and funds will be transferred to the exporter.

- An L/C that an importer has asked to be opened will become part of the importer's banking facilities and overall limits may need to be adjusted or increased to accommodate this liability.

CASE STUDY
Amber Computers

Amber Computers Ltd (Amber), based in Cambridge, uses specially manufactured cases in the production of personal computers which it makes for the construction industry. It sources these from Kyoto Industries (Kyoto) in Japan. It tends to purchase the cases every two months and uses documentary letters of credit (L/Cs) for Kyoto.

The average value of an L/C is between £200,000 to £250,000. For each large transaction Amber asks its bankers ABC Bank plc to open an L/C and these are always opened via Kyoto's bankers, XYZ Bank in Japan.

In June, it has an order for £225,000 for cases, where construction will take two weeks and shipping will take a further two months (goods to come by sea). Amber asks its bank ABC Bank to open a new L/C and ABC Bank will need to assess this request as it would any other request for finance. It will need to include this in the overall facilities for Amber.

Once the L/C is agreed, ABC Bank, via its international department, will open the L/C with XYZ Bank in favour of Kyoto. ABC Bank then has a liability of £225,000 that it must honour. Assuming all the agreed documentation is correct, when it receives the documents from XYZ Bank, following the shipping of the goods, they will debit their customer Amber under the L/C, send the funds to XYZ bank, who will then pay these to Kyoto. The documents will be released to Amber, which allows them to take delivery of the goods at a local port.

Once Amber have been debited, the limit that was set for the L/C can then be released.

Questions

1 What are the advantages to Amber Computers in conducting international trade via L/Cs?

2 How might Amber's bank deal with the new liability of the L/C?

Many foreign trade transactions for UK businesses will be in a foreign currency such as US dollars or euros. Dealing in foreign currency, whether making payments or receiving payments, gives UK companies increased risks as currencies such as the US dollar will fluctuate in value against sterling. The longer into the future a transaction is, then the greater the risk of a fluctuation in currency exchange rates.

To mitigate this risk a bank and a business can use **forward currency contracts**.

Forward currency contracts

In the simplest form a forward contract is an agreement between the bank and the customer for:

- a specific amount of a particular currency;
- at a specified exchange rate; and
- at a specified date in the future.

The case study for Amber Computers involves a sterling transaction in order to make it less complicated to explain; however, it is highly likely that the transactions between Amber Computers and Kyoto Industries could be in US dollars.

If we assume the L/C was for US $225,000 rather than sterling, Amber would have had to pay this amount of dollars to Kyoto when the L/C was paid. If the sterling against the US dollar had weakened (ie it would need more sterling to pay for the US dollars), between the time it ordered the goods and the time it paid for them, then it would cost more in sterling for Amber to pay for these goods.

A forward contract, by fixing the future exchange rate, takes away the risk of the fluctuations between the two currencies, and means that Amber have certainty about the payment that needs to be made.

Important points to note from a banker's perspective are:

- This is rather counter-intuitive, but if a business is paying out foreign currency the bank is selling the currency to the business in order for the business to fulfil the transaction.

- An overall limit will normally be given to customers to allow them to arrange forward contracts – standard practice where the currencies are between sterling and US dollars or euros is for a gross facility to be agreed and the actual net limit that is marked is usually 10 per cent of the gross limit (if the bank had to 'close out' all the forward contracts, exchange rates will not normally have moved by more than 10 per cent).

Foreign currency accounts

Businesses that trade regularly in foreign currency will often have current accounts denominated in specific currencies: these are known as **foreign currency accounts**. These operate in a very similar way to sterling current accounts and allow the business to receive and make payments in a currency without having to convert to sterling.

Forward currency contracts An agreement between the bank and a customer for a specific amount of a particular currency to be exchanged at a specified exchange rate, at a specified date in the future.

Foreign currency accounts An account denominated in a currency other than sterling (for a UK business), eg US dollars or euros. It can be a current or a deposit account and operates in the same way as a sterling current/deposit account, allowing a business to receive and make payments in a currency without having to convert to sterling.

ACTIVITY 7.4
International trade services

It is useful to understand what your own bank does to support customers who trade internationally. Research your own bank and explore the products and services that are offered to customers. If your organization doesn't provide this type of service have a look at one of your competitors.

Green finance

There is not the room in this book to explore **green finance** in any great detail and this section is designed to give you a brief introduction to it, pointing you in the right direction if you wish to explore it in greater detail.

Green finance Finance facilities that are predominantly aimed at reducing the carbon emissions of a business.

The Green Finance initiative in the UK defines green finance as: 'Funding any means of reducing carbon emissions or raising resource efficiency' (Green Finance Initiative, 2018). Banks and businesses all over the world are increasingly concerned about the impact commercial activities can have on the environment. The Governor of the Bank of England (Mark Carney) gave a detailed speech in September 2016 entitled 'Resolving the climate paradox'

(BBC News, 2016), so as you can see this is a topic which concerns the central bank in the UK, albeit the focus of this speech was very much at a larger institutional investor level.

What does this mean for commercial customers? Certain banks are focusing on key areas such as renewable energy and RBS plc supports businesses through the use of a small-scale renewable energy fund (SSRE), which it uses to support 'solar PV (photovoltaic), onshore wind, micro hydro, biomass and anaerobic digestion (AD)'. Using Asset Finance, it also supports businesses who wish to use, for example, LED lighting and heat pumps (air and ground source) (RBS, 2018).

ACTIVITY 7.5
UK banks and green finance

Research what initiatives your own bank is involved in to support green finance and compare it with the RBS example, and consider whether offering green finance gives a commercial bank a competitive advantage.

Chapter summary

In this chapter we have explored:

- key commercial lending products available to banks when they are lending to commercial customers;
- the advantages and disadvantages of each product;
- the rise of asset based lenders as an alternative to commercial bank funding;
- the use of international trade products to support commercial customers who engage in international trade; and
- the various alternative sources of finance that are available where banks are unable to lend.

This chapter is not intended to be an exhaustive list of what is available, but more a starting point for the key products and services that are available. It is important that you explore fully both what your own organization does and what competitors are also offering. You need to know where to look for funding, particularly if you cannot provide what the business is looking for.

Objective check

1 Outline the key characteristics of three commercial lending products, specify their individual advantages and disadvantages and then compare and contrast each product.

2 What is an asset based lender, in what ways do they differ from commercial banks and when might they be appropriate for commercial customers?

3 When would it be appropriate to use international trade products and how do they support commercial customers?

4 List three alternative sources of finance (apart from asset based lending) that are available and specify in what circumstances they might be used.

Further reading

Asset finance

For further information on asset finance go to the Finance and Leasing Association site, and under Asset Finance there are a number of useful guides:

https://fla.org.uk/index.php/asset-finance-2/
https://www.closeassetfinance.co.uk/about-us

Mentors

www.mentorsme.co.uk

Green finance

Carney, M [accessed 26 June 2018] Resolving the climate paradox [Online] www.bankofengland.co.uk/speech/2016/resolving-the-climate-paradox
The UK Green Investment Bank was sold by the UK government in August 2017 [accessed 26 June 2018] [Online]
https://www.gov.uk/government/organisations/uk-green-investment-bank
UK Business Angels Association [accessed 26 June 2018] [Online] https://www.ukbaa.org.uk/

References

BGF | Invested in Growth [accessed 26 June 2018] [Online] https://www.bgf.co.uk/
British Business Bank [accessed 26 June 2018] What we do – British Business Bank [Online] https://british-business-bank.co.uk/what-the-british-business-bank-does/
Carney, M [accessed 26 June 2018] Green bonds 'major opportunity' [Online] https://www.bbc.co.uk/news/business-37446120

Crowdfunder [accessed 26 June 2018] Crowdfunding, UK fundraising website for community, business and creative projects | Crowdfunder [Online] https://www.crowdfunder.co.uk/

Glenwyvis [accessed 26 June 2018] GlenWyvis Whisky Distillery, Dingwall Scotland [Online] https://glenwyvis.com/

Green Finance Initiative [accessed 26 June 2018] Facts & Figures – Green Finance Initiative [Online] http://greenfinanceinitiative.org/facts-figures/

P2pfa.info [accessed 26 June 2018] The Peer-to-Peer Finance Association [Online] http://p2pfa.info/

RBS [accessed 26 June 2018] Sustainable energy | Royal Bank of Scotland [Online] https://www.business.rbs.co.uk/business/turnover-2m-or-over/business-guidance/financial-expertise-by-sector/sustainable-energy.html

Santander [accessed 26 June 2018] Sources of finance and comparison | Santander Corporate & Commercial Banking [Online] https://www.santandercb.co.uk/financing/corporate-lending/guide-to-borrowing/sources-of-finance-and-comparison

UK Finance [accessed 26 June 2018] Unsuccessful Lending Applications and Lending Declines – UK Finance [Online] https://www.ukfinance.org.uk/unsuccessful-lending-applications-and-lending-declines/

What type of finance? – Reward Finance Group [accessed 26 June 2018] [Online] http://www.rewardfinancegroup.com/our-products/

YFM [accessed 26 June 2018] [Online] http://yfmep.com/about-us/

Answers for activities

Learners should devise their own answers for all the activities in this chapter. No model answers have been supplied.

Suggested answers for case study questions

Case study: Invoice discounting and the Cheesy Factory

1 What are the advantages for The Cheesy Factory having an invoice discounting facility?

2 What are the disadvantages of them having an invoice discounting facility?

3 How might this product help the overall sales strategy for the company?

Answers

1 Advantages:

- The business is growing, the bank will not fund the growth with an overdraft so an invoice discounting facility is an ideal solution.

- Drawdown of funds against new invoices The Cheesy Factory issue will be immediate, their cash flow will be significantly improved.
- The new customer is unaware of the funding arrangements.
- The trade receivable book (debtor book) continues to be run by the business.

2 Disadvantages:

- The debtor book can only be used to support the invoice discount facility.
- Interest rates and fees may be higher than a standard overdraft facility.
- This facility may not help fund much smaller trade receivables (eg small local shops and delicatessens).

3 The new facility may encourage the business to approach larger customers that they would not normally have considered.

Case study: Glenwyvis Distillery, Dingwall, Scotland

Q3 – Why do you feel customers are so keen to support this kind of project?

There are many reasons why customers want to support this kind of project:

- being part of a new business;
- investing in an exciting project;
- being part of an investment community (especially if you are local to the business);
- having access to the products from the business before other consumers; or
- investing in a product that is unusual or different to what may be available in the usual retail outlets.

Case study: YFM Equity Partners

1 Businesses that might benefit from investment: These need to be businesses with a strong unique selling point (USP) and need a strong brand or technology which they own. They need to have the ability to become the leaders in their niche market

2 Why approach YFM rather than the bank? Often businesses have ambitious growth plans which mean that higher risk funds are needed which is beyond the risk parameters of a commercial bank. Equity funds are needed.

Case study: Amber Computers

1 What are the advantages to Amber Computers in conducting international trade via L/Cs?

2 How might Amber's bank deal with the new liability of the L/C?

Answers:

1 Amber has greater certainty of being paid, knowing that its own bank and Kyoto's bank are involved in the process.

2 Amber's bank will need to either increase the overall facilities available to Amber, or reduce, say, the overdraft facility by the amount of the L/C.

08

Management and leadership

INTRODUCTION

The success or failure of a business is usually linked to the managers who run that business, but the reasons some managers are successful, and others aren't, is one of the most challenging areas for bankers to understand when they are assessing the abilities of management that they are lending to.

LEARNING OBJECTIVES

By the end of this chapter, you will be able to:

- assess the usefulness of relationship management in the context of lending to commercial customers;
- evaluate the benefits of customer/bank meetings at customer premises;
- identify the key areas of focus for banks when assessing the management capabilities of their commercial customers;
- define management and leadership;
- assess a variety of leadership styles;
- define emotional intelligence and explain why the best leaders have it; and
- assess the key attributes of entrepreneurs.

Assessing management

There are no 'blue-prints' for helping bankers assess the people they lend to. Banks do not ask the management of businesses to take tests to prove they can run their business, nor do they have personality tests they ask customers to take to ensure they fit a particular psychological profile which might somehow ensure the success of their business. Banks in the UK lend to thousands of different types of businesses with a huge variety of different managers and management teams that run them.

The difficulty with trying to have a standardized approach to assessing management is that there isn't a 'model' manager that a bank would want as a customer. There is evidence, however, to suggest that there are certain attributes that 'successful' managers have (we will explore some of these attributes later).

Whilst it is difficult to have a blueprint for assessing management, there are certain measures which can be used to view management. These often tend to be quantitative rather than qualitative, such as:

- Do they provide management information and any other information the bank requires against agreed deadlines?
- Do they perform against previous budgets and projections? If not, why not?
- How do they compare to other businesses in the sector?

If we don't have a blueprint, is it still possible to standardize the way we assess management? It's a very valid question and, depending on the type of business the bank is lending to, it is relatively easy to look for specific functions within the business that need management 'ownership'. These include finance, marketing and sales, and production. Some businesses may be too small to need a specific individual to cover one role and one member of the team may have more than one responsibility.

The relationship between bankers and business management

The importance of relationship managers

A relationship between two parties supposes that there is a connection between them, and in a business sense this should usually be mutually beneficial.

Banks often have a challenge when they look to allocate their own human resources and match them with the needs of their commercial banking customers. Most UK banks often have what they designate as 'relationship managers'. These are managers who look after a portfolio of customers that borrow (the numbers looked after will usually be determined by the size and complexity of each borrowing customer). Some portfolios may be specialist in nature (eg being made up of customers in a particular sector such as real estate or professionals).

> **Relationship management** The human resources given by a bank to maintaining a relationship between the customer and the bank. This normally involves the appointment of a specified individual in the bank who has overall responsibility for the relationship.

It is easy to overlook what the title relationship manager actually means. This is the person in the bank who arguably has the most important, and pivotal connection with a customer, and more specifically with the management of that business. A good relationship manager will spend time regularly with the management team, will have a better understanding of those managers, their individual strengths and weaknesses, how they work together and also how they work with the bank.

The benefits to the bank

There are a number of positive benefits to having a strong relationship manager looking after a business. From a risk perspective, this allows the bank to have a much deeper understanding of the management team and to cover a number of areas that we have explored in Chapter 4.

Building a relationship

From the customer's point of view, the relationship between the management of the business and their banker is one of the most fundamental and pivotal relationships that the business can have. This relationship is vital for the health of the business, at every level, and a good relationship with the bank will help the business to grow and develop in ways that might not be possible otherwise.

The first element of building a positive relationship is to establish a rapport. Building a rapport is about establishing common ground, and where, ideally, there is a close and harmonious relationship. Banks of course need customers to lend to (and to provide other services) and businesses need banks to lend to them, otherwise their future growth, and ability to operate effectively, will be stifled. The relationship, however, is potentially not one of equals, and the customer will not always appreciate the risk stance of the bank or be comfortable with the terms and conditions a bank may wish to impose.

One of the other key elements of the relationship between the banker and the customer is one of trust. The Concise Oxford English Dictionary defines the act of trust as, 'belief in the reliability, truth, or ability of' (Stevenson and Waite, 2011). This means that a relationship manager will be looking for elements in the relationship where the management do what they say they will, are truthful in their dealings with the bank and also have the collective abilities to perform the functions of their business effectively and efficiently. However, trust, as in any relationship, is a 'two-way street' and the public image that banks have had since the financial crisis has made the element of trust much more challenging, with customers much more distrustful of their bankers.

The final element is arguably respect. What is absolutely vital in the relationship between the banker and the customer, is that there is respect on both sides. From the banker, respect that the management team has the ability and drive to run their business and from the management team, respect that the relationship manager knows what they are doing, has a strong knowledge of the services that the bank provides and is able to meet their needs in a timely manner.

Does it also matter whether or not bankers like their customers (and vice versa!)? It can certainly help, particularly when a business is going through a challenging period (such as not performing against budgets or having lost an important customer), but it is not a prerequisite to a successful relationship.

The banker potentially has a challenge in dealing with a customer, and usually needs to wear two hats. One is for the bank, ensuring the bank's interests are protected, the other is for the customer. A good banker will need to have a high level of empathy with their customers. Empathy is an emotional intelligence skill (which we explore later) and is based on the principle of being able to put yourself in the shoes of another person and understand their feelings and, perhaps, even share them. Not an easy ask for a banker, who often needs to ensure the bank is protected, but it is a skill, if developed over time, that will differentiate between a good and a great banker.

Relationships naturally change over time and this is as true in personal relationships as it is in business relationships. Sometimes the nature of the banker and customer relationship will need to change, as it will be dictated by changes in the business. Businesses are very likely to grow over time, and as they grow will need to deal with, and adapt to, external and internal changes. Growth, whilst good for the business, often gives the management of the business issues to deal with that they may not have faced before. A business may wish to expand geographically, need new sites, a new factory, new machinery, more employees and have a myriad of other needs.

The challenge for the banker is to be able to recognize the nature of the change in a business and be able to adapt accordingly. Big step changes in a business are likely to create an environment where the demands from the customer are higher, more complex and certainly more time-consuming than the banker had experienced previously. The customer is likely to be facing a time of greater stress and the banker needs to be able to empathize with this and help in the best way that they can. The ability to draw on the experiences of other customers who have faced similar phases in their businesses will help inform the banker's actions.

Customer visits

This section may appear, at first glance, to be obvious and perhaps even common sense but there are clear and important reasons why the banker should visit the customer at their own premises. It is of course time-consuming to visit customers and if a banker has a busy and active portfolio (ie many of them are borrowing) seeing all of them regularly over a 12-month period can create an added level of pressure. All customers who borrow will have an annual review and are likely to have half-yearly reviews also.

THE FUTURE OF CUSTOMER INTERACTION?

Digital banking is an increasingly vital part of the ways that banks service the day-to-day banking needs of their customers. This isn't the only way that technology is changing the way banks and their commercial customers interact.

As technology changes, particularly with the increased penetration of smartphones and other devices, the ability to communicate with customers in different ways is changing too. Smaller businesses, such as those discussed in Chapter 1, are likely to be dealt with by a central team that is able to handle a large volume of business customer requirements –

this keeps cost down for the bank. An SME, particularly if it has larger borrowing requirements, requires more bank management time but not all interactions need to be physical, and monthly calls could very easily be made by using FaceTime or Skype.

Why bother at all? First, there are significant benefits from the customer perspective. It is not always easy for a customer to explain, for example, a complicated manufacturing process and being able to show their banker how something works, or why a new machine is needed because an old one is decrepit; this would be much easier in the factory than it would during a meeting at the bank premises. Commercial printing companies, for example, use large printing presses, and one of the more well-known brands in the industry is manufactured by Heidelberg. It is hard to envisage exactly what such a machine looks like unless you go and see it on the customer's premises. When the management of a business knows their banker has a fuller view of that business, because they've visited the premises, it helps to deepen the relationship.

Secondly, there are appreciable benefits for the bank in regularly visiting the premises of a business. If a bank wants to truly 'get under the skin' of a business, then they need to have a full view of how the customer operates. There is absolutely no substitute for meeting a customer on their own premises. Websites and other promotional material are important, but physically seeing a customer's factory and being able to see its state of repair and the conditions in which the work is carried out give a much more realistic picture of how the business is doing. This often enables a banker to corroborate what the customer is telling them.

An additional point to consider is that business premises, whatever the sector, without regular maintenance, can deteriorate quickly, and regular visits will alert the banker to potential issues with the business. Loan documents often have clauses in them where the customer agrees to maintain the premises so it's important to keep an eye on this.

Where businesses are located is always vital to their success or failure, and the local knowledge a banker has of their area should never be underestimated. Cities and towns change constantly so regular visits to the locality are advised. A retail business will normally look to be located where there is sufficient 'footfall' (customers who are walking past their shop), and this can be negatively impacted by a new development. A new city centre retail development that a banker may be aware of can have both positive and negative impacts as areas that were in need of investment become more desirable with this development; however, this can be at the expense of parts of the city or town which had thrived previously.

One of the key sectors where customer visits are vital for the bank are in real estate, particularly where the bank is funding a new commercial or residential development. Regular visits, and these are likely to be monthly, will allow the banker to see that development is progressing against the plan produced by the customer (the development will also be monitored by a monitoring surveyor). If it isn't (due to bad weather, for example), then the banker can see this for themselves. From a purely practical viewpoint, it allows a banker to see progress, and makes the internal reporting more meaningful. As a final note, it also stops unscrupulous customers using funds for a development for other purposes.

The final reason for making customer visits, from the bank's perspective, is to be able to protect the relationship against the competition. If a customer is performing well, then it is highly likely that the other banks are also talking to the customer (and the customer will not always share this information with their existing bank!).

Customer meetings and interviews

When a banker is meeting the management of a business there can sometimes be a sense that the managers are somehow being 'interrogated', particularly from the viewpoint of the management! This is unhelpful at best and damaging at worst. Meetings need to be participative and whilst a banker has a job to do (perhaps for a half-yearly or annual review), the process of a banker keeping up to date with a customer shouldn't be a painful process and some kind of endurance test for the management team!

To have real credibility, and to help meetings and interviews run smoothly, bankers really do need to know their customer. Busy management will not want to have to repeat information about their business that they have already shared with the bank. Bankers will need to be aware of developments, and threats in the customer's sector.

The relationship between banks and customers since the financial crisis has definitely been more strained and, as we explored in Chapter 7, many customers are turning towards alternative forms of finance. This makes the job for the banker even more challenging, and this is all the more reason why a banker needs to be informed, engaged and knowledgeable in order to demonstrate to their customer they do understand their business. The key 'balancing' act for any banker is knowing the right questions to ask.

There are two key areas for the banker to explore:

1 Financial – in Chapter 2 we looked at the techniques which are available to examine financial information. The vital part of any customer discussion is the analysis of the information and the implications of this for the future of the business. It will inform the key areas of where the management should be focusing, and where, for example, gross margin is dropping, the banker will want to know how this is being addressed. Whilst this is of course an important area, a banker who only focuses on the financial performance is likely to miss other key information.

2 Non-financial – these areas are the most important as changes in these will drive the financial results. We have explored how to strategically analyse a business in Chapter 5, and with the benefit of this knowledge, a banker can ask more searching questions about both internal and external issues the business faces. Issues to consider include:

- Recent successes, new customers and new products – management like to talk about their business. After all, it is very important to them, is the source of their livelihood for themselves, their families and their employees. It is very gratifying for a banker to know that the bank has been part of business success by providing finance.

- Strategy – for smaller businesses, certainly in the early part of their existence, this may be no more than wanting to survive! For more established businesses, however, bankers will need to understand what the longer terms plans are, and how the business intends to achieve them (the use of strategic tools is explored in depth in Chapter 5). A good question to ask management is where they see the business and themselves in five years' time?

- Succession planning – this will usually link very closely to the question on strategy and takes into account the ages of the management team and what their own personal aspirations are.

- Top three? – if a banker asks a manager of a business what their top three concerns are, they will usually tell them. Sometimes the answers may surprise the banker and it may not be something the banker had considered. The key is not to be afraid to ask, but at the same time to be prepared to deal with what the customer is prepared to share.

- The market – what is happening in the marketplace overall? What are the competitors doing? Are there new entrants?

- Management – it is important for the banker to consider a number of key practical areas in the management of the business and we will go on to explore these now.

Questions to ask about the management

Roles and responsibilities

All management teams are very different, and sometimes there may only be one individual who is running the business. Where there are two or more in the management team, it is important that the banker understands the roles of each individual. In some businesses, and professional services firms like solicitors are a good example, all members of the management team may be fee-earning, and therefore contributing to the profits of the business. Some firms may specialize in certain types of the law (eg criminal work) and this will have very heavy demands on the time of individual partners. A banker needs to understand how other responsibilities such as finance (billing, cash management, management information etc), or human resources are being dealt with. Often the support of other professionals such as their firm of accountants will be critical for the success of the business. This is where the knowledge by the banker of specific firms like accountants who support the banker's customers will be vital. Often the accountant may attend customer meetings to support the customer and be able to discuss in more detail financial performance. It is in the banker's interests to cultivate a relationship with these firms.

A banker needs to understand the different personalities within a management team. Some managers enjoy setting up new ventures, or running new projects, whereas others are more comfortable with ensuring operations run smoothly once a new project is up and running. A good example of this is a restaurant business, where with a two-manager team, one manager enjoys finding new sites, working with architects and builders to set up a new site, whereas the other manager enjoys running the restaurant once it has been completed.

The key area where a banker can really help a management team is to be able to explore with the management team the possible 'gaps' in the running of the business. An obvious thing to identify, and something that is often overlooked, is the person on the management team who is going to act as the main contact with the bank. If there is a finance director then this question is easily answered; however, if the business isn't big enough then one of the management team will need to take responsibility for this.

Where there is only one key individual running a business then the banker needs to understand how that individual can cope with all the demands on them. Do they have a partner who can help them? It is not uncommon for a husband or wife of a business owner to be involved in the administration of the business, including inputting financial information into accounting software packages such as Sage, Xero or QuickBooks.

Technical skills

The 'formal' skills needed for managers to run their business will depend on the size, complexity and sector the business operates in. A care home business, for example, will need a qualified individual (in nursing) who can look after the complex needs of the residents. An engineering business is highly likely to be run by individuals who have science degrees. We will explore entrepreneurs later in the chapter, but it is worth mentioning them here as many may not have formal qualifications to run a business, but will have taken an idea, or in some cases a hobby, and developed it into a business.

The banker's challenge is understanding and ensuring that all of the parts of the business have individuals, who as a group, have the capability to run the business, as well as the appropriate licences and qualifications. These are essential in highly regulated sectors such as care homes and waste management. A waste management business, for example, requires a stringent process before the directors can be granted the appropriate licences to operate the business.

The ability to take difficult decisions

Leading always comes with responsibility, and often that is when the 'burdens' of running a business can be the most acute. Closing down factories, making staff redundant and many other difficult (and emotional decisions) will sometimes be the lot of the leader.

This is often unknown territory for both those who run businesses and the bankers who lend to them and until these difficult situations are faced by a customer, it is difficult to determine how the difficult situations will be dealt with.

Experience

Previous experience is obviously important, particularly if it is in the same sector, and shows that a management team has a breadth of experience. It is important to remember, however, that experience, in itself, is not a guarantee of future success.

What is management?

We will now consider how bankers can use management and leadership theory to understand their customers in greater detail and also how to identify the different styles of management and leadership that may be employed by the management teams they lend to. The study of management is a discipline in itself and good bankers need to be able to understand a number of the key tenets of academic management theory. In the following section we will explore in more detail what management is and whether there is a definition for what a 'good' manager or leader looks like.

Views of management and leadership

Charles Handy, one of the most influential management thinkers of the twentieth century, said about management: 'management of people is like driving a car… Most of us do it at least adequately though perhaps we worry from time to time that we might do it better.' He also said about leadership: 'Is leadership… an innate characteristic? Can anyone be a leader, or only the favoured few?' (Handy, 1993).

Management usually involves the management of other people and the challenges of this task are encapsulated by a quote which is attributed to Abraham Lincoln, the sixteenth President of the United States (1861–1865): 'You can please some of the people some of the time, all of the people some of the time, some of the people all of the time, but you can never please all of the people all of the time.' This is very applicable in the world of business as managers continually strive to work effectively with employees at all levels of the organization.

Believing in those you manage is an incredibly powerful source of motivation for employees. Peter Grant (1935–1995), the manager of the rock group Led Zeppelin (*Led Zeppelin IV*, which contains arguably one of their most famous songs, 'Stairway To Heaven' has sold over 37 million copies), was once asked in a television interview in 1988, what the 'secret' of being a good manager was. He answered: 'Have great belief in your artist. Believe' (YouTube, 2018).

Self-belief by managers is also an important part of an examination of their 'make-up'. Leaders can be powerful forces to get the best from their team. Sir Simon Rattle, the classical conductor, is described in an interview as a '… galvanizer, an inspirer… ' (Jeal, 2017), where galvanizing is defined as a process of exciting or shocking into action. Rattle, however, said of himself in the same interview:

> Our world divides into people who are supremely confident and those who have doubts every day. I am on the doubts every day team. Probably just as well. It means you don't take too much for granted.

This neatly illustrates the dichotomy between how a leader can inspire those around them, yet simultaneously be more critical with themselves.

What are the key skills that management require – or, what's in the toolbox?

This next section examines the different styles that managers and leaders may use. It is useful for bankers to understand how to recognize the different styles and the circumstances they may be used in.

We often hear business leaders being described as *effective*. What do we mean by this? Being effective is usually characterized as *'doing the right things'*, which is very different to being *efficient* which is usually characterized as *'doing things right'*. Managers, and indeed businesses, can be very busy being efficient, but focusing on entirely the wrong activities, particularly if they are not important to their customers. Being effective does, of course, require the support of efficient practices but there does of course need to be a balance of focus. Being effective also means that managers and leaders need the skill-sets required to act in particular ways. We will explore further in this section some of the different styles that can be effective and we will also discuss when it might be appropriate to use these styles.

The toolbox – leadership styles

Good managers should develop a management and leadership 'toolbox' that they can reach for when dealing with different situations and also with different teams or employees. As we will see below, some of the most effective leaders may use more than one technique in conjunction with each other in order to achieve the best results.

There is sometimes a misconception about management theory and techniques, that there is some kind of personal 'one size fits all' style that managers or leaders of business may personally have, and that this is the style that he or she will always use. The 'real world' in business is significantly complicated, and multi-dimensional, requiring a variety of skills and responses. Many managers may have a 'preferred' style of leading the people within their business, and sometimes this 'default' style may be triggered when the business is under stress; for example, a manager may want to work more consultatively with staff, but their style, when under pressure, is to be much more directive, telling staff exactly what is needed. This style of manager may adopt a 'my way or the highway' approach when under stress, (ie do things as I want or leave!). This is perhaps not a particularly helpful stance to take when dealing with a difficult situation, although as an owner of the business, this is often felt to be justified!

Autocratic versus democratic

Charles Handy, who we have already mentioned, in one of his most influential books, *Understanding Organizations,* makes a very useful examination of the different types of management theory, which he maps out between two different dimensions:

- autocratic; and
- democratic (Handy, 1993).

An autocratic leader is seen as someone who dominates, with absolute authority and as we can see from Figure 8.1, the two styles are opposed to each other. Leaders adopting the **autocratic leadership** style can be seen as authoritative and 'strong' and can be of benefit if staff are inexperienced and need higher levels of guidance. This can work well in a hierarchical structure, which needs a uniform approach across the organization. This is very much a 'top-down' approach, where 'commands' come from the top of the organization and there is little discussion involved. The same style can be used no matter how large or small the organization. The downside of this kind of approach can be the demotivation of more experienced members of staff.

At the other end of the spectrum is the democratic leader who operates on a more consultative basis, wanting to involve the whole team in decisions. The **democratic leadership** style allows for different viewpoints and allows team members to all contribute. There can be a better chance of a team all accepting

Figure 8.1 Autocratic versus democratic

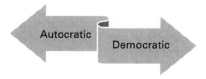

a change in direction, or challenging targets if they have all had the chance to participate. This approach works well in industries which are more knowledge based and need to leverage the skills and capabilities of their employees.

> **Autocratic leadership**   A leadership style where the leader dominates the decision-making process.
>
> **Democratic leadership**   A leadership style where the leader operates on a more consultative basis with their team.

THE DEVELOPMENT OF THE PLAYSTATION

The Sony Playstation, one of the main devices for playing computer games, was developed by a team led by Ken Kutaragi. The president of Sony at the time, Norio Ohga, recognized the potential of Kutaragi and his team, and had the foresight to remove them from the main Sony buildings to new premises in Aoyama (a suburb of Tokyo) previously occupied by Epic Sony. Computer games were not seen to be a priority within Sony and Ohga, despite opposition from senior management, felt that Kutaragi's team had huge potential. The team, given the freedom and space to work and supported by the belief of Norio and vision of Kutaragi, went on to develop the first Playstation games console, launched in December 1994. The Playstation is now one of the most successful games consoles in the world.

(Sutton, 2001)

The downside of this approach is that teams can feel that there is no real direction, decisions take an inordinate amount of time, and where there are diametrically opposed views, team members want a leader to make a decision, using their authority. Particularly with the democratic approach, employees can feel disenfranchised if they don't feel their contribution is valued or that their opinion is being heard. Employees can also become cynical if they feel the leader's stance is just for show or inauthentic.

'Good' leaders

There are many different views of what constitutes 'good' leadership. The following are phrases sometimes used to describe 'good' leaders: inspiring, decisive, visionary, charismatic, empowering, communicator, good learner, supporting, motivating, chosen, experienced, credible, coordinator, self-belief, responsible, thinks widely, critical thinker, good at compromising, professional, keeps momentum, aware of consequences, confident, makes decisions for the greater good, empathetic, diplomatic, gets best out of people, innovator, pulls in expertise, guides, unites, galvanizes, sees the bigger picture.

ACTIVITY 8.1
Types of leadership – Part 1

Using the above list as a starting point, what other words would you use to describe a good leader and what words might you use to describe a bad leader?

Consider the leaders in your own organization. How would you describe them? Are they people you want to follow? If you have moved office/department/team how would you compare your new leader with the previous leader?

The six styles of leadership

Daniel Goleman wrote in his seminal work *Leadership That Gets Results* of six distinct leadership styles which he believes should be deployed by leaders. These are considered in the context of different scenarios, rather than what may be the preferred style of the leader themselves. The **six styles of leadership** are as follows:

- the authoritative style;
- the affiliative style;
- the democratic style;
- the pacesetting style;
- the coaching style; and
- the coercive style.

We will go on to consider each of these below.

Six styles of leadership The different styles of leadership as established by Daniel Goleman: 1) the authoritative style, 2) the affiliative style, 3) the democratic style, 4) the pacesetting style, 5) the coaching style, and 6) the coercive style.

ACTIVITY 8.2
Personality and management style

As you will be aware, and without stating the obvious, we are all very different! A good leader has a level of self-awareness and self-knowledge that allows them to manage themselves and those who work for them. We will discuss emotional intelligence later in this chapter and before you continue, you may wish to take a well-known personality test. It has very strong links to an individual's leadership preferences and style.

1 Leadership self-examination – *16 Personalities* 'test' – takes 10–15 minutes to complete: https://www.16personalities.com/

2 Answer questions honestly.

3 Try not to leave any 'neutral' answers.

4 Read about the theory – https://www.16personalities.com/articles/our-theory

5 Compare your type with overall descriptions on the website: https://www.16personalities.com/personality-types

6 Do you feel it is accurate?

The authoritative style

This style is often used when a leader wants to galvanize a team around a common vision with clear goals. It is a style which can be used to accelerate enthusiasm within the team and works well where there is little or no interference by the leader into the work of team members but allows more autonomy.

This style is usually ineffective where there is a highly knowledgeable and experienced team which knows more than the leader.

The affiliative style

This style sees a leader putting team members first. It works well where there is a desire to build emotional bonds in the team and in situations where trust needs to be rebuilt (a good example would be where there has been trauma within the organization, such as redundancies, and team members are feeling vulnerable).

The downside to this type of approach is that the management tools used, such as praise and encouragement, are not conducive to addressing poor performance, which needs to be dealt with by the leader. This can cause resentment with other team members.

The democratic style

The leader using this style is looking to achieve consensus in the team. This is accomplished through giving team members the ability to be part of decision-making processes. It often achieves the result of employees being more accepting of new plans or goals. Flexibility is often achieved in the overall organization and, where new ideas are needed, this style can help create that environment.

The downside to this approach can be that there are too many meetings, with employees feeling that no-one is in charge, and that they just want a leader to make decisions. This is particularly acute when employees lack experience. It is also a style which is less effective when there are time constraints.

The pacesetting style

This is a style which can be very powerful where a leader embodies and exemplifies a high level of excellence, with their own high standards, which they also exhibit in the workplace (this is sometimes known as 'walking the talk' where leaders act in the way that is consistent with their communications). It requires a credible leader and is a very effective style where a team of employees is motivated and has the right skill-set. It works well where the leader is looking for quick results.

The downside is that this leadership style can become overbearing and overwhelming to certain staff, who perhaps do not 'buy-in' to the leaders' style. This can also stifle innovation and lead to internal resentment.

The coaching style

Compared to the other styles, this is a longer-term, future-looking approach which looks to develop the capabilities of individuals within a team. Coaching should take place based on the strengths and weaknesses of the individuals in a team, and there needs to be an awareness by the individuals themselves of their own strengths and weaknesses.

Coaching is often associated with sport, where a coach works with a runner, tennis player or footballer to improve their capabilities and performance. Business coaching helps build a team, where often the team as a whole can achieve much more than the individuals might on their own. It also helps to develop lasting strengths for individuals, which in turn creates a higher level of sustainability within the business.

The downside to this approach is that it will be ineffective when there is resistance to change by team members. This style can also be very damaging where the leader does not have the skills or credibility required to coach.

The coercive style

This is arguably one of the most 'toxic' of the six leadership styles, by virtue of the fact that coercion usually entails getting someone (an employee) to do something they don't want to do, either by force or threats.

It can be effectively used when there is a 'crisis' (a good example would be when a business is facing a financial crisis and management need to enact a turnaround plan – in this type of situation an employee, for example, may have a choice between taking on a role they don't want and being made redundant).

This style can sometimes be used as a last resort, invoked when other styles have not worked with an employee, and this may be the last course of action before, for example, disciplinary action is considered.

The six styles of leadership and emotional intelligence

Goleman's work on leadership styles was informed by his own, earlier work, on emotional intelligence (EI). In the past, measuring intelligence has been viewed in a more traditional sense, such as verbal, numerical and verbal reasoning, sometimes referred to as IQ (intelligence quotient). Emotional intelligence recognizes that there are other dimensions to a manager's or leader's ability to lead that are not just about that individual's IQ.

Emotional intelligence divides into four key attributes and EI theory recognizes that individuals can develop and hone these skills over time, developing the theme that good leaders are made and not born:

- Self-awareness – a leader needs to be aware of their own emotions, and the impact they have on those around them.

- Self-management – a leader needs to be able to control their own emotions that may have a negative impact on their employees.

- Social awareness – one of the key elements of this attribute is the skill of empathy, which is the ability of a leader to put themselves in the shoes of another, and to understand their feelings.

- Social skills – these are the skills that help a leader motivate and develop their teams. The key elements of this skill include the ability to create a vision, to communicate effectively, to manage change, to manage conflict and to improve teamwork and collaboration.

The understanding and development of a leader's EI capabilities is very strongly linked to the ability to use the different leadership styles, and being aware of the most appropriate and effective one to use.

Goleman concludes his analysis with the following:

> The business environment is continually changing, and a leader must respond in kind... executives must play their leadership styles like a pro – using the right one at just the right time and in the right measure. The payoff is in the results. (Goleman, 2000)

ACTIVITY 8.3
Types of leadership – Part 2

Having now considered in greater detail leadership theory above, and also considered your own personality type, consider the following:

1 For the leaders you identified earlier, can you now link them to any of the different leadership styles above?

2 For yourself, with the combination of the personality test and the theory above, do you have a sense of what kind of leader you are, or perhaps what kind of leader you aspire to be?

3 If you deal with customers, can you use any of the theory above to understand them in greater depth?

The managerial grid

This is a theory developed by Robert R Blake and Jane Mouton and sees management styles split into five categories, with these categories matched against two metrics: 1) concern for people, and 2) concern for production.

The five different types of management are:

- Country club management – this is a style which has a high concern for people in the organization and tries to create a comfortable and friendly environment.
- Impoverished management – this is where the minimum effort is expended both on staff and production processes.
- Task management – this sees a focus on getting the job done at all costs, with little consideration of the human side of the processes.
- Team management – this is where there is a commitment from both management and employees and where there is seen to be a heavy level of co-dependence between all parties.
- Middle of the road management – this tries to strike the balance between getting the work done, but at the same time as maintaining morale and ensuring that there is engagement at all levels.

The challenge for management can very often be that, if change is needed, and this change means that the culture is likely to move to a different one in the grid, then many of the employees will not be engaged with this change, particularly as they may have been attracted to the original culture of the organization.

Entrepreneurs

Before we look in depth at **entrepreneurs,** it is worth examining briefly what kind of structures may encompass businesses run by entrepreneurs.

Family and lifestyle businesses

Commercial bank businesses are sometimes run by high profile entrepreneurs; however, the majority of businesses that bankers deal with are relatively small businesses, many of them family concerns. Sometimes these businesses are 'lifestyle businesses', which means they are set up, owned and run by the original founders of the business in order to generate sufficient income to support a particular lifestyle. Be careful not to see this as a negative, however – it does not mean that the owners and managers are somehow running the business as a hobby.

It is very important for bankers to appreciate that the management styles and themes to be explored can be as relevant and applicable for smaller family businesses (which could be classed as lifestyle businesses) and SMEs as they may be for larger and more complex organizations.

> **Entrepreneur** A business person who sets up a business, taking all the risks that this involves.
>
> **Lifestyle business** A business that is run to generate sufficient income to support a particular lifestyle.

Family businesses are often very strong entities that can have much stronger ties between family members than might be seen where there is no connection between employees. There is often a common purpose shared between family members which can lead to a very positive level of support for the business. On the downside, family businesses can be riven with dissent and in-fighting which is very counter-productive. Non-family members who hold key positions within the business may sometimes feel precluded from the key decision-making processes.

What is an entrepreneur?

One of the key skills that bankers need to develop is a self-awareness around their attitude to risk and how this may differ from the managers they will deal with on a regular basis. Many entrepreneurs tend to be people who will take more risks and a banker who is by nature more risk-averse will need to both recognize this in themselves that their customer is different to them.

Many businesses start at the kitchen table, and this was literally what happened in the case of Levi Roots. Levi Roots, who makes Reggae Reggae Sauce (and famously appeared on the TV show *Dragon's Den*), began his business journey making his sauce in the kitchen. Chrissie Rucker (White Company) started her business as a mail-order business – she didn't go straight into owning all the shops she has now.

In Chapter 1 we discussed different types of business structure, but we haven't explored the 'make-up' of the different type of business owner, particularly the entrepreneur. The Concise Oxford English Dictionary defines an entrepreneur as, 'a person who sets up a business... taking on financial risks in the hope of a profit' (Stevenson and Waite, 2011).

We often find it difficult to define an entrepreneur without thinking of an example. Well-known modern entrepreneurs include Sir Richard Branson (the Virgin empire), Sir James Dyson (inventor of the Dyson 'bagless' vacuum cleaner), the late Dame Anita Roddick (co-founder of The Body Shop) and Chrissie Rucker (OBE) (founder of The White Company). There are now a number of newer entrepreneurs, such as Ella Mills (founder of Deliciously

Ella and 2017 Finalist, UK EY Entrepreneur of the year 2017), who have been able to use social media channels to start businesses.

Entrepreneurs don't always start as business people; they can be driven with an idea, or even a dream that they want to turn into a reality. The business part may come sometime after that. Also, entrepreneurs are not just a modern-day phenomenon. Many of the technological advances that we take for granted today were created by inventors who went on to become successful entrepreneurs.

These include developments such as the television (invented by the Scotsman, John Logie Baird, in the 1920s), the telephone (invented by another Scotsman, Alexander Graham Bell in 1876) and the electric light bulb (invented by Thomas Edison in 1878). All three individuals, following their successful inventions, went on to establish companies to develop these ideas commercially: Baird Television Development Company Ltd (Baird), Bell Telephone Company (Bell) and Edison Electric Light Company (Edison).

None of the entrepreneurs above took the same route to success, and Baird in particular suffered years of financial hardship being supported by his family and friends before his breakthrough development.

Characteristics of an entrepreneur

Are there characteristics that set entrepreneurs apart? Is it possible to articulate what drives an entrepreneur? No two entrepreneurs are the same; nevertheless it is possible to bring together some key themes. Attitude to risk is important and many entrepreneurs are prepared to take a high level of risks.

Initiative, as identified earlier in this section, is often seen as a prerequisite skill to being an entrepreneur, and in many cases means that new businesses are started. Many businesses that we can easily take for granted, such as Google, started life as the product of entrepreneurial drive.

Self-awareness is hugely important (which was discussed earlier as part of the 'The six styles of leadership and emotional intelligence' section), particularly of strengths and weaknesses. Richard Branson said of one of his early collaborators, Jonny Gems who ran with him their magazine, *Student* in the late 1960s, '... I've always needed somebody as a counterbalance, to compensate for my weaknesses and work off my strengths' (Branson, 2009).

Conviction and self-belief are vital, particularly when many entrepreneurs leave the relative safety of large organizations to start up on their own.

Persistence (James Dyson had more than 5,000 prototypes for the Dual Cyclone vacuum cleaner!), patience, the ability to withstand disappointments and set-backs, focus (sometimes to the point of obsession!), innovation and an ability to explore different avenues are also vital (as well as the electric light, Thomas Edison was involved with the film industry, mining and had even developed a battery for an electric car in 1904!) Hard work is usually mentioned by entrepreneurs as is serendipity or luck, and 'being in the right place at the right time'.

Strategic vision, and not just day-to-day activity is vital. Chrissie Rucker, when asked what was the biggest lesson she had learned, said:

> The most important thing is to always be forward looking and have a longer term vision for where you want the company to be in the future. We always have a five-year plan. When you are just going from day-to-day you can waste a lot of time. (Card, 2016)

CASE STUDY
Coal mines and public houses

In the 1980s there were many redundancies in what had previously been traditional primary industries, such as mining. As coal mines closed, miners used their redundancy monies to invest in businesses such as small hotels and guest houses (many on the coast), pubs and post offices. Some thrived and were successful, others sadly failed. The key themes behind some of the failing businesses was often nothing to do with the attitude of the new owners of the businesses. More than anyone else, they wanted their businesses to work. It was their new livelihood and in many cases, it was all the money they had. The leisure industry (which encompasses hotels, guest houses and public houses) is very different to working in a mine, requiring a different skill-set.

Whilst pubs in the 1980s were very different from many of the 'gastro' pubs we see today, they were very often low-margin businesses (due to arrangements with breweries which 'tied' the landlord to certain pricing arrangements for alcoholic drinks and often soft drinks). Cash flow management was always a challenge, and many of the new owners had never had to do this before. There was a huge amount of competition in the industry, and particularly where it was a couple who were running the pub, making sufficient money to pay two salaries made many new entrepreneurs realize that it was very difficult to replace the level of income that had been enjoyed previously.

Knowing when to give up?

Some entrepreneurs stretch themselves too far, and brand extension, which can be very effective, doesn't always work. Not everything that entrepreneurs do works and sometimes there has to be the painful recognition that a product or service needs to be discontinued. A balance is usually required between sheer determination, persevering (often against the odds) and intransigence. Failure is difficult and often hard to take, particularly where large amounts of time and money have been invested. As James Dyson said when discussing the discontinued CR01 washing machine: 'Failure is the best medicine as long as you learn something' (Dowling, 2013). Richard Branson launched Virgin Cola in the 1990s as a rival to the major brands of Coca-Cola and Pepsi-Cola. It had a number of years of success in the UK following its launch, but at the present time there is no holder of the licence to manufacture it in the UK.

Bankers supporting entrepreneurs

Do all entrepreneurs have to possess messianic qualities, be larger than life, glamorous business people? No, of course not, and the reality is that bankers will deal with many hard-working, passionate business people who have a good idea, don't want to work for someone else and have the drive to make a success of their businesses. These are the people that the banks will want to support, and many of these businesses will become the household names in the future.

ASSIGNMENT/EXAM TIP

You may be presented with information about managers or a management team in an assignment or an exam question– use this wisely! If the question or scenario suggests that there is a good relationship with the bank, that the customers are trustworthy and that they have honoured previous commitments then factor this into your answer. You need to analyse the information and take it on 'face value' to start with, that is, *don't imagine a position that isn't there!*

That doesn't mean that you shouldn't critically assess what you have been given, and one of the areas you may be concerned with, due to the lack of information in the question, may be succession planning. This would be a legitimate and valid area to question and is always an area that bankers are concerned with. Give justifications for your answer.

Chapter summary

In this chapter we have explored:

- the key strategy of relationship management and why it is a vital approach for commercial banks;
- the importance of meeting customers in their own premises;
- the important areas for banks to consider when assessing the management of commercial businesses they lend to;
- what defines management and leadership;
- what emotional intelligence is and why it is important when considering leadership and management; and
- the qualities that make a good entrepreneur.

Objective check

1 What are the benefits to the bank in using a relationship management approach with commercial customers?

2 What do you feel the benefits are to the customer and bank for having meetings at customer premises?

3 What three key areas do banks need to consider when assessing management?

4 What is the difference between management and leadership?

5 What are the six styles of leadership (as defined by Daniel Goleman)?

6 What is emotional intelligence and how is it beneficial for leadership?

7 List three characteristics that tend to be exhibited by entrepreneurs. How important do you feel these are for success?

Further reading

Watch the video *Employee Engagement – Who's Sinking Your Boat?* [accessed 24 June 2018], [Online] www.youtube.com/watch?v=y4nwoZ02AJM) and think how this might be applied to your own workplace.

References

Branson, R (2009) *Losing my virginity,* Virgin, London

Card, J (2016) The White Company founder: 'We've been through four recessions' [accessed 24 June 2018] [Online] https://www.theguardian.com/small-business-network/2016/nov/16/the-white-company-founder-weve-been-through-four-recessions-since-we-started

Dowling, S (2013) *Frustration and failure fuel Dyson's success* [accessed 24 June 2018] [Online] http://www.bbc.com/future/story/20130312-failure-is-the-best-medicine

Goleman, D (2000) Leadership that gets results, *Harvard Business Review* (March–April 2000)

Handy, C (1993) *Understanding Organizations,* 4th edn, Oxford University Press, Oxford

Jeal, E (2017) Simon Rattle: 'I would have been wary about taking the job had I known about Brexit' [accessed 24 June 2018] [Online] https://www.theguardian.com/music/2017/aug/04/simon-rattle-interview-london-symphony-orchestra-brexit

Stevenson, A and Waite, M (2011) *Concise Oxford English Dictionary*, Oxford University Press, Oxford

Sutton, R (2001) *Weird ideas that work*, Allen Lane, London

YouTube [accessed 24 June 2018] Peter Grant Interview 1988 [Online] https://www.youtube.com/watch?v=KM9bBu55EXE

Answers for activities

Learners should devise their own answers for all the activities in this chapter. No model answers have been supplied.

09

Businesses facing financial difficulties

INTRODUCTION

Businesses can sometimes face financial difficulties, perhaps through no fault of their own, and this chapter deals with the issues that banks and their customers face when this happens. It also discusses the choices and options facing both the bank and the customer and covers the various insolvency routes available.

The bank is one of a number of stakeholders that will be concerned when a business isn't performing financially as it should be. The risk, that you, as a banker, face is that the lending you have made will either not be repaid at all, or only repaid in part, resulting in a bad debt for the bank and where all or part of the monies lent will need to be written off.

The other stakeholders in the business will include staff, trade creditors (including suppliers), HMRC (tax and VAT), possibly other banks and, of course, the owners of the business themselves.

LEARNING OBJECTIVES

By the end of this chapter, you will be able to:

- assess the warning signs for banks that indicate a commercial customer is in financial difficulties;

- explain how businesses get into financial difficulties;

- evaluate the choices commercial businesses have to deal with their financial difficulties;

- assess the different choices and options that face the lending banker;

- define insolvency; and

- apply the main insolvency procedures for personal and commercial customers.

How do businesses get into financial difficulties?

There are many reasons why businesses get into financial difficulties and some of these can be due to external factors outside the control of the business. Sometimes as a banker, you may see the decline of a business due to the change in tastes of customers or, in many cases, new technology. Such changes can have enormous impacts on existing business models. We explore this issue in more detail in the box, 'Music – Changing Technology… and HMV'.

MUSIC – CHANGING TECHNOLOGY… AND HMV

Many people love music and the way this has been consumed has changed significantly over the last 40 years. Compact Discs (CDs) were introduced in 1985 which allowed digital versions of music to be stored and played. A major shift came in 1998 when MP3s were introduced, which were digital files of music which could be stored on computers and could also be shared with others.

The pace of technological change continued throughout the noughties, and one of the main routes many consumers now use to listen to music is via 'streaming' services such as Spotify, where for a subscription, music can be listened to on a mobile device, such as a smartphone or a PC, but the user does not buy the music.

It's worth now reflecting on the fortunes of a high street brand that many of you will know, HMV. For a period, HMV were the major retailer for CDs in the UK. They also sold DVDs and computer games.

Changes in technology had a number of impacts for HMV. Not only was the company affected by the changes discussed above but the growth of online retailers such as Amazon, who sold the same goods as HMV, but at discounted prices, with direct delivery to the customer's home had a huge impact. HMV were not able to adapt sufficiently quickly and went into administration in January 2013.

However, this was not the end of the story for HMV. Whilst a number of stores were shut, and jobs were lost, at the time of writing, HMV still has over 120 physical stores in the UK. It was bought out of administration by a company called Hilco and is currently the largest UK retailer of physical music (ahead of Amazon).

We will explore what administration is later in this chapter and why it is important for you, as a banker.

ACTIVITY 9.1
Businesses that have entered insolvency processes

Research businesses that have faced financial difficulties recently, and may have entered an insolvency process. These might be local businesses or national businesses.

Write down your answer and check it against the one at the end of the chapter.

The warning signs

Businesses don't often suddenly get into financial difficulties, although the reasons for a sudden decline in a business will be discussed later. One of the key skills that bankers need to develop is the ability to spot the warning signs that might indicate that a business is having problems.

Management information

You will recall that the importance of management information was introduced in Chapter 2 and that management information shows the financial performance of a business in a particular period of time, either for a month or a three-month period. It is a little like having a dashboard on a car which shows very quickly what is happening. The key measure of how a business is performing is the profit and loss account. This will show how much money it is making or losing in the last month or three months. The business will also be able to show how it is performing against the comparable period a year ago, against its budgets and also the cumulative position of the business during the financial year. As we have discussed throughout this text, many businesses are seasonal, and the budgets produced by the business will reflect this seasonality (eg a retail business will be building inventory up in the period leading up to Christmas) and the management information produced should reflect what has happened, taking into account possible seasonal variations.

If there are variances against budgets, then it is easy to see where these variances are occurring, particularly if these are basic indicators such as turnover falling, or gross and net profit margins falling.

Management information is there to tell the owners and directors how their business is performing but is also a way for the banker to be able to tell if they should be concerned about the ability of their customer to repay them.

Trends in management information

There is an old saying 'one swallow doesn't make a summer', meaning one good thing happening doesn't mean everything is getting better, and the inverse of this is also true! One month where a business has not performed financially as it projected doesn't mean that the business is facing financial difficulties but if this turns into a two or three-month period, or even longer, when the business is showing a deteriorating performance (particularly if losses are being suffered) then the bank has a very clear warning sign that it needs to discuss matters with the partners or directors to ascertain what they are doing about the situation.

Management information can be used to check key metrics, sometimes also called key performance indicators (KPIs), in the business which can be used quickly by the banker to check if there are performance issues which the bank should be concerned about. The bank will also benchmark the business against industry norms, and of course against its own past performance.

ACTIVITY 9.2
Warning signs in management information

Consider three businesses:

- an estate agency;
- a care home; and
- a property company (renting out residential flats and houses).

What are the KPIs which can be used to identify warning signs for each business?
Write down your answer and check it against the one at the end of the chapter.

Delays in receiving management information

When the bank lends money, it will normally set covenants (again as discussed in Chapter 2) to protect itself. Not only will the bank want to receive management information on a regular basis, to track the financial performance of its customer, but it will also want to ensure that information is received on a timely basis. Banks have a duty to treat customers fairly (you will recall this from Chapter 1) and, therefore, need to be 'reasonable' about the timescales of when they would expect to receive information. If the requirement is to produce monthly information, then the bank will usually stipulate that management information must be produced within a month of the month end (ie September management information must be produced by the end of October).

The bank should have a monitoring system for each customer and any delays in receiving information need to be followed up with the customer immediately. There may of course be legitimate reasons for management information being late, such as the owners being very busy with the running of the business or illness of one of the partners or directors. A more serious reason is that the business is not performing as it should financially, and the owners are concerned about sharing this information with the bank, for fear that the bank may take precipitous action and, therefore, delay sending information or not send it at all. Non-receipt of management information may therefore be an act of default on behalf of the borrower.

Regular excesses over overdraft limits

Bankers use 'limits' when deciding how much money will be lent to a customer as a method of restricting the risk to a particular customer. The limit given to a customer should be appropriate for the level of funding the business needs and should be used for funding the working capital cycle. Overdrafts allow businesses to go overdrawn up to a certain level.

As we discussed in Chapter 3, most businesses have periods within the month, the quarter or the year when they face greater cash flow pressures. This can be due to a variety of reasons, including salary payments, supplier payments, loan and rental payments and tax liabilities (corporation tax/ VAT) or perhaps the seasonal nature of the business. These can cause 'spikes' in the cash requirements of the business and may cause overdraft limits to be breached.

If this causes an overdraft limit to be exceeded then you, as the banker, need to investigate what is causing the excess. This will entail checking through internal records to ascertain what items are being 'presented' – this will include cheques which are in the clearing system that day. It will also entail contacting the customer to discuss what monies are due to be paid in either that day or very shortly. A decision is then made as to whether or not the payments going out that day will be allowed. A banker will be very careful about not paying supplier payments as this will have an impact on the future relationship between the customer and that supplier. There is also a danger the bank will be perceived as acting as a shadow director (the principles of being a shadow director are explored later in this chapter). Often excesses are of a temporary nature and are cleared that day or very shortly after that.

Management information, as discussed earlier, will be a rich source of information for the bank. It may be that the business is growing quickly and needs more working capital to fund an increase in inventory and trade receivables, or it could be that the business is suffering losses which is resulting in regular pressures on cash flow and therefore causing the business to breach the agreed overdraft limit. Understanding the operational impact that drives management information is important. There are some very easy 'cross-checks' that a banker can carry out, and one of these is to check the turnover through the bank account, to compare this to both what the customer is telling you should be going through the account (via their management information) and what the banker would expect to be seen.

A simple example of this would be a residential real estate business that has 50 houses and flats that are rented out to private individuals. Rental income should be received on a regular basis into the bank account and this can be cross-referenced against how many properties are rented out. A falling turnover or a month when no income at all is received will indicate that either fewer properties are being rented out or that the customer is paying rental income into another bank account. Sometimes this type of business employs estate agencies to collect rents for them, and there can be delays in the estate agencies remitting funds to the bank; regular checks will ensure that there are no issues with the operation of the bank account.

It is the trend on an account which is important and if excesses become a regular feature of the operation of a customer's account then this is when the bank needs to investigate more deeply to explore why these are occurring.

Hardcore borrowing

Hardcore borrowing is a term used to describe a situation when an overdraft for a business does not fluctuate between credit and debit. The overdraft is permanently being used and never falls below a particular level. Let's return again to *Amanda's Country Kitchen* to illustrate this.

> **Hardcore borrowing** The element of borrowing within a revolving facility, such as an overdraft, where the level of indebtedness never falls below a particular level. It is where an overdraft does not fluctuate between credit and debit.

Table 9.1 shows that the bank agreed an overdraft limit of £1,000 and at the end of March, this was being used to the level of £870 (debit). Hardcore borrowing would be where, during the year, the balance of Amanda's business account never fell below £450 (debit).

There can be many reasons why hardcore borrowing occurs. One may be that a business has used the overdraft to purchase fixed assets, and in Amanda's case she could have seen a new coffee machine for the business

Table 9.1 Amanda's Country Kitchen – as at 31 March

Facility	Limit (£s)	Exposure (£s)
Overdraft	1,000	870
Loan	15,000	14,875
Balance	16,000	15,745

for £600 which she felt she needed and simply used the overdraft to buy it. Overdrafts should normally be used for working capital and buying the coffee machine then distorts the operation of the overdraft.

Often, however, a hardcore position is caused by losses in the business and the overdraft is then used to absorb these losses. If losses continue to be suffered then the hardcore position is likely to increase, and this means that the business will have less 'room' in the overdraft facility and the gap between the hardcore position and the overdraft limit becomes smaller, the result being that excesses will be much more likely.

Falling turnover

If the banker sees the sales turnover of a business is falling, then this is a strong indicator that the business is facing trading difficulties. The business will require a certain level of turnover in order to generate the profits required to repay its borrowing. The banker will want to know why turnover is falling and what the partners or directors are doing to reverse the situation.

Unplanned events

These can take the shape of anything sudden and unexpected that is likely to affect the ability of a business to perform.

External events, and certainly political events, can have a detrimental impact on businesses. The decision for the UK to leave the European Union, for example, had an immediate impact on businesses that imported to the UK as this 'weakened' sterling against other major currencies such as the euro and the US dollar. It then cost companies who were importing more to import goods. The immediate impact of this was for businesses who were importing to have to reduce their profit margins (by absorbing the extra costs), or increase their prices.

Other external events that may not be anticipated are severe weather events that either stop businesses being able to operate, or significantly slow down operations. In both instances, sales and profitability are likely to be impacted.

The reputation of a business can be very quickly affected by information that becomes public. A food 'scare' for example can impact significantly on sales of certain products. Cadbury had to recall more than a million chocolate bars in 2006 due to worries about salmonella infecting a number of products (news.bbc.co.uk, 2006).

Internally, the sudden departure of a key partner or director can have a very detrimental impact on the ability of a business to continue to perform effectively, particularly if that individual takes key clients and customers with them (this can be a high risk in creative industries such as advertising agencies where strong personal relationships are developed etc).

Breach of covenants

You will recall in Chapter 4, that we discussed why the bank would put in place covenants that are effectively a 'safety net' for the bank and allow them to manage the risk and be able to get an early warning if a company isn't performing as it should. If, for example, there is a covenant in a loan agreement for interest (on borrowing) to be covered a number of times from profits (eg three times) and information is given by the customer via the regular management information to show cover is only two times, then this is a breach of the terms of the loan agreement, known as a **breach of covenant**. The bank needs to deal with this breach (which we will discuss shortly).

> **Breach of covenants** The breaking of specific terms and conditions within a loan or overdraft agreement.

What are the routes a business might take to remedy challenges?

The directors in a company that isn't performing well financially can take any actions they wish to improve the trading position of the business and this may mean tackling a number of different areas of the business. The actions that directors might take will also depend on whether or not the business is insolvent (see later in the chapter for a discussion of the implications for directors) and the availability of capital/cash resources.

Usually these actions will be taken as part of wide-ranging discussions with the bank. Some of the decisions may be relatively easy to make, whereas others, particularly where they involve factory closures or having to make redundancies, will be significantly harder.

Cash position

This is likely to be critical and everything the business does in the short term will need to be focused around this issue.

Directors' support

Directors and/or shareholders/members can support their company by putting funds into the business. This may be particularly pertinent if there has been a high level of dividends over the last few years which may have contributed to the current financial difficulties.

Falling turnover

This is fundamental to the performance of the business and depending on the types of activities that the customer engages in will drive how this issue is tackled. Marketing is often the key part of a strategy to increase sales.

Costs

Cutting costs is often the place where businesses feel they can make very quick improvements to the financial performance. Initially this will involve reviewing all parts of the operations to see where efficiencies might be made. It may not be possible to influence some input costs, such as energy costs, as oil prices may be high which makes it difficult to make any immediate cost savings. The business will also need to seriously consider whether or not it will look to make redundancies.

Suppliers

A review of suppliers is likely to take place and consideration will need to be made to whether any contracts are moved to cheaper suppliers or those with preferential payment terms. The business will need to be careful not to sacrifice quality, however.

Inventory

If a business holds high levels of inventory, a critical review may help. Obsolete inventory needs to be sold as quickly as possible to release cash (although it may not be worth what is shown in the balance sheet!). Reducing stock levels won't immediately make more money for the business but it will ease the immediate cash requirements.

Trade receivables

The business will need to review all its trade receivables, ensuring that monies owed are being collected as quickly as possible, and that older debts are chased robustly. This should improve the cash position in the short term. The business also has the ability to have an invoice discount facility which, as we have discussed in Chapter 7, should provide the business with the ability to improve its cash flow.

What are the choices and options facing the lending banker and how does it protect itself?

This is possibly one of the most difficult times for the relationship between the bank and the customer. You will recall that in earlier chapters we set out the rights and duties that existed between both the bank and the customer and we also developed this through Chapter 6, 'Securities for lending'.

A banker has certain rights when they take security, such as a debenture or a legal charge over property. You, as the banker, do not always have to exercise these rights but you need to be aware of how these rights may be used and how they are used to help the bank to recover funds it has lent.

The actions that a bank may take are partly influenced by a number of factors, including:

- what actions the customer can take to improve the business (discussed above);
- what security the bank holds (and when it was taken);
- what actions have been taken by third parties such as creditors, and, potentially most importantly, is the business they are dealing with fundamentally viable?

Transfer of the business to a specialist high-risk unit

Many of the major clearing banks in the UK have teams who have responsibilities for what the bank considers to be higher risk lending. The trigger points for when a customer is to be transferred will depend on each individual organization.

The responsibilities that the high-risk team will undertake will very much depend on the 'model' that the individual bank prefers. In some banks the whole relationship is moved to a new team who have overall responsibility for the day-to-day banking as well as looking after the credit function (eg writing internal credit reports and managing all elements of the lending relationship with the customer). Other banks only move the responsibility for the lending to the customer to the high-risk team, with all other parts of the relationship remaining with the existing relationship team. The high-risk team will usually have responsibility for all lending that has been made to the customer throughout the bank (eg if there is lending from the asset finance division for machinery).

Once a customer has been moved to a high-risk team there are a number of potential routes that can be taken and these are usually:

- restructure; or
- insolvency.

The customer does of course always have the option to refinance and if the business is not so distressed that another bank with a different risk appetite will consider taking over the debt then this could be a route for the customer to take (it does not, however, address the fundamental issues that the business may need to deal with).

ACTIVITY 9.3
Transfer to a specialist high-risk unit

Find out within your own organization what the internal triggers are for moving a customer to a high-risk team.
What does this team do?
What is their operating model, ie do they just take responsibility for the credit function?

Restructure

The bank will have an overriding priority to proactively manage the risk and what it will look to do, if possible, is to work with the customer for a restructure to take place. A **restructure** usually has two elements to it:

- restructure of the business; and
- restructure of the lending.

Restructure of the business

Earlier in the chapter we discussed the possible actions that the owners of a business can take, and these actions will be part of the customer's plans to improve the performance of the business. This can include improving turnover, reducing costs, improving profitability and cash flow. The customer may also include proposals to reduce debt and ask the bank to reduce repayments on existing borrowing.

> **Restructure** The process which can involve, often in conjunction with its bankers, the reorganization of a business including its finances.

Information

The customer will usually provide a detailed business plan incorporating a strategic plan with the key changes that are planned. This will include detailed financial projections, including profit and loss figures and critically, cash flow projections over a three-month period (on a weekly basis) and also for a 12-month period (anything longer for cash flows is unlikely to be very reliable). The business may be able to produce this itself or may use its accountants to help.

Restructure of the lending

Information

Using information provided by the customer (detailed above), the banker may sometimes ask for an **independent business review** (IBR). These are usually carried out by a firm of accountants that has experience in restructuring businesses. The IBR will examine all aspects of the business, including the management, the products or service provided by the business and critically test all of the strategic plans put forward by the directors including sensitizing all the projections. It will also include a view of the potential losses that will be faced by the bank should the business fail and go into some form of insolvency process.

> **Independent business review** Carried out by a firm of accountants that has experience in restructuring businesses.

Following this review there is often the possibility of either the appointment of a non-executive director or a **turnaround consultant** who can help the business through what is often a very difficult and stressful period. The bank will usually be the party who drives this appointment and the appointee will need to be an individual who ideally has experience in the industry the customer operates in.

> **Turnaround consultant**   An individual (or individuals) who can help a business as it goes through a restructuring process. They are usually appointed by a bank for a specified period and ideally have expertise in the industry the customer is involved in.

Security

A banker will want to know what the security they hold is currently worth. This will involve using professional valuers to value assets (such as property) that the bank holds a charge over and lawyers to check that the security is valid and when it becomes enforceable. The bank may also be able to approve its security position; for example, a customer may have certain assets that are currently subject to the bank's floating charge, but the bank may be able to take a fixed charge.

Options/strategies

A banker will be prepared to restructure the bank's lending if they feel there is a better chance of the bank being fully repaid by taking this route rather than leaving loans and other lending on the original terms. Also, if the bank feels there is a higher risk lending to a particular company then the bank may wish to see some short-term reductions in debt to reduce their risk. It is useful at this point to explore the structure of existing borrowing:

- Overdrafts.
  - Hardcore borrowing – if there is hardcore borrowing on the current account (as discussed earlier), one of the bank's strategies could be to reduce the overdraft limit and place the hardcore element of the overdraft on a short-term loan. For example, if the overdraft limit is £1 million, with a hardcore level of £500,000, the overdraft limit would be reduced to £500,000, and a new loan of £500,000 provided, to be repaid over, say, 12 or 18 months. Initially the bank is still lending the same amount of money, but in a relatively short period of time the borrowing will start to reduce.
  - Invoice discounting – we discussed in Chapter 7 the comparison between a straightforward commercial overdraft facility and an invoice discount facility. If the business has a good trade receivable book, then an invoice discount facility might be a positive way to use one of the current assets of the business more effectively and to release more cash into the business at a time when cash flow is under pressure.

- Loans.
  - Debt reduction – if one of the offered strategies of the business is to reduce debt by asset sales (perhaps property or fixed assets such as machinery), then one option for the banker is to place part of an existing loan onto an interest-only basis until the asset is sold. In this way, cash pressures on a short-term basis will be lessened.
  - Loan extension – extending the loan term may also be a course of action that the bank will consider if it feels this will help the survival of the business. The business may be paying higher capital and interest payments than it needs to. It is possible that the original loan term was based on an aggressive repayment plan, where the customer was looking to repay the loan in a shorter period and the bank would have been comfortable lending funds for a longer period of time.

It is worth pointing out at this point that the bank will only wish to carry out any restructuring of the facilities if it is reasonably confident of the viability of the business and that there are no insolvency events.

Failure to pay

A loan agreement between a bank and the customer will set out the loan payments that need to be made over a specified period. The most obvious way that a customer can be in default of a loan agreement is to miss one or more scheduled loan payments. This is then a very clear-cut breach of an agreement and also means that the bank can then potentially take more serious action against the customer.

Insolvency

In many cases the banker will have worked closely with the customer to arrange a restructuring of both the business and the lending and in some cases it is still not possible to save the business. In these circumstances, one of the **insolvency** options will be taken as a next step. We will explore the different insolvency choices in the following section.

Insolvency

What is the definition of insolvency?

The insolvency regimes under English and Welsh law are different to other parts of the world, eg the United States, and often it is very easy for bankers to confuse terminology from different territories. In the United States you may often see the phrase 'bankruptcy' used when the media is discussing the insolvency of a corporate entity. Under English law, it is incorrect to use the phrase 'bankrupt' relating to a limited company or LLP entity (which you will recall from Chapter 1 are separate legal entities and able to enter into contracts in the same way that an individual can). Only individuals can become bankrupt under English and Welsh law (this will be discussed later in this chapter). You will also see that in the United States the media refers to chapters of the US bankruptcy code, for example Toys R Us USA is 'in Chapter 11'. This terminology is not used in English law.

> **Insolvency** The inability of a business to pay its liabilities as and when they are due. It can also be where the liabilities of a business are more than its assets.

Before we explore the subject of insolvency in greater depth and particularly how it might impact you as the banker, it is important to be clear about what we mean by the term 'being insolvent'. The tests for insolvency are set out in Section 123 of the Insolvency Act 1986.

REGULATION
Insolvency

The key legislation in England and Wales that relates to insolvency is the *Insolvency Act [1986].* See also Insolvency (England and Wales) Rules 2016. It has been impacted by the *Enterprise Act [2002]* and the *Small Business, Enterprise and Employment Act [2015].* The *Law of Property Act (1925)* impacts on Law of Property Act receivers.

The *Companies Act [2006]* is also relevant, particularly relating to the duties of directors.

Keeping up to date: There are many firms of lawyers and accountants who provide regular updates on insolvency issues. For example, the international firm Pinsent Masons prepares regular updates and publishes a quarterly magazine, *Restructuring Business*, available at: https://www.pinsentmasons.com/en/expertise/services/banking—finance/restructuring/

Usually a business is considered to be insolvent when it is unable to pay its debts (as and when they fall due). This is known as the 'cash flow test' and is the most commonly used test to assess insolvency. A business that has bank loans and hire purchase agreements (with monthly payments), trade payable payments and tax liabilities, only needs to have sufficient funds available to make these payments when they are due (in the same way that if you have a mortgage, you only need to have sufficient funds available to meet your monthly payments and not have to be able to repay the *full* amount of the mortgage in one amount).

The other test of insolvency is the 'balance sheet' test, where if a company's liabilities are more than its assets then it is insolvent (under the Insolvency Act). A company can be cash flow and/or balance sheet insolvent for the insolvency procedures to apply; it does not need to be both.

There are many implications that insolvency for a company brings:

- Directors' duties:

  - Once a company is insolvent, the directors have a duty to put the interests of the creditors (who are owed money by the business) before other parties; you may often see this referred to as trading in the 'twilight zone'.

  - They need to be mindful of 'wrongful trading' (under Section 214 of the Insolvency Act 1986) where, if they continue to trade the business with no reasonable prospect of avoiding entering into an insolvency process (eg administration – to be discussed later in this chapter), they could be held personally liable for some of the company's liabilities. From the point that the directors realized, or ought to have realized, that there was no reasonable prospect of avoiding insolvent administration/liquidation, they must take every step to minimize the losses to the company's creditors.

  - If the business of the company is carried out with the intent to defraud creditors or for any other fraudulent purpose, known as fraudulent trading, the directors may be subject to criminal sanctions; directors could also be personally liable if they are guilty of misfeasance or act in breach of their duties (known as fiduciary duties) to the company.

- Creditor action – An insolvent company is highly likely to be facing increased pressure from many of its suppliers and also HMRC:

  - Any creditor who is owed more than £750 and has not had their debt paid can then ask the courts to issue a 'winding-up petition' against the company. The creditor may issue a formal demand (known as a 'statutory demand') for payment. Failure of the company to pay the sums demanded within three weeks of the demand creates a presumption that a company is insolvent, but it is not formally required to issue a winding-up petition. The court needs to be satisfied that the company is in fact insolvent; therefore, it is common for statutory demands to be issued prior to winding-up petitions.

Winding-up petition

If a **winding-up petition** has been issued by a creditor then it is highly likely that the next steps will be for some form of insolvency proceedings to take place. The company cannot trade, cannot dispose of any assets and will have its bank accounts frozen whilst the winding-up petition is outstanding. In these circumstances the banker will have to take action to preserve the bank's position and not allow the debt the company has to get worse by paying further items out of the main trading account. The bank will 'break' or stop the current account – this is the principle under *Clayton's Case* which was discussed in detail in Chapter 1.

> **Winding-up petition**   A petition presented to the court by a creditor (who is owed more than £750 and has not had their debt paid) to wind up a company.

> **CLAYTON'S CASE REMINDER**
> *Clayton's Case [1816]*
>
> The actual legal case is *Devaynes and Noble [1816]* but is often referred to as *Clayton's Case*. It requires banks to stop current accounts on partnership or sole traders to ensure the bank doesn't incur further liability and is able to protect any outstanding lending position.
>   It requires some form of 'trigger event' such as bankruptcy or death in order for the bank to have to take action.
>   A winding-up petition is also considered a 'trigger event'.

Liquidation of the business is likely to be the next step (to be discussed in greater detail later in the chapter).

Can a company be saved?

If a company can be saved then it has to be in the interests of all the key stakeholders to do everything in their power to make this happen – this will include the directors, the staff, the creditors and the bank.

As we have explored in an earlier part of this chapter, the fundamental question for the banker to ask will always be: is this fundamentally a viable business? Many businesses that have faced restructuring come through the other side of the process; however, they will not usually survive the process looking the same 'shape' as they did before going through it. A retail business, for example, with, for example, 30 stores in the South of England may find itself with 15 stores after a restructuring.

Options and choices

The available options to a company will be dictated by how much pressure the company is under and what actions any of the stakeholders may be taking. The next two options, company voluntary arrangements and administrations have been in existence since they were introduced as new processes under the *Insolvency Act [1986]*, although the administration regime was significantly changed by the *Enterprise Act [2002]* which has applied since 2003. All of the insolvency processes that we will discuss in this chapter need to be administered by an individual (there may be more than one for a larger business) called an insolvency practitioner who is fully licensed; and are commonly referred to as the 'office holder'.

A third option is a scheme of arrangement under the *Companies Act (2006)*. A scheme is not technically an insolvency process and a company does not need to be insolvent to propose one; however, schemes are commonly used to restructure insolvent companies and they are, therefore, usually listed alongside the formal insolvency procedures as an option.

Insolvency processes

Survival

Some of the insolvency processes that we will discuss in this next part of the chapter are designed to ensure the survival of the business rather than be 'terminal' stages where the business will not survive.

Company voluntary arrangements

We have discussed earlier that a business will need to be insolvent before these options are explored. **Company voluntary arrangements** (CVAs) are a way of a 'distressed' company being able to make arrangements with its unsecured creditors, and usually in these circumstances, there is an inability to make contractual payments to some or all of the creditors. This allows the business to continue to trade normally, preserves the value in the business and preserves jobs.

The directors (usually with the assistance of the **insolvency practitioner** (IP) who intends to administer the CVA and who is known at this point as the 'nominee') will submit a proposal to shareholders and creditors. If more than 50 per cent of shareholders and 75 per cent of the creditors (both in value not number) agree to the proposals then the arrangement is approved, provided that objections are not received from more than 50 per cent of independent creditors (ie those that are not associated with the company). The IP then becomes the 'supervisor' of the CVA. The existing directors or management team continue to run the business, under the supervision of the IP, to ensure the CVA terms are adhered to.

> **Company voluntary arrangement**   A formal insolvency arrangement between a company and its unsecured creditors (binding on all parties). It allows a business to continue to trade normally. It preserves the value in the business and jobs. Once agreed it is controlled by an insolvency practitioner who is the supervisor.
>
> **Insolvency practitioner**   A licensed individual who is authorized to carry out specific duties in relation to insolvent companies and bankrupt individuals.

A CVA is a formal arrangement between the company and the unsecured creditors which is binding on all parties; the CVA is binding on creditors who did not agree to it (often referred to as 'cramming down') and even those that were unaware of it. The creditors cannot approve a CVA which restricts the rights of a secured creditor (which the bank usually is) without the secured creditor's approval. A CVA is a mutual agreement whereby existing liabilities may be partly written off and agreements reached for future payments. These creditors can be made up of a number of different types: some may be suppliers to the business, others may be landlords, who lease properties that the business trades from.

Many retail businesses, for example, operate from leased premises, and in both high street locations and out of town shopping centres these rents can be very high, and also the retail business may have entered into long leases over a number of years. Landlords might agree to write off half the amount they are owed, and then agree to reduced rental payments in the future. This will be on the proviso that the company pays back the monies that are owed.

The critical point that bankers need to understand is that the company which has entered into this agreement must adhere to it or the CVA will fail and another insolvency process will be used.

The key weakness of a CVA is the lack of a moratorium (as discussed below in relation to administration) for all companies, other than 'small' companies. Unless a secured creditor has agreed not to enforce its security or the company benefits from the small company moratorium, the secured creditor will be able to enforce its security by appointing administrators, liquidators or receivers which will effectively bring the CVA to an end. In practice the company should have engaged with the bank and have its support prior to the directors proposing a CVA. A CVA can also be proposed by an administrator or a liquidator, but not a creditor or shareholder.

Administration

Administration is an insolvency process that is designed to find a way for a business to survive as a 'going concern' (ie it doesn't stop trading). It is of particular use to a bank, where it wishes to see value in the business preserved, rather than trading stopping with a resultant drop in the value of the business itself and any assets it holds (and that may be held as security by the bank). An important point to note for learners is that administrations are for the benefit of *all* creditors and not just banks.

The *Insolvency Act (1986)* sets out a number of guiding principles for administrations under Schedule B1 of the Act (which was introduced by the *Enterprise Act (2002)*). Administrations are carried out by an **administrator** (who must be a licensed insolvency practitioner). An administration must be likely to achieve one of the following purposes:

1 rescuing the company as a going concern; or

2 achieving a better result for the company's creditors as a whole than would be likely if the company were wound up (without first being in administration); or

3 realizing property in order to make a distribution to one or more secured or preferential creditors.

The administrator must follow these in a logical order starting with the first purpose unless this is not possible, then moving to the second purpose and if this is not possible, moving to the last purpose.

Administration   An insolvency process designed to find a way for a business to survive as a 'going concern' (ie it doesn't stop trading).

Administrator   An appointed individual (usually a licensed insolvency practitioner), who will be responsible for running an administration.

Appointment of administrators

There are different methods to achieve appointment:

1 Court appointment – a director or a creditor (there may be more than one creditor) can ask the court to appoint an administrator.

2 Qualified floating charge holder – if the bank holds a debenture then it will hold a floating charge over the assets of the company. The vast majority of floating charges will be qualifying floating charges (QFCs) and this will give the bank the power to appoint an administrator. If there are any other holders of QFCs (ie usually other banks) that also have QFCs which rank in priority, they must be given notice (known as 'notice of intention to appoint' or 'NoIA') prior to an administrator being appointed. This gives the prior ranking QFC holder the chance to appoint its own choice of administrator.

3 The directors or the company itself (you will recall it is a separate legal entity) can appoint without a court order. However, this will not be possible if:

- the company has previously been in administration;
- a voluntary arrangement (see below for more details) has ended earlier than it was scheduled to;
- a moratorium ended without any kind of voluntary arrangement being agreed by creditors;
- a winding-up petition has been issued and remains outstanding; and
- the directors or company must also give NoIA to the holders of any QFC to allow the QFC holder the opportunity to appoint its own choice of administrator. In practice the company or directors will have discussed this with the bank beforehand and it will consent to the appointment as most banks prefer the appointment to be consensual where possible.

Once an administrator is appointed he or she takes over the running of the company and the directors relinquish their responsibilities. They may still be employed by the business.

Benefits of an administration – moratorium

One of the major benefits to the company is that it achieves something called a moratorium – this stops certain creditors taking enforcement action against the company without the agreement of the administrator or consent of the court. The most common use of the moratorium is to prevent landlords from forfeiting leases of property that the company occupies, as the property will be needed to trade the business.

Pre-packaged sales

A **pre-packaged sale** involves the pre-arranged sale of the business and assets of an insolvent company often to its existing directors immediately following the appointment of a licensed insolvency practitioner (usually an administrator). It is sometimes known as a 'pre-pack' due to the pre-arranged element of the process. The assets will usually be transferred into a new company.

It can also be referred to as a 'phoenix' process and some banks are uncomfortable with this as often a number of key trade creditors (and sometimes also HMRC) can be left in a weaker position than they were previously.

> **Pre-packaged sales** The pre-arranged sale of a business and assets of an insolvent company (often to its existing directors) immediately following the appointment of a licensed insolvency practitioner (usually an administrator). It is sometimes known as a 'pre-pack' due to the pre-arranged element of the process. The assets will usually be transferred into a new company.

Advantages of a pre-pack

- As we have seen in some of the other insolvency procedures where the survival of the business is of paramount importance, the pre-pack aims to preserve value by ensuring that there is not a long sales process that would reduce the going-concern value.
- Finance is in place before the sale completes.
- There is less disruption for staff, and this should also help to retain staff.
- Suppliers/landlords have little time to affect the process and stop it.
- Running the whole process through an insolvency practitioner ensures the process is fair for all stakeholders.

Disadvantages of a pre-pack

- There is an argument that if the existing management have led the business into its current insolvent position, then should they benefit from a sale of the business back to them?

- As the process is undertaken in a relatively short period of time, there is the potential criticism that assets are not sold at their true value, which could be challenged at a later date by a liquidator.

- The reputation of the business and its directors may be damaged by what may be perceived as the secret and not transparent nature of the sale.

- The pre-pack could be classed as an insolvency event in lending agreements (via covenants) and with suppliers which could have a detrimental impact on the future of the business.

- Given the concerns around pre-packs, IPs act under strict guidelines (known as statement of insolvency practice 16 (SIP 16)) and the 'pre-pack pool' (PPP) was established in 2015. The PPP is an independent body of experienced professionals who offer an opinion on the pre-pack sale of assets to connected parties. However, referral to the PPP is optional and it has received fewer referrals than expected.

Schemes of arrangement

Schemes of arrangement are similar to CVAs in that they create a binding agreement between the company and its creditors. Unlike a CVA, a scheme must be approved by the court and it can bind secured creditors (provided that the required number has voted in favour). Schemes are predominantly used in large complex restructurings and are often used by overseas companies provided that they can show a 'sufficient connection' with the UK, as many foreign jurisdictions do not have an equivalent to the scheme of arrangement.

> **Scheme of arrangement**   An insolvency arrangement that creates a binding agreement between a company and its creditors. The scheme must be approved by the court and it can bind secured creditors.

The end of the road?

Administrative receiver

Appointment

In a similar way to an administrator being appointed, an **administrative receiver** can be appointed by a floating charge holder (such as a debenture held by a bank). The one difference, however, is that this option is only open to holders of debentures which were taken *before* 15 September 2003. The *Enterprise Act [2002]* changed the powers of banks (held via a debenture) so that any debentures taken after that date would only give banks the power to appoint an administrator.

> **Administrative receiver** A licensed insolvency practitioner appointed by a floating charge holder (such as a debenture held by a bank). It is only open to holders of debentures which were taken *before* 15 September 2003.

An administrative receiver must be a licensed insolvency practitioner.

Powers of an administrative receiver

The administrative receiver will take over the control of the company from the directors, acting as an agent of the company and their primary responsibility is to the bank, which you will notice is a subtle difference to an administrator, where the administrator has responsibilities to all creditors.

The administrative receiver has similar powers to a liquidator (discussed in detail below) and they have the power to turn assets into cash and to repay fixed charge holders first (fixed charges were discussed in Chapter 6; the bank is also likely to be a fixed charge holder over assets such as property) and then share funds with floating charge holders. Their role is to obtain the best price for the assets of the business, and in a similar way to an administrator, the best way to do this could be by selling the business as a 'going concern' to third party buyers. If this is a potential strategy, then the administrative receiver will continue to trade the company for a short period whilst searching for buyers.

Law of Property Act receiver

This is a type of receiver which can be appointed under the *Law of Property Act [1925]* and specifically relates to assets, predominantly property, which are subject to fixed charges. The **Law of Property Act receiver** is sometimes known as an LPA receiver or fixed charge receiver and will be appointed over freehold and leasehold property which is owned by an individual or a company.

> **Law of Property Act receiver** A type of receiver appointed under the *Law of Property Act [1925]* and specifically to assets (predominantly property) subject to fixed charges. They will be appointed over freehold and leasehold property which is owned by an individual or a company. They are not usually a licensed insolvency practitioner but are likely to be a qualified surveyor.

Unlike the administrative receiver, they are not usually a licensed insolvency practitioner but are likely to be a qualified surveyor. A peculiar quirk of insolvency law is that when the fixed charge holder appoints the LPA receiver there are usually individual appointments over individual properties so if a customer has 50 separate houses and flats there will be 50 different appointments, which can be administered by the same or 50 different LPA receivers!

The LPA receiver, in the same way as the administrative receiver, has a responsibility to the fixed charge holder (usually the bank) and needs to obtain the best value for the property they have a responsibility over. If the properties are rented out, the LPA receiver will enforce the rental agreements where tenants are not paying and will devise a very careful strategy with a portfolio of properties, taking into account repairs that may need to be made. Whilst the eventual aim will be to dispose of property until the bank is fully repaid, in order to obtain best value this may only be achieved over a protracted period of one or more years.

An LPA receiver derives his or her power from the *Law of Property Act (1925)* and the terms of the charge over the particular property. The powers under the *Law of Property Act [1925]* are very limited and do not include, for example, a power to sell. It is, therefore, extremely important that the bank checks (or asks its lawyers to confirm) that the charge contains all the powers an LPA receiver will need. If this is not the case the bank will need to apply to court.

Liquidation

The basic definition of **liquidation** is a process where the assets of a company are turned into cash and distributed to the shareholders and/or creditors (depending on the particular type of liquidation).

> **Liquidation** A process where the assets of a company are turned into cash and distributed to the shareholders and/or creditors.

Compulsory liquidation

In a situation of **compulsory liquidation**, the company is insolvent, and by order of the court (after the issuing of a winding-up petition as discussed earlier in this chapter), will have its assets turned into cash (liquidated) by a liquidator and this will be distributed depending on charges that third parties (such as banks) have on the assets of the company. Any fixed charges will take priority (eg where a bank has a fixed charge on property) and the liquidator will have to account to the bank for the sale proceeds. After any fixed charge holders have been dealt with then any remaining funds will be shared amongst the remaining creditors on a 'pari passu' basis – this means that the monies will be distributed on a pro rata basis.

Creditors' voluntary liquidation

With a **creditors' voluntary liquidation,** the company is insolvent, as defined earlier, and by definition cannot pay all of its creditors. The shareholders of the company (and sometimes they are described as members) will have a meeting and in it will need to pass a 'special resolution' to 'wind up' the company and also to appoint a liquidator. A majority of 75 per cent of the shareholders is needed. The shareholders may choose to pass the resolution in writing, rather than hold a physical meeting.

Once this is passed a decision will be sought from creditors within 14 days of the passing of the resolution to ascertain whether they approve the liquidation and the proposed choice of liquidators. This decision used to be made at a meeting of creditors commonly referred to as a 'Section 98' meeting. This was replaced in April 2017 by the deemed consent procedure or a virtual meeting. However, 10 per cent of creditors in number or value or 10 creditors (the 10/10/10 rule) can still require that a physical creditors' meeting is held.

Members' voluntary liquidation

A **members' voluntary liquidation** happens when the company is solvent. There can be many reasons for this type of liquidation: it may be due to the shareholders wanting to retire and not wishing to sell the business or it may be that the company was set up for a specific purpose which has now been fulfilled. A good example would be a property company that has been set up for a specific purpose (sometimes known as a special purpose vehicle) such as building a block of flats. Once the building project has been completed, and the flats have all been sold then all creditors can be paid off and the profits shared amongst the shareholders.

The directors need to sign what is called a 'statutory declaration of solvency' which is a legal confirmation that they believe the company is in a position to pay all of its debts (this may be bank debt and creditors) and any interest within 12 months of this declaration. There are serious consequences to signing this document falsely, which include fines and imprisonment.

In a similar way to the creditors' voluntary liquidation, a special resolution is then passed (requiring 75 per cent of the members to agree) to wind up the company and to appoint a liquidator. At this point in time, whilst the company will not stop trading immediately, any further trading activity must be for the purposes of achieving the eventual winding up.

If the members' voluntary liquidation fails, because the company is in fact insolvent, it can be converted into a creditors' voluntary liquidation.

Compulsory liquidation A type of liquidation process. A process where an insolvent company, by order of the court, will have its assets turned into cash (liquidated) by a liquidator and this will be distributed depending on charges that third parties (such as banks) have on the assets of the company.

Creditors' voluntary liquidation A type of liquidation process. The company is insolvent and the shareholders of the company (and sometimes they are described as members) will have a meeting and in it will need to pass a 'special resolution' to 'wind up' the company and also to appoint a liquidator.

Members' voluntary liquidation A type of liquidation process. The company is solvent in this situation (there is no suggestion that all outstanding creditors will not be repaid).

ACTIVITY 9.4
Administrations

Why might a bank wish to pursue an administration and what is the main aim of an administrator?
Write down your answer and check it against the one at the end of this chapter.

Order of repayment – creditors

This is the usual order of repayment, subject to the liquid funds available for distribution. This can be either under a liquidation or an administration. Funds are paid out in a 'waterfall' arrangement until there are no funds left. Any funds left from fixed charge asset realizations will be used towards paying any creditors who are further down the 'waterfall':

1 Secured creditors (against their fixed charges).

2 Insolvency practitioner fees/expenses linked to administration/liquidation.

3 Preferential creditors (this will include employee claims for wages/salaries).

4 Prescribed part – this is part of the funds set aside for unsecured creditors and is based on a formula of 50 per cent of the first £10,000 of assets, and 20 per cent of all remaining assets, up to a maximum limit of £600,000. Funds are distributed pro rata to the unsecured creditors.

5 Secured creditors (under floating charges).

6 Unsecured creditors.

7 Shareholders – usually unlikely.

As set out above, creditors within the same class are paid on a pro rata basis, known as the pari passu rule. For example, if the unsecured creditors are owed £1 million in total, but the officeholder only has funds of £250,000 left after paying the items at 1 to 5 in the waterfall, each unsecured creditor will be paid 25p for each £1 it is owed.

Individual insolvency

This book is very much aimed at how you, as the banker, need to deal with insolvency issues relating to your commercial business customers. However, it is worth us touching very briefly on issues relating to individual insolvency.

Individual voluntary arrangements

An **individual voluntary arrangement** (IVA) is very similar to the corporate CVA, where an arrangement is made with the creditors of an individual, so that the debts outstanding are not necessarily repaid in full and will necessitate some or all of the creditors having to write off part of their debt. An insolvency practitioner will take over the individual's financial affairs and will effectively supervise the process, which may be over a period of two or three years. The arrangements must be agreed to by 75 per cent of the creditors (in value) (50 per cent of these creditors must also be unconnected with the individual proposing the IVA) and all creditors will be bound by this final agreement. The individual in the IVA risks becoming bankrupt if they do not adhere strictly to the repayment schedule.

Bankruptcy

Bankruptcy is an insolvency process aimed at individuals who are unable to pay their debts. It is the personal equivalent of a liquidation. The individual themselves can apply to an adjudicator to be made bankrupt or a creditor, in a similar way to the corporate insolvency rules, can issue in court a bankruptcy petition, where the creditor has a debt which is unpaid.

The *Small Business, Enterprise and Employment Act [2015]*, from October 2015, amended the threshold to £5,000. Unlike in compulsory liquidation, referred to above, a statutory demand is generally a prerequisite to a creditor issuing a bankruptcy petition.

The official receiver becomes a trustee in bankruptcy. However, if the individual (then known as the 'bankrupt') has assets, it is usual for an IP(s) to be appointed as trustee(s) in bankruptcy. The assets of the bankrupt 'vest', with some exceptions, in the trustee (this is known as the bankruptcy estate). The trustee will arrange to liquidate (often referred to as 'realizing') the estate and share the funds with the creditors. If the bankrupt has a house for example, where there is a fixed charge to a bank or building society, then the fixed charge holder will be able to exercise their rights over the asset they have charged, selling it and repaying their borrowing. Any surplus will then be paid to the trustee in bankruptcy to distribute to unsecured creditors.

Usually the bankruptcy period lasts for 12 months, and after that period the bankrupt is discharged. The bankrupt's debts are written off (with some exceptions, including secured debts) and he/she can start afresh. However, as the assets vest in the trustee, the bankrupt does not automatically get these back after the 12-month period unless all creditors have been repaid.

Individual voluntary arrangement An arrangement is made with the creditors of an individual, so that the debts outstanding are not necessarily repaid in full and will necessitate some or all of the creditors having to write off part of their debt. An insolvency practitioner will take over the individual's financial affairs and will supervise the process (which may be over two or three years).

Bankruptcy An insolvency process aimed at individuals who are unable to pay their debts. The personal equivalent of a liquidation. The individual themselves can apply to an adjudicator to be made bankrupt or a creditor, in a similar way to the corporate insolvency rules, can issue in court a bankruptcy petition, where the creditor has a debt that is unpaid.

Debt relief order

Debt relief orders (DROs) were introduced in 2009 and are aimed at those with little or no income or assets and are a cheaper alternative to bankruptcy. In order to qualify for a DRO an individual must be (i) unable to pay their debts, (ii) have unsecured liabilities of less than £20,000, (iii) have assets of less than £1,000, and (iv) disposable income of less than £50 per month.

> **Debt relief order**   Introduced in 2009 and aimed at those with little or no income or assets; a cheaper alternative to bankruptcy.

Related insolvency issues

We have touched on the duties of directors and there are three other issues that might have an impact on these duties if a company becomes insolvent – these are often known as 'antecedent transitions' or the office holder's power of 'claw back'. There are also the equivalents of these in personal insolvency.

Transactions at an undervalue

A **transaction at an undervalue** is when a company disposes of assets either for no 'consideration' at all (ie it gets nothing for the asset) or sells it for significantly below its market value. A court can reverse the transaction and rule that the director(s) who helped facilitate this transaction be involved in making up the difference when:

- there is an existing liquidation/administration;
- the transaction took place within two years of when the liquidation/administration commenced; and
- the company was insolvent when the transaction took place, or became insolvent due to the impact of the transaction.

If the transaction in question was to a connected person then there is no onus to prove the company was insolvent. A connected person is defined as a director or someone who is associated with that director (this can be employees, partners, close relatives or another company that is controlled by the director or an associated person).

> **Transaction at an undervalue**   A situation where a company disposes of assets either for no 'consideration' at all (ie it gets nothing for the asset) or sells it for significantly below its market value. This can be reversed by a court when: 1) there is an existing liquidation/administration, 2) the transaction took place within two years of when the liquidation/administration commenced, and 3) the company was insolvent when the transaction took place or became insolvent due to the impact of the transaction.

Preferences

This is where one creditor is placed in a more favourable position than others. This can include paying one creditor when others are not being paid and paying off company overdrafts (or other liabilities) which are guaranteed by the directors.

Again, a court can reverse the transaction if:

- there is an existing liquidation/administration;
- the transaction took place within six months of when the liquidation/administration commenced (two years if it is to a connected person);
- the company was insolvent when the transaction took place, or became insolvent due to the impact of the transaction.

The courts will review preferences with reference to whether or not it was the company's intention to put another party in a better position (the 'desire to prefer'), and did this have an impact on the final decision. The desire to prefer is presumed where the transaction is with a connected party.

Granting security to a bank could be challenged as a preference; however, it is highly unlikely that the desire to prefer the bank would be established.

Preferences Where one creditor is placed in a more favourable position than others. This can include paying one creditor when others are not being paid and paying off company overdrafts (or other liabilities) which are guaranteed by the directors. This can be reversed by a court when: 1) there is an existing liquidation/administration, 2) the transaction took place within six months of when the liquidation/administration commenced (two years if to a connected person) and 3) the company was insolvent when the transaction took place or became insolvent due to the impact of the transaction.

Transactions defrauding creditors

This is where there is a transaction at an undervalue where the purpose is to put assets beyond the reach of creditors (current or future), or anyone who is making (or may make) a claim against the company. The purpose of the transaction is key. The company does not need to be insolvent at the time of the transaction, does not need to become insolvent as a result of it nor does it need to be in an insolvency process. There is no time limit.

Avoidance of floating charges

A further consequence of a company entering administration/liquidation is that certain floating charges can be avoided under the *Insolvency Act [1986]*. If the bank is relying upon its floating charge to appoint administrators and/or to receive payment as a floating charge creditor under the insolvency waterfall referred to earlier in this chapter, it is critical that the floating charge cannot be challenged by the office holder. A floating charge is invalid except to the aggregate value of the monies paid by the bank or debt reduced by the bank if:

- the charge was granted in the 12 months before the commencement of the administration/liquidation; and

- the company must be unable to pay its debts at the time of the transaction or become unable to pay its debts as a consequence of the transaction under which the charge is granted.

The banker as a shadow director

One of the issues that impacts on banks and their staff is that via the banker's dealings with a company that is in financial difficulties, the banker or the bank itself becomes a shadow director. Once a business is either in default of its lending agreements, or faces a potential default, the bank is likely to be more involved in the business, for example, in monitoring and vetoing payments out of bank accounts. The status of shadow director is defined in Section 251 of the *Insolvency Act [1986]*:

> 'Shadow director' in relation to a company, means a person in accordance with whose directions or instructions the directors of the company are accustomed to act...

Case law is not settled regarding whether a lender is capable of being held liable as a shadow director, therefore there is a risk. However, to date no cases have been reported where a lender has been found to be a shadow director and it is accepted that a creditor is entitled to protect its own interests, without necessarily becoming a shadow director (*Re PFTZM Ltd*).

We discussed independent business reviews earlier in this chapter, and these reviews can lead to actions that the company takes which are not only part of the recommendations of the report but are also part of the bank's conditions for continued support. The company does, of course, have the option not to implement these actions and then deal with the issue of the bank taking more serious actions in order to recover its lending. This 'choice' goes some way to countering a claim that the banker is acting as a shadow director.

> **Shadow director** As defined by the *Insolvency Act [1986]* – 'a person in accordance with whose directions or instructions the directors of the company are accustomed to act...'

Chapter summary

In this chapter we have explored:

- the main reasons that commercial businesses find themselves in financial difficulties;
- warning signs banks need to be aware of that indicate a business is potentially facing financial difficulties;
- remedies businesses have available to them to tackle the challenges of poor financial performance;
- the choices and options the bank has when dealing with a business facing financial difficulties;
- the definition of insolvency and the key insolvency processes.

Objective check

1 Detail three warning signs that show a business may be struggling financially.

2 Detail some of the reasons businesses get into financial difficulties.

3 What are some of the remedies that businesses may use to tackle their financial issues?

4 What choices does the bank have when dealing with a business in financial difficulties?

5 Define insolvency.

6 Detail some of the key insolvency processes that are available for personal and commercial businesses.

Further reading

HMV stages £17m comeback [accessed 25 June 2018] [Online] http://www.telegraph.co.uk/finance/newsbysector/retailandconsumer/11125772/HMV-stages-17m-comeback.html

Pinsent Mason (Solicitors) produce a number of guides on insolvency and also produce an excellent magazine to keep up with up-to-date insolvency issues [accessed 25 June 2018] [Online] www.out-law.com

Options when a company is insolvent [accessed 25 June 2018] [Online] https://www.gov.uk/government/publications/options-when-a-company-is-insolvent/options-when-a-company-is-insolvent

References

BBC NEWS | UK | Cadbury salmonella scare probed [accessed 25 June 2018] [Online] http://news.bbc.co.uk/1/hi/5112470.stm

Corporate insolvency: the basics [accessed 24 June 2018] [Online] https://www.out-law.com/en/topics/financial-services/restructuring/corporate-insolvency-the-basics/

Legal case references

Devaynes v Noble (Clayton's Case) [1816] 1 Mer 572

Re PFTZM Ltd, [1995] 2 BCLC 354

Suggested answers for activities

Activity 9.1 – Businesses that have entered insolvency processes

At the time of writing a number of high profile businesses have become insolvent – where administrators have been appointed includes Carillion, Maplins and the UK arm of Toys R Us.

Activity 9.2 – Warning signs in management information

The learner was asked to consider key performance indicators for three businesses and how these could be used to identify warning signs:

- An estate agency – this type of business sells properties and will have a minimum number it needs to sell each month/quarter in order to repay its bank borrowing. Any drop in numbers sold will be an indication that there may be issues.

- A care home – this type of business will need to have a minimum number of residents and due to the high running costs and finance costs, minimum occupancy will need to be more than, say, 85 per cent. For a home with 35 residents this will require minimum residency of at least 30 residents at all times.

- A property company (renting out residential flats and houses) – a useful KPI here would be the level of 'voids' that the business has. The ideal scenario would be for all properties to be rented out all the time, but as tenants change, this is unrealistic and if the normal experience of the business is to have 5 per cent voids at any time, any change away from this will be a concern for the bank as it indicates a potential drop in profitability in the short term.

Activity 9.4 – Administrations

The learner was asked to consider the advantages of an administration and the role of the administrator.

The main advantage of an administration is that it:

- helps preserve the value of the business;
- stops other creditors taking action against the company once the administrator has been appointed; and
- the role of the administrator is to act on behalf of all the creditors.

Learners should devise their own answer for Activity 9.3. No model answer is supplied.

GLOSSARY

Ability The specific capabilities of a business to carry out its core activities and therefore be able to repay its borrowing.

Accounts [pre FRS 102 term] The financial statements for a business.

Acid test ratio Another term for liquidity ratio.

Acquisition The purchase by one business of another.

Administration An insolvency process designed to find a way for a business to survive as a 'going concern' (ie it doesn't stop trading).

Administrative expenses These are fixed costs incurred (and will include head office costs if applicable).

Administrative receiver A licensed insolvency practitioner appointed by a floating charge holder (such as a debenture held by a bank). It is only open to holders of debentures that were taken before 15 September 2003.

Administrator An appointed individual (usually a licensed insolvency practitioner), who will be responsible for running an administration.

Alternative use This is used to examine how specialized a property is and whether there would be other uses for it.

Amortization The reduction over time in the value of intangible assets.

Amount The total funds that are being lent.

Annual accounts The financial statements for a business covering a year. A statutory requirement under Companies Act legislation.

Artificial intelligence The use of computers and machines that can think for themselves, without human intervention.

Asset based lenders A category of lender that provides specialist financial services, primarily lending against an asset or assets that a business has.

Assumptions The factors that have been used to build a set of projections or forecasts.

Autocratic leadership A leadership style where the leader dominates the decision-making process.

Automation The replacement of humans by robots and other machines, which carry out the tasks that humans used to perform. Used extensively in manufacturing processes.

Balance sheet [pre FRS 102 term] A financial statement that details the assets and liabilities of a business.

Bank instructed bank addressed valuation A valuation that a bank asks to be conducted, where the purpose of the valuation is for security purposes.

Bank mandate A standard bank document used to detail the relationship between the bank and the customer. It sets out the signing arrangements for the sole trader, the partners or the directors (in the case of a limited company). For a limited company or a partnership, it may specify how many partners or directors need to sign banking instruments such as cheques.

Bankruptcy   An insolvency process aimed at individuals who are unable to pay their debts. The personal equivalent of a liquidation. The individual themselves can apply to an adjudicator to be made bankrupt or a creditor, in a similar way to the corporate insolvency rules, can issue in court a bankruptcy petition, where the creditor has a debt that is unpaid.

Base case scenario   The initial model for business projections, which usually contains the most conservative figures.

Boston Consulting Group (growth/share matrix)   Sometimes also known as the Boston Star Matrix. A strategic tool that assesses the products/services of a business based on market growth and market share. There are four categories: 1) stars, 2) question marks, 3) cash cows, and 4) dogs.

Breach of covenants   The breaking of specific terms and conditions within a loan or overdraft agreement.

Bricks and mortar value   The value of a building that is used for business purposes where the value of the business is discounted from a valuation.

British Business Bank   Owned by the British Government (established in 2013), the British Business Bank supports UK businesses via a combination of finance and guarantees to banks and investors who will then deal directly with the business that is looking for the support.

Business angels   Wealthy private individuals who wish to invest in private businesses. This may be either through loans or via purchasing part of the shares of the business.

Business credit cards   A version of a credit card which is used by a director or employee for business purposes only.

Business Growth Fund   An independent organization set up in conjunction with the major UK clearing banks. Its purpose is to make minority equity investments of between £2 million and £10 million in businesses that have turnover of between £5 million and £100 million.

Capital expenditure   The purchase of fixed assets used to continue to run the business. Sometimes shortened to Capex.

Capital and reserves [pre FRS 102 term]   The share capital and profit reserves that a business holds.

Cash [new FRS 102 term]   The cash a business holds (in bank accounts or in petty cash).

Cash at bank and in hand [pre FRS 102 term]   The cash a business holds (in bank accounts or in petty cash).

Cash flow available for debt service (CFADS)   The calculation used to ascertain whether a business can afford to repay its borrowings.

Cash flow forecast   A prediction of the forward requirements for cash.

Certificate of Incorporation A document issued by Companies House, which shows when a limited company began and is the proof of the company's existence.

Character The trustworthiness of the principals behind a business

Charge This is where the bank takes a controlling interest in an asset. It restricts the owner of the security dealing with the asset without the consent of the bank (it is important to note that *ownership* of the asset does not transfer to the bank).

Chargee A party taking a charge over security.

Chargor A party giving a charge over security.

Companies House The government body in England and Wales that maintains a central register of all information pertaining to limited companies.

Company voluntary arrangement A formal insolvency arrangement between a company and its unsecured creditors (binding on all parties). It allows a business to continue to trade normally. It preserves the value in the business and jobs. Once agreed it is controlled by an insolvency practitioner who is the supervisor.

Composite corporate cross-guarantee Guarantees given between companies in the same group (*see* also 'down-stream guarantee').

Compulsory liquidation A type of liquidation process. A process where an insolvent company, by order of the court, will have its assets turned into cash (liquidated) by a liquidator and will be distributed depending on charges that third parties (such as banks) have on the assets of the company.

Conditions precedent Specific conditions a business must comply with before funds are lent to them.

Corporate guarantee A guarantee given by a limited company.

Corporate social responsibility (CSR) 'The commitment by organizations to behave ethically and contribute to economic development whilst improving the quality of life of the workforce and their families as well as the local community and society at large' (World Business Council for Sustainable Development).

Cost of sales Costs the business has incurred in order to generate turnover (these include the variable costs incurred such as purchase of inventory, wages and other costs).

Covenants Specific clauses built into loan agreements that provide the ability of the bank to monitor the performance of a business after monies have been lent.

Credit policy A formal set of rules adopted by a bank or financial institution that set out the circumstances under which it should lend to businesses.

Credit risk The risk that a customer (sometimes also defined as a counterparty) will default and not pay back their borrowing.

Creditors' voluntary liquidation A type of liquidation process. The company is insolvent and the shareholders of the company (and sometimes they are described as members) will have a meeting and in it will need to pass a 'special resolution' to 'wind up' the company and also to appoint a liquidator.

Current asset ratio The relationship between current assets and current liabilities.

Debenture   Security given by a limited company to a bank. This gives the bank a fixed charge over fixed assets and a floating charge over floating assets.

Debt interest cover   A measurement of how many times interest is covered by the profits of the business.

Debt relief order   Introduced in 2009 and aimed at those with little or no income or assets; a cheaper alternative to bankruptcy. In order to qualify for a DRO an individual must be: 1) unable to pay their debts, 2) have unsecured liabilities of less than £20,000, 3) have assets of less than £1,000, and 4) disposable income of less than £50 per month.

Debtors [pre FRS 102 term]   Funds owed to a business that arise when a business sells goods or services on credit terms. These funds are due to be paid at a future date.

Democratic leadership   A leadership style where the leader operates on a more consultative basis with their team.

Depreciation   The measurement of a reduction in value of a fixed asset owned by business.

Desk-top research   Research carried out on a business using publicly available information.

Directors' duties   Statutory duties imposed by the *Insolvency Act [1986]*.

Discounting factors   The percentage used to write-down an item of security that a bank has.

Disruptive technology   Technology that allows new entrants into a marketplace, where they are able to offer products and services at a lower price or in a simpler way than existing businesses.

Distribution costs   Costs incurred to distribute the goods of a business.

Dividend policies   This is the process a business uses to distribute profits of the business to the shareholders.

Dividends   The payment of profits to the shareholders.

Documentary letter of credit   A method of securing an international trade transaction (exporting/importing), where trade documents are used. The banks will often be involved in 'guaranteeing' the finance for the transaction.

Domino effect   The effect that occurs when one event happens that usually has ramifications on the ability of a business to repay its borrowing.

Down-stream guarantee   A guarantee given by a parent company in favour of a subsidiary company (*see* also 'Composite corporate cross-guarantee').

Earnings before interest, tax, depreciation and amortization (EBITDA)   The profits for a business before further items including interest, tax, depreciation and amortization are deducted.

Emotional intelligence   A measurement of intelligence which is different to IQ and is based on four attributes: 1) self-awareness, 2) self-management, 3) social awareness, and 4) social skill.

Enterprise Finance Guarantee scheme   A UK government-backed scheme providing support to UK businesses via the British Business Bank.

Entrepreneur   A business person who sets up a business, taking all the risks that this involves.

Equitable charge   This is sometimes also known as an 'equitable mortgage'. This is when a holder of security signs a document that is an agreement between the bank and the holder of that security, allowing the bank to take a mortgage over that security if certain events happen (such as borrower default).

Equity [new FRS 102 term]   The value the shareholders have, usually expressed as the share capital owned.

Exposure   The level of lending to a business.

Facility   A specific line of credit provided to commercial customers (eg overdraft/ loan etc).

Factoring   A type of invoice funding. A variation on an invoice discount facility, the major difference being that the funder buys the outstanding debt and effectively steps into the place of the business that has the debtor.

Finance costs [new FRS 102 term]   The costs incurred by a business in a specific period.

Finance income/investment income [new FRS 102 term]   Interest paid to a business for any deposits it may have had in the period in question. Any other investment income is also recorded here.

Finance lease   A type of leasing agreement. Usually for a longer term than an operating lease and will often link to the life of the asset being funded. The asset is normally shown on the balance sheet of the business.

Financial Conduct Authority   The UK regulator of conduct of 56,000 firms and financial markets in the UK.

Financial information   Information about a business that is purely based on the financial performance.

Financial Reporting Standard 102   An accounting standard that affects businesses that have accounting periods commencing after 1 January 2016. It replaces a number of other accounting standards. It introduces new accounting terminology.

Financial statements [new FRS 102 term]   The financial accounts for the business, usually covering a 12-month period.

Financial strength   The financial resilience of a business. It shows the actual or potential vulnerabilities that a business has in relation to its ability to repay bank and other borrowings.

Financial year [pre FRS 102 term]   The 12-month period covered by the financial accounts prepared by a business.

First charge   When a bank takes security, this is when the bank has priority over any other lender.

Fixed assets   These are assets that the business owns, which are used to run the business and are divided into intangible assets and tangible assets.

Fixed charge   A charge given by a limited company, which attaches to certain assets that are classified as fixed (eg machinery, land and buildings, etc).

Floating charge   A charge given by a limited company, which attaches to certain assets that are classified as floating (eg trade receivables, inventory etc).

Foreign currency accounts   An account denominated in a currency other than sterling (for a UK business), eg US dollars or euros. It can be a current or a deposit account and operates in the same way as a sterling current/deposit account, allowing a business to receive and make payments in a currency without having to convert to sterling.

Forward currency contracts   An agreement between the bank and a customer for a specific amount of a particular currency to be exchanged at a specified exchange rate, at a specified date in the future.

Freehold   The owner of land or property (real estate) who has an absolute right to deal with the property in any way they wish including selling it. Ownership stays with the owner of the property without any time limitations.

Gearing   It measures the relationship between what the bank (and any other lenders) have committed to the business and the financial commitment of the shareholders/directors/owners.

Generic strategies   A strategic approach by Michael E Porter that focuses on low cost and differentiation as tools of competitive advantage. The three strategies are cost leadership, differentiation and focus. Focus is then split further into: 1) cost focus, and 2) differentiation focus.

Gilts   Issued by the UK Government, these are a savings product issued for a fixed period of time and are redeemable at 'par' (ie at face value), with a fixed interest rate (or coupon) on them.

Green finance   Finance facilities that are predominantly aimed at reducing the carbon emissions of a business.

Gross profit   The profit the business has made after the deduction of variable costs.

Gross profit margin   This is a ratio of gross profit to sales. It is a measurement of how much money a business makes after it has taken into account the variable costs incurred for achieving the sales in that period.

Guarantee   The promise by one party to repay part or all of the liabilities of a third party, if the third party fails to repay the borrowing, they are contractually obliged to.

Hardcore borrowing   The element of borrowing within a revolving facility, such as an overdraft, where the level of indebtedness never falls below a particular level. It is where an overdraft does not fluctuate between credit and debit.

Hire purchase   A finance agreement where when a business wants to purchase a capital item it will enter into an agreement with a hire purchase (HP) provider, where the asset is purchased by the HP provider and the business then pays for the asset over a set period. At the end of the agreement period the business that is the hirer will have the option to purchase the asset for a nominal figure from the HP provider.

Income   The profits generated by a business, which can be used to repay borrowing.

Independent business review   Carried out by a firm of accountants that has experience in restructuring businesses. It examines all aspects of the business, including the management, the products or service provided by the business and critically tests all of the strategic plans put forward by the directors including sensitizing all the projections. It will also include a view of the potential losses that will be faced by the bank should the business fail and go into some form of insolvency process.

Independent legal advice   Where a solicitor explains the legal implications of documentation that is being entered into and also explains the consequences of what may happen if loan agreements are not adhered to, and how this will impact on security (such as guarantees).

Individual voluntary arrangement   An arrangement is made with the creditors of an individual, so that the debts outstanding are not necessarily repaid in full and will necessitate some or all of the creditors having to write part of their debt off. An insolvency practitioner will take over the individual's financial affairs and will supervise the process (which may be over two or three years).

Insolvency   The inability of a business to pay its liabilities as and when they are due. It can also be where the liabilities of a business are more than its assets.

Insolvency Act [1986]   The key legislation in England and Wales that governs the insolvency of companies.

Insolvency practitioner   A licensed individual who is authorized to carry out specific duties in relation to insolvent companies and bankrupt individuals.

Insurance (security)   See 'Security'.

Intangible assets   Items such as intellectual property (eg patents/software). They are called intangible because it is not possible to touch them or see them.

Interest payable and similar charges [pre FRS 102 term]   This relates to all interest-bearing borrowings in an accounting period.

Interest receivable and similar income [pre FRS 102 term]   Interest paid to a business for any deposits it may have had in the period in question. Any other investment income is also recorded here.

Interest roll-up   The process of adding interest to a loan as it is being drawn down over a period of time (often to fund property development).

Inventories [new FRS 102 term]   The raw materials, work-in-progress and finished goods that a business has to sell (but hasn't yet sold).

Inventory turnover   This is the number of times that inventory turns over in a particular period.

Invoice discounting   Sometimes also referred to as confidential invoice discounting. A type of invoice funding.

Invoice funding (*see* also 'Factoring' and 'Invoice discounting')   A hybrid type of financing and usually considered as an alternative to overdrafts. A financing option where a bank or other finance institution will use the invoices issued by a business to its customers and discount these, providing upfront (immediate) funds before the invoices are paid by the customers.

Iron triangle (the) (also known as the triple constraint)   The business concept that it is not possible to achieve every aim without having to sacrifice one element in the 'triangle' (eg it is not possible to achieve high quality and quickly without a high cost).

Joint and several guarantee   A joint personal guarantee given by more than two or more guarantors. Each guarantor is individually responsible for the full amount of the guarantee and if the guarantee is called on by the bank, the amount outstanding can be recovered from the guarantors in any ratio acceptable to the bank.

Key person protection policy   A life policy that a limited company will take out on the life of a key employee.

Key ratio analysis   The important financial ratios that are used to analyse the financial performance of a business.

Land Registry   A central government department covering all registered land in England and Wales.

Law of Property Act receiver   A type of receiver appointed under the *Law of Property Act [1925]* and specifically to assets (predominantly property) subject to fixed charges. They will be appointed over freehold and leasehold property that is owned by an individual or a company. They are not usually a licensed insolvency practitioner but are likely to be a qualified surveyor.

Leasehold   The owner of the freehold property grants a lease over the property, giving the leaseholder the ability to use the property as if it were their own. The ownership of the property stays with the freehold owner. This will be for a specific period of time and can be up to 999 years. The leaseholder must comply with the terms of the lease including making the lease payments.

Leasing   A finance agreement using business assets, with a lessor (the owner of the asset) and the lessee (the party using the asset). The lessee effectively rents the asset throughout the agreement period.

Lending mnemonic   A set of initials that set out the key headings with which a business should be analysed when it is borrowing money.

Lending proposition   A proposal prepared by a bank containing all of the information and analysis on a business that requires borrowing facilities. This is prepared using specific headings to ensure that all key risks are considered and discussed.

Lien   This is the right by one party to hold an asset belonging to another party until an outstanding debt has been repaid.

Life policies   A product issued by an insurance company on the life/lives of an individual/s. The policy will pay out on the death of the life insured.

Lifestyle business   A business that is run to generate sufficient income to support a particular lifestyle.

Limited liability partnerships   Introduced in April 2001 (via the *Limited Liability Partnerships Act [2000]*) they are a hybrid of private limited companies and partnerships. They have members rather than shareholders and directors. The personal liability of members is limited.

Liquidation   A process where the assets of a company are turned into cash and distributed to the shareholders and/or creditors.

Liquidity   A measure of liquid funds that a business can access to cover current liabilities.

Liquidity ratio   The relationship between current assets (having subtracted inventories from current assets) and current liabilities.

Loan   An amount of money lent to a business over a term period (usually a number of years). Interest is charged on the outstanding capital amount and repayments are set at a level that will repay the outstanding borrowing and the interest over the agreed term.

Management information   Financial information produced on a regular basis by a business (often monthly or quarterly). It shows the financial position of the business in a 'mini' version to the annual accounts. It will show the profits or losses in the month (or quarter) and show the assets and liabilities of the business.

Managerial grid (the)   A management theory by Robert R Blake and Jane Mouton where management styles are split into five categories: 1) country club management, 2) impoverished management, 3) task management, 4) team management, and 5) middle of the road management. The categories matched against two metrics: 1) concern for people and 2) concern for production.

Margin   The rate of interest charged above either base rate or London Interbank Offered Rate (LIBOR).

Members' voluntary liquidation   A type of liquidation process. The company is solvent in this situation (there is no suggestion that all outstanding creditors will not be repaid).

Micro-enterprise   A business that employs fewer than 10 persons and has a turnover or annual balance sheet that does not exceed £2 million.

Mid-sized businesses   Entities that have turnover of between £25 million and £500 million.

Mortgage   This is sometimes also known as a 'legal mortgage'. A holder of security signs a document that is an agreement between the bank and the holder of that security, allowing the bank to take control of that security if certain events happen (such as borrower default).

Mortgagee   This is what the bank becomes when it lends money and is the party TAKING an interest in the security (the bank).

Mortgagor   The entity borrowing the funds and is usually the party giving the security (the customer).

Net profit   The profit made after all costs have been deducted from sales income (the costs include interest, tax and dividends).

Net profit margin   This is a ratio of net profit to sales. It is a measurement of how much money a business is making, after the deduction of all costs including interest, tax and dividends.

Non-financial information   Any information about a business that excludes financial information (this can be from a variety of sources including media reports).

Open market value   The value of real estate where a sale might take place under normal market conditions (ie not in a distressed situation).

Operating lease   A type of leasing agreement. It tends to be for much shorter periods than a finance lease (the leasing company takes all the risk for owning the asset that is being leased and therefore the asset would not show on the lessee's balance sheet).

Operating profit   The profit a business has made after the deduction of all of its costs and before the deduction of finance costs and taxation.

Operating profit margin   This is a ratio of operating profit to sales. It is a measurement of how much money a business makes after it has taken into account the variable costs and fixed costs incurred for achieving the sales in that period.

Other operating income   Any other income.

Overdraft   An ability to borrow on a current account up to an agreed limit.

Overriding interest   When a party (or parties) other than the borrower has an interest in a property (usually a domestic residence). This will usually be a spouse/common law partner and/or dependents (including children) who would lose their home if the bank took control of it. The interests of the other parties are seen to be more important than those of the banks.

Overtrading   The rapid growth in turnover where there is a weak financial base in the business.

Partnership   Two or more individuals working together in a business to make a profit.

Peer-to-peer funding   An intermediary service that allows the direct investment in businesses (an alternative to more traditional funding by banks).

Person   The entity that is being lent to.

Personal guarantee   A guarantee given by an individual in favour of another individual or a limited company.

Pledge   An undertaking that an asset may be used as security and potentially disposed of by a bank if funds are not paid out under a transaction (often involving international transactions).

Political, Economic, Social, Technological, Legal, Environmental (PESTLE)   A strategic analysis tool used by organizations to review their external environment.

Porter's Five Forces   A concept developed by Michael E Porter that examines the forces exerted on business: 1) the threat from new entrants/barriers to entry, 2) the power of suppliers, 3) the power of customers/buyers, 4) the threat from substitutes, and 5) the marketplace-competition/rivalry.

Preference   Where one creditor is placed in a more favourable position than others. This can include paying one creditor when others are not being paid and paying off company overdrafts (or other liabilities) which are guaranteed by the directors. This can be reversed by a court when: 1) there is an existing liquidation/administration, 2) the transaction took place within two years of when the liquidation/administration commenced, and 3) the company was insolvent when the transaction took place, or became insolvent due to the impact of the transaction.

Pre-packaged sale   The pre-arranged sale of a business and assets of an insolvent company (often to its existing directors) immediately following the appointment of a licensed insolvency practitioner (usually an administrator). It is sometimes known as a 'Pre-pack' due to the pre-arranged element of the process. The assets will usually be transferred into a new company.

Pricing for risk   The adjustment of the price charged by a bank when it lends based on the level of risk that the bank is exposed to.

Private equity   The investment in a business by the purchasing of part of the share capital of the business by an external investor.

Private limited company   A legal entity, owned by a shareholder or shareholders. The liability of the shareholders is limited to the amount of the share capital. It has the same rights as a person and can enter into contracts as a person would. There must have at least one director and one shareholder.

Product life-cycle   A model which tracks the life of a product, through its four stages: inception/growth/maturity/decline.

Profit and loss accounts [pre FRS 102 term]   The profit or loss a business has made in a particular period.

Profit on ordinary activities before taxation   Profit before taxation is paid.

Profit for the period/year   The final profit after all costs have been deducted.

Profitability   The measure of how much profit a business generates, being the difference between income generated and the costs incurred.

Projections   Management forecasts of the future financial position of a business. They will forecast profits/losses, asset/liability position and the cash position.

Property   Another phrase for real estate.

Property finance   See 'Real estate finance'.

Public limited company   A company that must have share capital with a nominal value of no less than £50,000. The shares can be purchased by the general public. Public limited companies are usually quoted on the Stock Exchange.

Purpose   The reason the lending is needed.

Real estate   Land and buildings. This can be domestic (private residences – house/flats etc) or commercial (offices/factories/industrial units).

Real estate finance   The lending of money to businesses that deal in property (residential or commercial).

Registered land   Any land or buildings (domestic or commercial) in England and Wales that is registered at the Land Registry. Title is evidenced by a land certificate.

Relationship management   From a bank's perspective, the human resources given internally to maintaining a relationship between the customer and the bank. This normally involves the appointment of a specified individual in the bank who has overall responsibility for the relationship.

Repayment   The ability of a business to repay the monies it is borrowing.

Reporting period [new FRS 102 term]   The time period covered by the financial statements.

Restructure   The process that can involve, often in conjunction with its bankers, the reorganization of a business including its finances.

Revolving credit facility   An alternative to an overdraft and is usually only offered to larger commercial and corporate businesses. As a lending product it sits somewhere between an overdraft and a loan. Usually agreed over a two- to five-year period.

Risk cycle   The process of identifying, assessing, considering mitigants and finally monitoring risks.

Risk-weighted assets   Assets held by a bank that require a certain level of capital held against them. Higher risk assets require higher levels of capital.

Sanctioning process   The internal processes a bank goes through when agreeing to lend money, particularly to a commercial business. This will usually involve having a separate credit department as part of this process.

Scenario planning   A planning technique used particularly by Shell (the oil company), which examines future states of the world and formulates strategic responses to these possible scenarios.

Scheme of arrangement   An insolvency arrangement that creates a binding agreement between a company and its creditors. The scheme must be approved by the court and it can bind secured creditors.

Seasonality   The impact during the year of certain events (such as Christmas for retail businesses).

Second charge   When a bank takes security and there is already another lender in place (eg a personal mortgage).

Sector appetite   The level of willingness that a bank has to lend to a specific industrial sector.

Security   The assets taken by a bank, which are owned by the business. These are used to repay borrowing if the business defaults (sometimes also referred to as collateral).

Sensitivities   The changes that have been applied to a set of projections or forecasts to reflect risks that the business may face in the future.

Shadow director   As defined by the *Insolvency Act [1986]* – 'a person in accordance with whose directions or instructions the directors of the company are accustomed to act...'.

Six styles of leadership   The different styles of leadership as established by Daniel Goleman: 1) the authoritative style, 2) the affiliative style, 3) the democratic style, 4) the pacesetting style, 5) the coaching style, and 6) the coercive style.

Small- and medium-sized enterprise   A business that has less than 250 employees, turnover of less than £25 million and gross assets of less than £12.5 million.

Sole trader   A single individual who runs a business in their own name. They have full personal liability for any business debts. They may have a trading name.

Spikes   The points in a cash flow cycle when there is a greater requirement for cash due to payment of items such as wages/salaries, rent, tax and loan payments.

Stakeholders Individuals/organizations that have an interest in a business.

Statement of comprehensive income The profit or loss a business has made in a particular period. It details all of the costs incurred in that period including depreciation, amortization, interest, tax and dividends.

Statement of financial position [new FRS 102 term] The assets and liabilities of the business, stated at a particular point in time (usually the year end).

Stocks [pre FRS 102 term] The raw materials, work-in-progress and finished goods that a business has to sell (but hasn't yet sold).

Stocks and shares Quoted investments in securities that are traded on the Stock Exchange.

Strategy A long-term view in business, which allows the achievement of medium- and long-term aims.

Strengths, Weaknesses, Opportunities and Threats (SWOT) A strategic analysis tool used by organizations to review their internal position (strengths/weaknesses) and their external environment (opportunities/threats).

Tangible assets [pre FRS 102 term] These are assets the business has (eg property – such as factories/offices/shops) that are used to run the business.

Tax on profit on ordinary activities The tax payable for a specific accounting period based on the profits in that period.

Term The length of time funds are being borrowed.

Trade creditors [pre FRS 102 term] These arise when a business buys raw materials or other goods on credit terms from its suppliers. It is monies owed by the business.

Trade payable days The number of days it takes a business to pay monies that it owes.

Trade payables [new FRS 102 term] These arise when a business buys raw materials or other goods on credit terms from its suppliers.

Trade receivable days The number of days it takes monies that are due to the business to be paid.

Trade receivables [new FRS 102 term] Funds owed to a business, which arise when a business sells goods or services to its customers on credit terms. These funds are due to be paid at a future date.

Transaction at an undervalue A situation where a company disposes of assets either for no 'consideration' at all (ie it gets nothing for the asset) or sells it for significantly below its market value. This can be reversed by a court when: 1) there is an existing liquidation/administration, 2) the transaction took place within two years of when the liquidation/administration commenced, and 3) the company was insolvent when the transaction took place, or became insolvent due to the impact of the transaction.

Triple constraint (the) See 'Iron triangle (the)'.

Turnaround consultant An individual (or individuals) who can help a business as it goes through a restructuring process. They are usually appointed by a bank for a specified period and ideally have expertise in the industry the customer is involved in.

Turnover   Sales of a business.

Undue influence   The influence that one party is presumed to have over another, often in a domestic situation (eg a husband over a wife or vice versa).

Unit trusts   Investment products that consist of a pool of stocks and shares to spread the risk.

Unregistered land   Any land or buildings (domestic or commercial) in England and Wales that is not recorded at Land Registry. Title is evidenced by a set of deeds.

Up-stream guarantee   A guarantee by a subsidiary company to a parent company.

Winding-up petition   A formal demand issued by a creditor (who is owed more than £750 and has not had their debt paid). This is issued through the courts.

Working capital cycle   The capital a business needs on a day-to-day basis to run itself effectively.

INDEX

Note: Page locators in *italics* denote information contained within a Figure or Table.